Contents

KU-538-355

NEWCASTLE-UNDER-LYME
COLLEGE LIBRARY
301 LAW 32049
DC000805.

To Hal Westergaard, Bill Sugrue, Ann Clynch and the Seniors.
Better than the Leicester Riders.

Introduction

The introduction of a new AEB Advanced level syllabus in 1991 provided new challenges for sociology students at A level. Three developments during the 1980s had made a revision of the A level necessary.

Firstly, sociological knowledge had moved on as events in Britain and the wider world unfolded. New sociological arguments and debates had emerged and there was a renewed emphasis on the essential unity of the sociological approach.

Secondly, the introduction of GCSE produced students whose experience was very different from that of O level students. For example, most students reading this book will have had some experience of coursework and will be familiar with examination papers which rely more on structured questions and answers than on traditional essay-style responses.

Thirdly, many people in the 1980s were arguing for a different type of post-16 education, based on students acquiring skills as much as knowledge in Advanced level study. They argued that A level students, rather than being required to learn more and more items of information, should be rewarded for developing sociological skills with which they could more clearly understand the social world around them.

The 1991 A level syllabus therefore introduced important changes, of which the most important, from the students' standpoint, was the introduction of the sociological skills of knowledge and understanding, interpretation and application, and evaluation, which are now systematically assessed in the examination.

In addition, there has been an up-dating of the issues which the syllabus covers and a specific allocation of subjects to each of the papers. Paper One consists entirely of structured questions, while Paper Two consists of traditional essay-style questions. Finally, the new syllabus includes a coursework option.

These changes are in line with the increasing emphasis in the 1990s on various types of experiential, supported self-study or flexible-learning programmes. Students will be expected to take much greater responsibility for their own learning, showing that they have developed the three skill domains of knowledge and understanding, interpretation and application, and evaluation.

Because of these changes, new types of resource need to be developed which will be fundamentally different from the traditional textbooks like Haralambos and Holborn, Bilton *et al.,* etc. (see p. 1). It would be pointless to produce another book full of sociological studies, even if it contained the most recent sociological work, because the knowledge dimension of the new syllabus is adequately provided for in the main texts. This book is an attempt to prepare students for the skill domains of the AEB syllabus and, as such, represents a new type of text.

To gain a good pass in the new syllabus, students will have to have engaged in sociological study and be trained in the skills of understanding, interpretation, application and evaluation. This book, then, does not reproduce descriptions of empirical studies or sociological perspectives. Firstly, it gives an up-to-date overview of the issues and arguments which sociologists have examined in looking at the social world. The students' prime task will be to use the references provided, or their own notes, to furnish their own evidence. In deciding the relevance of the studies for the arguments in the text, and whether they support or undermine a particular point of view, students will be developing the skills of application and evaluation.

Secondly, by learning about the concepts in the text, students will be adding to their sociological knowledge in a useful way. Thirdly, in doing the questions and exercises in the text, students will increase their powers of interpretation and understanding, and at the same time provide themselves with examination experience. Fourthly, in looking at the coursework suggestions, students will develop their practical skills in doing sociology.

And fifthly, by trying to connect sociological debates to both individual lives and the social policy issues which these arguments inform, it is hoped that students will regard sociology as more than just another A level. Rather, by trying to place individual experiences in their wider structural settings and by exploring the relationships between individuals, social policies and society as a whole, it is hoped that students will better understand the society in which they live. This understanding should be all the more pertinent to them because they themselves have been involved in achieving it in an active way. If they also enjoy the process, then the intention of the book will have been fulfilled.

How to use this book

(*or* how to get a good grade at A level)

This book is unlike any other sociology textbook that you are likely to see. It *does not* give you sociological studies. It *does not* give you detailed descriptions of perspectives. It *does not* tell you what the answers are.

It *does* expect you to do most of the work yourself. It *does* expect you to think about issues. It *does* expect you to keep up to date with contemporary events by reading newspapers and watching current affairs programmes on television. It *does* also expect you to maximise the grade you achieve in the examination by developing your own skills of knowledge and understanding, interpretation and application, and evaluation. These are the skills which you are required to show in the examination and they need to be practised if they are to be developed by you.

So, what this text does is to describe, in a structured way, the debates and arguments going on in the various substantive areas of sociology. The main focuses of the text are:

1 recent and contemporary developments in sociology;
2 the relevance of sociology for individuals' everyday lives;
3 the experiences of various social groups in the contemporary world, especially those based on class, gender, ethnicity and age;
4 the social policy implications of sociology and sociology's response to policy developments.

Each chapter begins by providing a summary of the major areas that will be covered within it. Also, at the beginning of each chapter, your attention is drawn to some of the sources of information appropriate for the subject being covered. You will be expected to have studied and taken notes on at least one of these sources before you attempt any of the exercises designed to increase your sociological skills. You should also use the notes your teacher will have given you about the subject.

At strategic points in the text, you will find activities and exercises contained in boxes. These are designed to develop the sociological skills which are required for the AEB examination and are set out below.

Knowledge and understanding

You will have to show that you are familiar with and understand sociological concepts, empirical studies and approaches, and the main arguments of sociological debates. The important task here is to be accurate in the details of work you reproduce.

Interpretation and application

You need to show that you can interpret material correctly in a variety of forms. This may include graphical and numerical formats as well as different types of text. For example, with statistical information you might be asked to identify a particular percentage, perform a simple calculation, or work out the trends in a graph. You must also be able to apply sociological information in relevant ways to a set question. For example, this might include drawing on ideas, explanations and arguments from other areas of the syllabus and applying them to a particular question. Or it could involve using relevant examples to illustrate a point. The important task here is to select appropriate studies, or key points from them, and use them in ways which are directly relevant to the question asked.

Evaluation

You need to show that you can make balanced judgements about sociological issues and debates. This will include setting out the arguments and evidence both for and against particular points of view and coming to a conclusion about them. The important task here is to make sure that your assessment emerges from a balanced consideration of different points of view about an issue and can be supported by the evidence and arguments you have included. Evaluation should also be contained in a distinct section of any examination answer.

To develop these skills, you will need to practise them. The activities which are contained within boxes in the text are designed to give you that practice and to assist you in recognising which skill is being developed. Look for the appropriate symbol in the box.

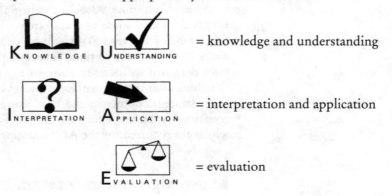

KNOWLEDGE UNDERSTANDING = knowledge and understanding

INTERPRETATION APPLICATION = interpretation and application

EVALUATION = evaluation

At times you will find that interpretation is separated out from application and only the appropriate half of the symbol will appear.

You will also find practice questions so that you can try out the skills you have developed in an examination context. There are also longer exercises to help you develop your skills further. You may need to ask your teacher to look at your answers or reports and perhaps to mark them for you. There are also coursework suggestions in each chapter but, adhering to the spirit of the book, they do not tell you how to do the projects. Rather, they suggest certain areas of interest and give pointers for you to think about when planning your research.

There is also a key concepts feature in each chapter to draw your attention to the sociological ideas you should be able to use. Each of the key concepts sections has an activity attached to check your understanding of them. Chapter by chapter, these key concepts build up into a glossary of important sociological terms. You might find it useful to record these on a card-index system, as arranging the concepts alphabetically will help you to remember them. A section at the end of each chapter points out some of the features of the area which are worth remembering and applying when answering questions in the examination. These include common misunderstandings which candidates in the examination often include in their answers.

Some general points in using this book

1 Look on this book as providing a two-year course. Do not try to do everything at once but build up your skills gradually. You can do this either by doing the boxed exercises after completing a topic or by picking out, for example, all the evaluation exercises from areas you have covered. Practise your skill of evaluation especially, for this is often the most difficult to apply. Be prepared to make judgements on the basis of evidence.

2 Do not just learn huge chunks of your textbook or notes in the hope that by reproducing them in an exam you will somehow get a good grade, but use them to develop your skills of interpretation and application.

3 Take some responsibility for your learning and for honing your skills yourself. You will still need to know sociological material, but it is best if you know it in an active not passive way.

4 Know the arguments and debates both from the past and the present in sociology, and have some supporting evidence, in the shape of relevant studies, ready to use.

5 This book gives you references for a number of the major textbooks and also for the *Social Studies Review* and the *Sociology Review,* which should be available in your school or college library. (Full details of all referenced articles appear on pages 337–8.) However, if you do not have access to these, you can refer to your notes or any other text you have, using the index appropriately.

6 Use the sections on key concepts as a check list of the terms you need to know to be able to perform well. If you do not know the concepts, or cannot do the tasks associated with them, take steps to find out their meanings and how sociologists apply them.

Acknowledgements

The author and the publishers are grateful to all copyright-holders who have granted permission for the reproduction of their material in this book.

Throughout this book there are a number of extracts from the *Guardian* which have been reproduced by kind permission. Readers are advised that, in many instances, these extracts appear in an abridged form only and so may not fully reflect the views of the writer. For the full original texts, readers are referred to the *Guardian*.

CHAPTER 1

Theory and method

In this chapter we will examine the arguments surrounding:

1 the discipline of sociology;
2 the claims of science;
3 sociology and science;
4 the anti-positivists;
5 science and the real world.

Before you begin any of the exercises you should have studied and should be familiar with at least one of the following texts:

Bilton, T., Bonnett, K., Jones, P., Stanworth, M., Sheard, K. and Webster, A. *Introductory Sociology*, 2nd edn, (Macmillan 1987), chapters 1, 12 and 13.
Giddens, A. *Sociology* (Polity 1989), chapters 1, 21 and 22.
Haralambos, M. and Holborn, M. *Sociology: Themes and Perspectives*, 3rd edn (Collins Educational 1990), chapters 1, 12 and 13.
McNeill, P. *Research Methods* (Routledge 1990).
O'Donnell, M. *A New Introduction to Sociology*, 3rd edn (Nelson 1992), chapters 1, 2 and 22.

In addition, you should have your notes on theory and method in good order.

Introduction

Sociology is one of a group of disciplines, known as the social sciences, which have emerged to become a central part of the post-16 curriculum in education. Along with the other social sciences such as economics, politics and psychology, sociology grew tremendously during the 1970s and 1980s and attained a position where it is now one of the major subjects for students outside the national curriculum. Its influence extends beyond the social sciences into such subjects as geography and history among many others, and, in its turn, it has been influenced by them, so that the traditional boundaries between these subjects are often crossed. Yet, in the 1960s, sociology had hardly been heard of in schools

APPLICATION

You will be required to show certain skills in the examination and it is, therefore, important that you develop them by practising. To do this, you should carry out the exercises in the boxes, taking note of which skill you are employing by identifying the logo attached to it. For example, in the following exercise, you will be applying your knowledge of different subjects through categorising them appropriately and providing a reason for your decisions.

Different types of academic subject		
Arts	**Social science**	**Natural science**
History	Sociology	Biology
Geography	Psychology	Physics
English literature	Economics	Chemistry

In which column, would you place the following subjects?
Religious knowledge, Geology, Anthropology, Astronomy, Mathematics, Technology, Law.
Justify your choices by writing down your reasons for each decision.

and was often greeted with mistrust and suspicion. However, the sociological enterprise goes back much further than the 1960s and has a long and honourable history.

1   The discipline of sociology

The emergence of sociology as a distinctive academic discipline occurred in the nineteenth century, although individuals have always thought about the nature of the society in which they live. What was distinctive about nineteenth-century sociology was its claim that it could scientifically analyse society's institutions and structures and the relationships of individuals in groups which made up that society.

Early disagreements

But from the very beginning of modern sociology, differences emerged over the proper focus of sociological investigation and the type of science that sociologists were pursuing. The first area of difference concerned the

One of the ways that you can develop your skills is by summarising important issues in a particular way. For example, the following exercise asks you to interpret reading you have done and to apply it in a specific way.

From your reading, contrast structural and interactionist theories, point by point, in two columns. You might begin for example like this:

Differences between structural and interactionist theories	
Structural	**Interactionist**
1 Examines collectives	1 Examines individuals
2 Stresses numerical data	2 Stresses qualitative data
3 etc.	3 etc.

level of analysis which should be attempted: the level of society or the level of the individual. Some sociologists argued that it was collective phenomena of social structures and institutions such as the family, the education system and economic activity, which sociologists should be investigating. Others argued that sociologists should begin with individual intentions and actions, and the individual's relationships with other people.

Another difference concerned the basic nature of society and how it should be looked at. Some suggested that the basic characteristics of society were its stability and the fact that individuals, by and large, worked together peacefully in an integrated way to achieve their goals. Alternatively, some argued that the major feature of society which sociologists should focus on was the conflict between groups within society, as this was the major means by which societies change and progress.

For this exercise, you will need to have access to *Social Studies Review*, vol. 4, no. 5, pp. 195–7. (See [1], p. 337.)

1 Summarise the ideas of Giddens presented in the article.
2 Provide an alternative example to the family (to show your skills of application).

Evaluation is about judgement and you need to practise this by doing such activities as deciding which are the most important points about an issue. In this exercise you will be asked to interpret and evaluate some perspectives.

1 From your reading decide which are the three most important points about functionalism, Marxism and interactionism. Record your points in three columns appropriately labelled:

Three perspectives		
Interactionist	**Marxist**	**Functionalist**
1	1	1
2	2	2
3	3	3

One way of evaluating a perspective is to compare it to real life and see if it accords with your experience and understanding of social reality.

2 From your reading choose one perspective and highlight the points which convince you that the perspective is useful in explaining social reality. For example, if you choose interactionism, you might be convinced by it because, among other things, it always begins from the experiences of individual people.

Another area of dispute concerned the depth at which sociologists should pitch their investigations. Some argued that it was important to probe beneath the surface of events to gain their true or underlying nature. This idea of a basic structure to society suggests that individuals have few real choices or decisions to make and that their actions are the product of an underlying structure of society or logic of ideas. Others suggested that there is no underlying logic to the social world, but only the surface level at which events happen. This surface world is chaotic and meaningless and individuals can try to make sense of it through imposing an order upon it. Sociology itself is one of the 'discourses' we use to try and make sense of the kaleidoscopic world. (See Coursework Suggestion 1.1 on p. 35.)

Modern variations

These differences still exist among sociologists but it is important to notice that they are not hard-and-fast distinctions. Very few sociologists can be fitted easily into any one of these positions. Indeed, individual sociologists may draw upon any combination of these traditions for their

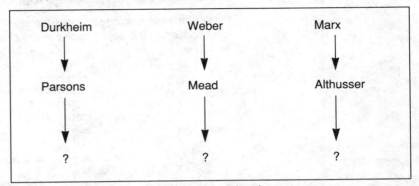

For this exercise you need to interpret the traditions suggested in the table and apply the correct perspective.

Where would you place conflict theory, action theory, consensus theory?

You can begin to practise evaluation by suggesting what problems there may be with this type of exercise. For example, you might explore the suggestion that the model of the perspectives presents far too neat a version of what sociology is really like.

From your reading you should be able to extract the basic information for this exercise.

Using two columns, juxtapose the differences between positivism and interactionism. The first points are done for you.

Differences between positivism and interactionism	
Positivism	**Interactionism**
1 Uses laboratory methods where possible	1 Uses observational methods where possible
2 etc.	2 etc.

work. They may also change their views over the course of their careers, in response to new events and investigations. This happens because sociologists are human beings and are difficult to categorise in any systematic way precisely because they are involved in the social process of investigating society.

To practise the skill of application you need to take things that you know and use them in new and unfamiliar circumstances. That is, you need to think how to utilize your knowledge relevantly.

Place ethnomethodology, symbolic interactionism, Marxism and functionalism in the appropriate corners of the following diagram.

1

Society
Structure
Erklaren

2

Radical
Change

Conservative
Order

Conflict

Integration

Verstehen
Action
Individual

3

4

In terms of how to investigate social behaviour scientifically, some sociologists argued for a purely objective approach, concentrating on *social facts* – the description of society as a collective 'thing' with an independent existence apart from the individuals composing it. They supported this by reference to the fact that individuals are 'born into' a society and, when they die, society continues without them. Others

For this exercise, you will need access to *Social Studies Review*, vol. 4, no. 2, pp. 68–71. (See [2], p. 337.)

1 From the article, identify the problems which sociologists have in applying science to the social world. It might help if you divide the problems into 'theoretical', 'practical' and 'moral', but do not assume you will address all three.
2 You will need to go further in the examination and also assess issues. So, write a paragraph on whether these problems mean that sociology cannot be a science.

argued that this was to 'reify' society, making something which exists only in people's minds into a real thing with a life of its own

Contrarily, others suggested that the science of society needed to investigate the motives of individuals, as well as their objective behaviour, through the practice of empathy or *Verstehen*, so that sociology would be 'adequate at the level of meaning'. (*Verstehen* can be defined as the process of putting yourself into someone else's shoes to see the world as they see and experience it.) Others have more recently suggested that, in the postmodern world, there can be no certainty of knowledge, no absolute science in a world where the image is more important than the reality.

The importance of science

However, any consideration of the relationship between sociological theory and sociological method must begin with the word 'science'. 'Science' literally means knowledge but we use it in more commonly to mean the 'natural sciences' of chemistry, physics and biology. These are the disciplines which seek to describe, understand and explain the natural world in a systematic and logical manner (theory) and by adopting specific techniques and procedures (method). Science developed over a long period of time as an attempt to provide rational and objective explanations of phenomena, either in nature (the formation of rocks, the growth of plants or the operation of the human body, etc.) or in society (the formation of individuals' minds, the growth of collectivities like the 'nation', the operation of organisations and so on).

Science is therefore an attempt to create knowledge which we can trust because we know for certain that it is true in all circumstances and at all times. By 'knowing something for certain', we can then predict the future accurately. For example, if, by following the scientific method, we can know for certain that a particular drug always successfully treats a particular disease, we can control the effects of that disease and change the future. Before the drug was developed the disease would, presumably, have run its course. Now, with this discovery, we can alter this chain of events. Thus, science is a powerful weapon for influencing what happens in the world. This is why governments and industrial firms employ large numbers of both natural and social scientists in research and development or in industrial relations and other capacities. It is this potential relationship between sociology and social policy which, in part, accounts for the growth of sociology over the past century.

However, if science is easily capable of producing 'knowledge for certain', we could solve all the social and economic problems which face societies and look forward to a 'golden age' of prosperity and peace. Clearly, our experience tells us that science cannot 'deliver the goods' in all areas. And yet, many of the great and undoubted advances made in the modern world – clean water, electricity, prevention of disease – are claimed to be the outcome of the use of the 'scientific method'.

EXERCISE

Poll tax may be key to census shortfall

The population of England and Wales has fallen for the first time since the modern census began in 1801, if preliminary results of the 1991 survey are to be believed.

However, the apparent failure to count some million people means the figures will be revised upwards to produce a growth figure more accurately reflecting the trend known from birth, death and migration statistics.

The words "poll tax" or "community charge" do not once appear in the report, but there can be little doubt that fears that census data would be used to track down defaulters were a principal cause of non-cooperation.

Strenuous efforts were made to reassure people that such fears were groundless. But Peter Wormald, the Registrar General, admitted at a press conference in April: "A lot of people are worried that census returns will be used to monitor community charge registrations . . ."

Before the count on April 21, however, he said he was looking for a response rate at least as good as the 99.5 per cent achieved in 1981 – a target he now accepts is out of reach in view of the failure to make contact with 130,000 households . . . He wrote, "The success of the census depends very much on the willingness of the public to complete the form . . . We encountered greater difficulty than in 1981 in contacting some householders, particularly in inner cities. Several measures were taken to tackle the problem, including leaving a pre-paid envelope to return to the local census office."

Although the under-counting will present awkward problems in producing precise population figures for some areas, the general trends shown by the preliminary results will hold good.

(Source: adapted from the *Guardian*, Tuesday 23 July 1991)

Newspaper reports often provide a valuable source of information for A level students, but they also provide an opportunity for students to develop their skills of interpretation and application, and can help students to evaluate sociological issues. Application can take a variety of forms.

Firstly, you can apply information such as that contained in the *Guardian* report to methodological issues.

APPLICATION

1 What are the implications of this information for the compilation of the electoral register?
2 Write a report on the implications of the information above for the reliability and validity of official statistics of population. In your report you should provide detailed evidence for the points you make and include references to:
   a) why death, birth and migration statistics are used by sociologists;
   b) what measures the collectors take to achieve reliability;
   c) the importance of the response rate;

d) whether the census can be seen as valid and reliable at all – that is, you should provide an evaluation of the census. This evaluation should identify the strengths and weaknesses of census procedures and census information, and come to a conclusion as to how valid or reliable it is.

Secondly, you can apply knowledge from other areas of sociology to specific issues, such as those identified in the *Guardian* article.

3 Which social groups are likely to be under-represented in the electoral register and why?

Thirdly, you can apply sociological insight to other areas of social life.

4 What might the political implications be of the information in the *Guardian* article?

2 The claims of science

So, on what basis does science claim to be superior to other forms of knowledge like common-sense or theological (religious) knowledge? The problem with these other two forms of knowledge is that they are based on the individual's perceptions and beliefs. I may believe that the earth is flat (which was common knowledge – something everybody 'knew' – at one time), or that the earth was created by God at some point in time (theological knowledge), but these are partial and subjective viewpoints.

Sociology needs to look at issues in the real world if it is to be relevant.

So in two columns, list four major advances made by 'science' since the Second World War and the problems which have been associated with them.

Progress and pitfalls of science since 1945	
Scientific advance	**Associated problems**
1	
2	
3	
4	

APPLICATION

For each of the following 'routes to truth', provide an explanation and example. Some have been completed already to assist you in the task.

'Routes to truth'		
Type of knowledge	**Explanation**	**Example**
Intuition		Hunch
Common sense		
Tradition		
Theology	Is given by God	
Science		

There is no evidence which I, the believer, can present to you, the unbeliever, to prove what I believe. All I can offer is my faith that it is so. The problem then is: how can I convince other people that what I believe to be true is not just subjective faith but is the objective truth of the matter?

The positivists

Positivists are people who believe that science, and science alone, can provide unbiased knowledge which is generalisable (it is true in many situations, not just in one specific case) and problem-solving. The aim of positivism is, thus, to produce scientific 'laws' about any phenomena, natural or social – laws which accurately describe the causes, functioning and consequences of phenomena.

How are such laws developed? Over the centuries, although positivism has taken different forms, it has usually been associated with a 'model' approach to research. That is to say, it has provided guidelines

It is also important that you use material from non-sociological sources and apply it to your understanding of sociology. Newspapers, in particular, are a rich source of examples which might be applied to sociological accounts.

So, look for newspaper accounts of scientific advances and answer the following points.

INTERPRETATION

1 What areas of research do the newspaper reports concentrate on?

EVALUATION

2 Give reasons why this may be so.

APPLICATION

3 How might the inclusion or exclusion of types of scientific research affect our views of what science is about?

on the way scientists are supposed to carry out their work. This model approach involves the following:

1 a certain logical procedure;
2 the use of a specific technique;
3 the adoption of a particular position towards the subject matter under study.

The procedure

Although this can be called many things, the procedure is usually thought of as a set of logical steps (the number and type might vary) which describe the order in which an investigation is supposed to be conducted. A typical order might be:

1 observation – a phenomenon or problem is observed to exist and deemed to need explanation;
2 hypothesis – a possible explanation is put forward;
3 experiment – that hypothesis is subjected to testing to see if it can be proved;
4 theorising – if confirmed by the experiment, a law is created which explains all identical phenomena or problems.

The technique

In the testing of hypotheses, the laboratory experiment is the preferred technique of the positivist. The reasons for this are complicated but they boil down to two essential points. Firstly, a laboratory is a controlled environment, in which all factors that might affect or cause a phenomenon

It is also legitimate to apply your own experiences to support substantive sociological points.

Write a paragraph on your own experiences in the chemistry, biology or physics laboratory which illustrates the problems of keeping experiments controlled. This may give you some insight into the problems of conducting controlled experiments.

can be maintained constantly. Then, by altering one factor (and one factor only) and comparing the consequences with an identical, unaltered phenomenon, the scientist can establish what effects are caused by that variable. For example, if a block of ice is kept in a controlled environment and heat is applied, the scientist can deduce that increasing the temperature of ice turns it into water because nothing else has happened which might explain the change of state. Further controlled experiments may determine the exact temperature at which the change occurs.

The second, and crucial, reason why positivists prefer the laboratory experiment is that such experiments may be replicated – that is, repeated under exactly the same controlled conditions. If the results obtained are identical this satisfies the criterion of convincing other scientists of the 'truth' of whatever knowledge is produced.

The position

Positivists believe that only by adopting a position of total objectivity towards the subject matter or phenomena can unbiased knowledge or theories be produced. This detachment is necessary to prevent 'contamination' by subjective influences such as emotions, preconceived ideas, prejudices or even dishonesty. Thus, the typical scientist is the dispassionate, white-coated individual, whose only motivation is the search for truth. Neither institution nor personal consideration, neither threat nor bribe, can deflect this exemplary person from the quest for objective knowledge.

Thus, adopting a positivist position towards the search for knowledge implies a certain type of methodology. But the social sciences will clearly have difficulty in putting such ideas into practice if only because, unlike the rocks, plants and animals of the natural sciences, the subject matter of the social sciences – human beings – think. This awareness, or conscious-

Sociologists often challenge this view of the scientist. List four reasons why scientists may not be as dispassionate as presented in the above paragraph.

Notice that you have to interpret the view before you can apply your knowledge to it.

From your reading, identify the similarities and differences between laboratory experiments and field experiments. The first points have been done for you.

Similarities and differences between field and laboratory experiments		
	Laboratory experiments	**Field experiments**
Similarities	1 Changes a variable	1 Changes normality
Differences		

Note that although this will provide you with the basis for an evaluation, you have not been asked to evaluate.

ness, about what is happening to them makes human beings extremely difficult to control. Sociologists cannot, for moral or practical reasons, carry out laboratory experiments very easily. Nor, given that sociologists are also human, can they divorce themselves from the people or from the issues they are studying. It is not easy to be detached from the 'family' when you have been brought up in one or are living in one on an everyday basis.

These difficulties have led some sociologists to question whether it is possible to adopt positivistic procedures or methods, and others to suggest that the subject matter of sociology is so very different from the natural sciences that it is not desirable to follow them at all. The former hold that a full 'science of society' must also explain the subjective motivations of people through the non-positivistic approach of *Verstehen*. They argue that no scientific approach could be established which would adequately explain the social world.

A good way of interpreting information is to condense it to an appropriate form.
So, from your reading, summarise Weber's distinctive contribution to the debate over whether sociology can be a science or not, in no more than 150 words.

STRUCTURED QUESTION

This information is taken from the *Guardian* but it can be applied to sociological debate. Answer this question. What are the implications of the information in this item for the idea that sociology is a science?

APPLICATION

Item A

Social science comes out fighting

Is the retreat of social science at an end? For more than a decade, social scientists have been on the defensive. But yesterday, a social scientist, Sir Claus Moser, presided over the most prestigious gathering of the nation's scientists – both natural and social – at the annual meeting of the British Association . . .

There was nothing apologetic about Sir Claus's speech. He robustly condemned the ministerial removal of the word "science" from the Social Science Research Council's title, criticised the tiny proportion (5 per cent) which social science receives from research council money, and pointed to the growing links between the natural and social sciences. He had no problem justifying the term "science": a search for truth, not a particular set of methods. Unlike in natural science, there were no certain constants, like the speed of light, but social science shared with natural science the same quest for discovery and understanding, the same dependence on empirical data, the same attempt to measure, seek causal findings and make predictions.

(Source: adapted from an editorial in the *Guardian*, Tuesday 21 August 1990)

Item B

The 1991 census
The date of the census:
Sunday 21 April 1991

Application does not necessarily need long answers. For example: why are these 'topics', like sex, date of birth, etc., sometimes called 'variables' by sociologist?

APPLICATION

The census is designed to collect information from each household about each person who lives there. By law, people have to supply the required information. However, the purpose of the census is not to produce data about individuals so much as statistical facts about the community, and groups within the community, as a whole. It is against the law to disclose facts about individuals or single households on the basis of data collected through the census.

The topics covered by the 1991 census include for each person: sex, date of birth, marital status, country of birth, ethnic group, address a year ago and extent of any long-term illness suffered by residents.

(Source: adapted from *Sociology Update*, 1991)

Item C

Interactionists have been critical of social surveys precisely because they concentrate on statistics and ignore the individual. They argue that statistics are not 'facts' but are socially created through a process of negotiation by individuals. It is, thus, the individual, in relationship to other people, who should be the focus of sociological research, through the adoption of 'non-scientific' techniques. Statistics are, therefore, seen by interactionists not to provide a valid description of social life but, rather, a distortion of reality.

This part is asking you to interpret information in the item.

a) What is the 'particular type of method' (Item A, line 24) usually associated with the natural sciences? (1 mark)

b) Using Item B and other information, identify the features of the census which make it a reliable survey. (4 marks)

c) Suggest TWO non-scientific techniques which might be adopted by interactionists. (2 marks)

You must refer both to Item C and other sources to maximise marks.

d) With reference to Item C and other sources, assess the interactionist critique of statistics. (9 marks)

e) To what extent do sociologists agree with Sir Claus Moser's view of the relationship between social and natural science (Item A)? (9 marks)

Objectivity in the natural sciences

However, many natural scientists have themselves dismissed the idea that research into chemistry, physics, biology, etc. is carried out in the way that the positivists suggest. It has been pointed out that the detachment demanded by this model of inquiry is difficult to achieve even where the subject matter is *not* human.

The problem is that natural scientists are also human beings, usually carrying out their work within social organisations, and subject to much the same social and economic forces that all members of organisations

Your reading in sociology should be focused, i.e. it should be geared to answering particular questions or to looking for evidence surrounding debates or issues.

For example, if you read Haralambos and Holborn, pp. 756–61, you can practise your skills by answering the following questions:

APPLICATION

1 What are the implications of the information in the extract for the idea that natural science is objective?

EVALUATION

2 Which point do you find most convincing and why?

It is important that you know what sociologists have written, accurately and with relevant detail. So, for each of the following, find out the major point each has made concerning natural science: Popper, Kaplan, Kuhn, Hessen, Knorr-Cetina, Albury and Swartz.

experience. The product of their work, their knowledge, is, therefore, socially constructed and not obvious or natural. For example, natural scientists are concerned with their own status and career prospects which may depend on successful publications or achievements.

The history of science is littered with premature publication, the discarding of 'inconvenient' results and also downright cheating! The direction of research may be determined by the institutions providing the funding for research; they will certainly influence the questions which the natural scientists ask in their research. The institutions of the nation-state fashion the shape of all scientific research, if only through the enormous amount of money which is channelled into the development of weapons.

Moreover, the design of laboratory experiments and the interpretation of results are not objective processes but involve great imagination, human ingenuity, hunches and a good deal of luck. The development of penicillin illustrates the role of fortune in scientific progress. Scientists are members of a scientific community which not only scrutinises the individual's work but also helps to determine which questions are asked in the first place.

Indeed, most scientific work seems not to follow the strict procedure laid down by the positivist model. A number of the natural sciences, such as astronomy, are not conducted in the controlled environment of the laboratory but are based almost entirely on observation and calculation. Also, even in the natural sciences, conflicting theories are often put forward by scientists to explain a particular phenomenon. This is because the 'truth' is not always obvious or easily discovered by slavishly following the rules of the positivist.

Some of the conventions of sociological usage will be new to you. For example, do you know how to apply concepts from a non-English source correctly in your answers?

Write a sentence which correctly employs the word *Lebenswelt* in it.

If you do not know how to do this, where can you find out?

3 Sociology and science

If neither the social nor natural sciences measure up to positivistic standards in the search for 'truth', are they equally non-scientific? The social and the natural sciences have more similarities than is often recognised. Both have problems with objectivity, competing perspectives and replication, though natural scientists tend to agree on much more than sociologists do. However, the ideas of positivism represent how research would be carried out in a 'perfect' world. Positivism is a model, or ideal, which researchers strive to achieve with varying degrees of success.

The natural sciences, by and large, come closer to achieving the demands laid down by positivism, largely because their subject matter is more manageable than the awkward, contrary and illogical human beings which sociologists must deal with. But the model remains as a measuring rod for the conduct of research against which the methods and procedures of sociology may be compared. Science, therefore, influences how sociological research is seen and it is in the context of the positivistic model that the relationship between theories and methods in sociology must be understood.

Often, perspectives have groups of characteristics which go together. In the following diagram, you need to apply your knowledge of perspectives to a categorisation exercise.

	Structure	Action
Society		
Characterised by		
Primary data		
Secondary data		
Characteristic of method		
Stress on		

APPLICATION

Fill in the cells of the diagram above with the appropriate response: objectivity, external to the individual, observation, surveys, quantitative, validity, reliability, qualitative, diaries, created by individuals, statistics, subjectivity.

Information is often easier to understand if presented in diagrammatic form. Creating diagrams also helps you to practise the skill of application.

From your reading produce a diagram which illustrates the three main sociological perspectives and their associated variations.

Two broad positions

It is generally recognised that there are two broad theoretical outlooks in sociology with regard to science. For the sake of convenience, sociologists tend to refer to supporters of the scientific position as positivists and opponents as anti-positivists, although there are many different names for them. Functionalists are viewed as somehow associated with the positivists' position and the interactionists with the anti-positivists' position. Marxists are usually ignored in this debate or assumed to be 'scientific' but in a different, and often unspecified, way from the functionalists. The world, of course, is never as straightforward as this, but these two broad positions will be looked at to see how they affect the methods that sociologists adopt.

The positivist method

For the sociological positivist, the methods and techniques applied in research should preferably exhibit certain crucial features. They must be objective, are possibly quantitative (involving numbers or statistics), and must be replicable and under the control of the researcher. They should satisfy the criteria for reliability. This means that the method of collection of the data is systematic and standardised so that, regardless of who actually collects it, the same findings would always emerge. The findings produced using any method should also be generalisable so that laws, even if only partial laws, can be established.

To satisfy these criteria positivists have suggested a variety of strategies and techniques. When looking at secondary data (the massive amount of raw material which organisations in society produce and which makes a source of information for sociologists), positivists tend to emphasise official documentation and statistics as the most reliable. For example, they might point to statistics on deaths as 'hard' data – that is, data in which there is little opportunity for error or subjectivity to affect the

Evaluation has to be done directly, and one way to achieve this is by asking yourself direct questions. To practise this, answer the following question in a paragraph.

How far can social phenomena be represented quantifiably?

Some concepts are basic to a particular topic, so you need to know clearly what they mean. For example, what do sociologists mean by validity?

The first step towards evaluation is often to examine the strengths and weaknesses of a phenomenon, before going on to assess it. So, begin by making a list of the points in favour of, and a list of the points against, the use of official statistics by sociologists.

truth of the information. As there is a legal requirement to record deaths, the positivists argue that such data fulfil the conditions for qualification as scientific information.

By using statistics to compare social groups, countries or individuals (the comparative method), sociological positivists can claim to be following the logic of the laboratory technique in which the experimental group (where one variable is changed) is compared to a control group (where nothing is changed) in order to identify differences between the groups and thus establish 'causes'. (See Coursework Suggestion 1.2 on p. 35.)

As regards primary data (information which sociologists have collected themselves), various possibilities are open to positivists. Because its use emulates the natural sciences, the controlled laboratory experiment remains attractive. It seems to fulfil all the criteria laid down by the positivistic model and has the added advantage that it gives sociologists the appearance of being scientific, right down to the white laboratory coat, if desired. However, there are limits to what can be investigated in the sociological laboratory, and positivists have turned instead to techniques and strategies like the social survey, which also offer the promise of quantifiability, objectivity, etc. What these approaches have in common is standardised questioning in which responses may be reduced to numbers or types of answers, to be codified and, finally, analysed by computers.

From your reading identify the difficulties there might be in using the comparative method. This will help your skill of interpretation.

You need to be able to apply examples to support points made. To this end, discover an example of where a sociologist has used laboratory experiments.

From your reading you will need to interpret information correctly and know its proper uses. So, consider the following:

For each type of sampling, identify when it may be used by sociologists most effectively.

You need to know the basic concepts of sociology so that you can use them appropriately. Therefore, what do sociologists mean by 'population', 'sampling frame' and 'sampling unit' in survey work?

Formal, or structured, interviews and questionnaires of various sorts constitute the bulk of positivist-type research techniques. They are argued to be objective in so far as the presence of the researcher should not influence the answers that respondents give. They are replicable in that other researchers should be able to carry out the same question-naire schedule with the same respondents to produce the same results. They are generalisable as long as appropriate sampling techniques are used to gather a group of respondents who are representative, or typical, of the 'population' the sociologist is interested in. These, then, are reli-able techniques, used by social scientists to uncover information about the social world in a systematic and unbiased manner.

Critique of the positivist method

However, the positivists have been challenged over their methods and techniques on a variety of grounds. Most importantly, they have been criticised because such strategies do not measure up to the criteria of objectivity. This is not because they are bad techniques but simply because no technique can be completely unbiased. It has been pointed out, for example, that official statistics are the product of social processes of negotiation and construction in which people decide whether to include or exclude any particular event in the statistics. They also decide into what category any recorded event should fall.

It has been shown that, whatever the formal rules are for standardised procedure, common-sense judgements (or rules of thumb) are always employed by compilers of statistics, and different compilers apply differ-ent criteria, according to their experience, preconceptions, beliefs, etc.

Similarly, information from questionnaires may be expressed in a quantitative form, but it is made up from answers to questions which the sociologist, and not the respondent, believes to be important. Researchers are, therefore, imposing their *frame of reference* or 'under-standing' onto the respondent. This, necessarily, is a subjective influence.

Interviewers, by their manner and body language, may prompt a par-ticular response in a face-to-face interview. Alternatively, interviewees

As well as using the 'listing technique', evaluation needs to be explicit in a separate paragraph. From your reading on questionnaires:

1 list the advantages and disadvantages of them;
2 come to a conclusion as to whether or not sociologists should use them.

may be antagonistic towards interviewers for no reason other than, say, a dislike of the clothes they are wearing.

Thus, subjectivity is an inevitable part of any social interaction, including that involved in interviews, experiments and questionnaires, which techniques are, in any case, not easily replicable. When separate opinion polls offer very different pictures of voting intentions, it is not enough to explain away such differences by reference to sampling procedures and errors, slight differences in wording or huge shifts of opinions in very short spaces of time. We must also accept that respondents may lie or evade the question in varying proportions, at varying times, depending on a whole range of factors which cannot be controlled (the weather, respondents being in a hurry or tired of being hounded by opinion pollsters, and so on).

In the case of laboratory experiments, ethical doubts have been raised about the morality of subjecting people to controlled experiments, especially if they are unaware of the real nature of the experiment. But more damaging, in the eyes of the anti-positivist, is the sheer artificiality of the laboratory experiment. The critics of the experiment argue that it is not possible to generalise from the closed world of the laboratory to the rich, varied and uncontrollable real world outside. The presence of the subjects in a laboratory guarantees that they will not be acting in a normal manner or as they would in their home environment. It is this concern with naturalness which is at the heart of the anti-positivists' choice of method and technique.

You will need to interpret information from non-sociological sources and apply it to a sociological context.

So, from any newspaper report of an opinion poll, note down the sampling error and use it to explain, in one paragraph, the importance of sampling error in sociological research.

You need to practise supporting your views with appropriate arguments and evidence. Your reading will suggest that there are problems with laboratory experiments.

Does this mean that they are useless in investigating society? Construct an argument to support your viewpoint.

STRUCTURED QUESTION

You need to think about the information given in the items. For example, why do you think the Youth Track Survey picked these locations?

INTERPRETATION

Item A

A survey published today says that schoolchildren would back Labour or the Greens rather than the Tories if given the vote, and that *Neighbours* is their favourite TV show and the *Sun* their favourite newspaper. Eight to 18-year-olds embrace their parents' values and are dominated by ideas received from the media, which feed them role models unlikely to breed discontent.

The Youth Track Survey, by the research company Young Direction, was based on 2,074 questionnaires from pupils at primary and secondary schools and sixth form colleges in Glasgow, Manchester, Birmingham, London and the Southeast between March and May . . .

The punk nihilist philosophy of the late 1970s and early 1980s has been replaced by a determination to succeed in respectable professions such as computing, finance, teaching and nursing. But these ambitions are strictly gender-defined: the boys see themselves in business, the girls in service.

(Source: adapted from David Sharrock, "Pupils go for Labour, Sun and Neighbours", the *Guardian*, Tuesday 21 August 1990)

Other questions you can ask yourself have a different skill attached to them. For example: how might Sylvia Langham's gender have affected her research?

APPLICATION

Item B

My own research was based on interviews carried out with 16 women police constables with experience ranging from 11 months to over 10 years, aged between 21 and 37 years.

These women were all too aware of the difficulties which they face in working in a 'man's world'. However, they showed remarkable optimism about their own future promotion prospects.

One woman officer said that she thought a change in policy a few years ago had improved women's chances of promotion, at least to sergeant and inspector level. She said, 'All of a sudden, in the last few years, there's a big thing about getting women more prominent, [having] senior women officers. I've been told if I take my promotion exam, and pass it, I'd be promoted straight away.'

(Source: Sylvia Langham, Research Roundup, *Social Studies Review*, vol. 6, no. 5)

Item C

Simon Holdaway decided to study his own colleagues in an attempt to show the way that the police force really operates. However, as other policemen so strongly objected to his research, he had to do it in secret. He says, 'I found I was fortunate because I was in a unique position in carrying out research: before I studied sociology, and during the course of undergraduate and graduate work, I was a police officer.'

(Source: adapted from Stephen Moore, *Sociology Alive,* Stanley Thornes 1987)

EVALUATION

'Relative' merits means that you must directly compare and contrast the two techniques and evaluate them.

You need to apply the information from the items and anywhere else to the issue of researchers' choice of technique. For example, what does the last paragraph in Item C suggest is an important reason?

APPLICATION

a) Look at Item A. Suggest two reasons why the survey might not be representative of all eight- to 18-year-olds in Great Britain.   (2 marks)

b) With reference to Item C, what do sociologists call the methodological technique employed by Holdaway?   (1 mark)

c) Assess the relative merits of the techniques adopted in Items B and C in investigating the police force.   (8 marks)

d) To what extent can questionnaires such as the one in Item A produce valid information?   (6 marks)

e) Using information in the items and elsewhere, discuss the reasons why researchers choose the techniques they do.   (8 marks)

4 The anti-positivists

In rejecting scientific procedures and methods, anti-positivists argue not only that positivistic methods fail to find out the truth about people's actions and beliefs but also that they actually obscure what needs to be examined. Because positivists insist on objectivity they reject all subjective explanations of individuals' behaviour, even when it is the individuals themselves who are offering them.

The subjective dimension

Anti-positivists suggest that it is precisely because the sociological subject matter has consciousness and free will that the subjective dimension must be explored and explained if sociology is to achieve a full understanding of the social world. When individuals act, or behave in certain

INTERPRETATION

EVALUATION

For this exercise you will need to read *Social Studies Review*, vol. 3, no. 5, pp. 190–3. (See [3], p. 337.)

1 What do sociologists mean by ethnography?

2 To begin to evaluate ethnography you should compare it to other sociological approaches. What advantages does this approach have over others?

Some ideas are basic to an understanding of sociology and you therefore have to know them. So, write a paragraph on what Weber meant by his phrase 'adequate at the level of meaning'.

ways, they also have motivations and intentions which accompany or inspire those actions. Behaviour is neither random nor totally intuitive but may be planned or thought out beforehand so that people try to achieve their ends by taking what they see to be appropriate action. Anti-positivists argue that sociology must necessarily investigate these motivations and intentions if it is to be *adequate at the level of meaning* as well as at the level of visible behaviour.

This does not mean that the sociologist must necessarily accept an individual's own explanation of the behaviour which is being investigated. (Individuals may be lying or they may not fully understand their own intentions or motivations.) Rather, the sociologist must practise *Verstehen*. Only by 'living the natural life' can we attempt a true understanding and explanation of people's lives as they live them. How, then, in practice can this *Verstehen* be achieved?

In using secondary data, anti-positivists turn to accounts which the participants have recorded themselves, such as diaries, letters and even

One way you can begin to judge the balance of merit of anything is to set out its strengths and weaknesses.

For example, list the advantages and disadvantages of personal documents as sources of data using the format below. The first points have already been done to assist you.

Personal documents	
Advantages	**Disadvantages**
1 Records a person's own experiences	1 Are biased
2	2

You can also do this for any other methods to create a file of evaluation material. Remember, you still have to come to a conclusion about each one.

One activity you may be asked to engage in is to work out the meaning of something from its context. This is part of the skill of interpretation. So, if you can obtain access to *Social Studies Review*, vol. 6, no. 1, pp. 6–10 (see [4], p. 337), answer this question.

What do sociologists mean by 'authentic', 'credibility', 'representativeness' and 'meaning'?

novels, and they adopt a critical stance towards them. There are, of course, thousands of different 'life documents' now available to sociologists through which they may explore the cultures and subcultures of a society. While accepting that such documents are inevitably biased and subjective, they argue that, with careful handling, these documents can peel back the surface appearances of society and reveal the *Lebenswelt* – the day-to-day and minute-by-minute activities of the millions of people who make up what we call society.

As well as using primary data, the anti-positivists have adopted various observational techniques as part of their particular methodology, in addition to the informal, or unstructured, interview. There are several different types of observation available to them, depending upon the degree of participation the sociologist chooses to engage in (from total participation to none at all) and the degree of openness adopted with the subjects under study (from totally overt, or open, to entirely covert).

Any combination of these can be used because each claims to study people in their natural habitat, behaving as they normally do and expressing themselves in their usual manner. By using observational techniques, the anti-positivists argue that sociologists can experience the world as their subjects do and, therefore, produce *valid* knowledge about society. Validity refers to how *true to life* the information collected is and, thus, how far those investigated would, if they were honest with themselves, recognise the sociological account as an authentic account of their own lives.

Using a strengths and weaknesses chart like the one you did for personal documents on p. 24, move on to do a direct evaluation of participant observation by attempting the following.

In a paragraph, evaluate participant observation in describing social life. Use the following phrases in your answer:

1 so, in looking at its strengths, we can see that participant observation is useful in . . .
2 but its weaknesses suggest that there are limits to its usefulness, namely . . .
3 therefore, we can conclude that participant observation . . .

For this exercise you will need to read Haralambos and Holborn, pp. 762–4.

1 Identify four sociologists in the extract and summarise their beliefs.

2 State whether each of your chosen sociologists is in favour of objective sociology or against.

Criticisms of the anti-positivists

The positivists attack this approach for several reasons. They argue that it is so subjective, and so entirely based on the observations and interpretations of the researchers themselves, that it is little different from fictional accounts of social life found in novels or journalistic accounts in newspapers. It fails to provide a systematic and unbiased look at social life and, thus, is unlikely to convince anyone else that it is true.

Anti-positivists respond by arguing that interactionist research methods can be as systematic as the questionnaire or interview. For example, diaries can be investigated by means of a formal content analysis. Observation can be undertaken with a stopwatch and strict timings so that material can be standardised and quantified, if that is what is required. But the point is to get to the heart of the matter and not to impose false order on the real world.

Apply your knowledge of different sources of data by doing the following exercise:

Which of these are primary sources of data and which secondary?

Participant observation, diaries, videos, letters, observation, field experiments, life histories, newspapers, ethnographic study, artefacts.

Record your answers in the following form:

Types of data	
Primary data	**Secondary data**

The anti-positivists also say that the observer can be as objective as the scientist, by treating the world as anthropologically strange – as if he or she had never come into contact with society as before – and by subjecting everything to critical scrutiny. In these ways, they argue, non-positivist techniques may be made more reliable while retaining the ability to see life as it is truly lived (validity). What is interesting here is not so much whether these arguments are convincing or not, but that the debate is carried out using *scientific* criteria as the measuring rod against which different techniques must be compared.

Positivists also attack the validity of interactionist techniques. They suggest that the very presence of the observer will alter the behaviour of those being observed (the so-called *Hawthorne effect* which is, ironically, normally used as a critique of sociological experiments) and so prevent an examination of the very naturalness interactionists claim to uncover. Moreover, while the Hawthorne effect may be partially offset by hiding the sociologist's true identity, the very presence of the researcher will alter the balance of relationships within a group, thus producing a different situation from one in which the researcher is not present. Only by covert, non-participant observation can this issue be resolved but, then, only at the cost of the morally dubious position of effectively spying on people as they live out their lives.

5 Science and the real world

While the positivist – quantitative, anti-positivist – qualitative links set out the supposed relationship between theory and method, the *real world* of research does not exhibit those neat certainties. If the links were solid, positivists would always choose questionnaires and anti-positivists observation as their research methods. However, real research is often a mass of contradictions, exhibiting little logic and much opportunism. For example, there are many examples of Marxist sociologists who are highly critical of modern-day capitalism and who base their critique of society on the official statistics produced by the same capitalist state they wish to abolish. There are also functionalists who use observation, and interactionists who employ computers. Some sociologists use a variety of research methods which encompass statistical analysis, forms of observation and questionnaires, all in the same study!

EVALUATION

From your reading you will have come across a variety of reasons why sociologists choose a particular method. To evaluate the importance of any one reason, you will need to compare it to other factors. Therefore, choosing one factor in one choice of method, state how important it is compared to other reasons. State why you believe it to be more or less important than the other factors you mention.

EXERCISE

Population of regions
percentage change 1981–91

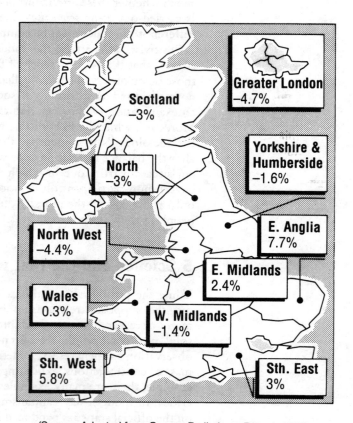

In evaluating you may be required to assess particular methods or types of data. So how accurate do you think these figures are? Give reasons for your answer.

E VALUATION

(Source: Adapted from Census Preliminary Report, 1991)

Using your skills of interpretation, describe the changes in population shown in the above map. Do not just reproduce the figures in the map but describe in your own words the regional and national changes from the figures.

Suggest reasons for the changes you identify.

The practice of sociology

So, it is not just a question of the principled positivist carefully choosing a structured questionnaire or another quantifiable research technique, or the interactionist opting for some form of observational analysis. Sociologists are human beings too, and, like natural scientists, they have career ladders, status considerations, financial limitations and peer-group pressures to deal with. They also have 'flashes of insight' (often in the pub!) and they use their imaginations sometimes ingeniously. In addition, they make wrong or hasty decisions and produce boring copy which no-one in their right mind would publish.

Thus, the relationship between theory and method is tempered by practical considerations such as how much money and time are available, what is the nature of the group to be studied and how amenable the group is likely to be to different forms of study. Of course, interactionists are likely to be highly disposed towards observational techniques. But if you are a 50-year-old female sociologist interested in football hooliganism, it is going to be difficult for you to perform a participant observation study of the topic. Similarly, if you are a positivist wishing to investigate illiteracy, a written questionnaire is not an option you should take.

Constraints on research

Like all other human beings, sociologists are constrained by the social structures they inhabit. The decisions they make are necessarily affected by tact and calculation of interest. If a researcher's head of department is a strong anti-positivist, it may be prudent for him or her not totally to rely on structured interviews in research. Women researchers, particularly feminists, interested in studying other women, have often found themselves to be disadvantaged in the male world of scientific research. Some women have been inhibited from using the more unstructured methods they regard as appropriate because of pressures from their male bosses and colleagues and the general ethos of 'academic machismo'. Some sociologists would go further and argue that all research, whether in the natural or social sciences, represents the cutting edge of capitalism and is carried out in the service of powerful financial interests in society.

Some ideas or concepts seem so obviously true that it is difficult to see any problems with them. However, sociologists should always have a critical attitude, if they are to evaluate ideas properly.

What difficulties can you suggest with the concept of 'triangulation'? You will need to think about this very carefully.

EVALUATION

Good evaluation is supported by sociological studies/evidence applied relevantly.

1 To what extent do you agree with the idea that science serves powerful financial interest?

2 What sociological evidence is available to discuss this issue?

Indeed, in one sense, research and theory hardly meet at all, in that those sociologists who think about society and develop theories (theoreticians) tend to be different people from those who actually get out in the world to investigate it (and are often accused by theoreticians of being empiricists). This is not to say that they do not influence each other, but they do have different interests and methods.

The uses of sociology

Does this mean that sociologists are just a group of unprincipled careerists who can tell us nothing about the truth of the society we live in? Of course not. Sociologists can never generate definitive explanations of the social world in the manner in which natural scientists seem able to for aspects of the natural world. Indeed, as societies themselves adapt to the course of events, our knowledge about them must always come under review. Rather, sociologists aim to increase our understanding about the society which we all inhabit. In trying to do so, they recognise that there must be limits to this understanding. The world is so complex and interconnected that no one person can hope to illuminate and understand its entirety. But that should not prevent the attempt to do so.

Such attempts do try to investigate the social world using an *objective* and systematic approach. It is generally accepted that values and subjectivity are an unavoidable part of the research process. Merely to choose a topic to study is to attach importance to it. But recognising the influence of subjectivity does not mean that we must abandon objectivity. This remains an ideal which sociologists strive for in a variety of ways – either by adopting *scientific* procedures, by declaring one's own values, or by treating the world just as an alien might. Once published, however, any piece of sociological research becomes the *property* of an intellectual community and is subject to critical scrutiny by other sociologists.

But the use of sociology goes beyond increasing the understanding of those who study it. While some sociologists would reject a connection between sociology and social policy, arguing that the influence of sociological studies on the real world has been minimal and even harmful, much of the history of sociology has been concerned with changing the

APPLICATION

You can apply your knowledge in a variety of ways, some of which can even be fun.

Influences on sociological ideas have always come from many non-sociological sources. Match up the modern theorists on the left with their main area of study on the right. The first one is given as an example.

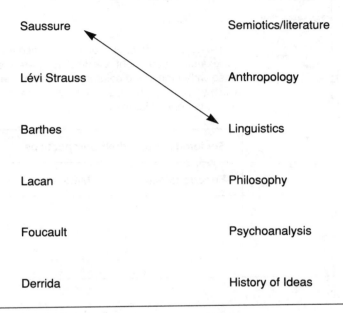

Saussure	Semiotics/literature
Lévi Strauss	Anthropology
Barthes	Linguistics
Lacan	Philosophy
Foucault	Psychoanalysis
Derrida	History of Ideas

social world. Sociologists of many different perspectives have been driven to attempt an understanding of the social world in order to change it for the better.

Sociologists' influence has sometimes been direct, for example, where they have been employed by the government, but often also indirect, creating a climate of opinion in which social policies have emerged.

From your reading you will have come across the work of Giddens, a major British sociologist. If you have not, look at Haralambos and Holborn, pp. 814–22. To interpret material correctly, you often have to select the appropriate part. So, answer the following:

INTERPRETATION

1 Does Giddens believe that individuals are free to act as they choose?

APPLICATION

2 Support your answer with appropriate arguments.

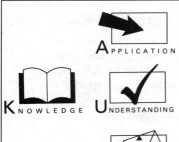

Place the following sociologists in the column they most closely fit.

G. H. Mead, Gramsci, Poulantzas, Schutz, Husserl, Berger and Luckman, Strauss, Spencer, Henderson, Merton, Coser, Marcuse, Goffman.

Add any others you know of.

You should also be critical of this exercise if you find that it is problematic. For example, you might ask whether there are any differences between those within the same column, or whether there are any other columns which you would add. Could it be said that any one individual belongs in more than one column?

Sociologists and their perspectives		
Functionalism	**Marxism**	**Interactionism**

Nevertheless, the continued support for sociological work, both by government and by private institutions, suggests that the discipline is seen by many to provide useful insights into the workings of society and to provide a starting point, at least, for the development of social policies.

Conclusion

Sociology has often been divided by competing perspectives but sociologists also agree on many things and are united by the belief that what happens on the societal level intimately affects what happens to the individual. While it may seem that sociologists are forever arguing (and, indeed, it would be foolish to deny that there are divisions within sociology), they are also all concerned with the search for truth and understanding in the same way as natural scientists are. To establish that sociology is a human activity, involving human frailties and disputes, is not to condemn it but to vindicate sociology's desire to establish how the social world works and the essential contradictions of the human condition.

Important points to bear in mind

1 Sociology is not a *new* discipline but emerged from the same revolution in thought which produced the natural sciences.
2 Knowledge, both of the natural and the social world, is always produced by someone. It does not lie around waiting to be discovered.
3 While sociologists disagree as to whether sociology can be a science or not, they would like to attain the same status for sociology that, say, chemistry or physics has.
4 Sociologists have to deal with the objective and subjective dimensions of the human experience.
5 The way in which research is in fact carried out very rarely corresponds to the way in which it is described in published accounts.

KEY CONCEPTS

It is important that you are familiar with, and are able to use, the concepts in this section in appropriate ways if you are to apply them effectively in the examination. Check your understanding of the concepts by carrying out the exercise. For each definition, choose the concept from the list which most closely matches it.

Institutions	Structures	Social construction
Science	Conflict	Consensus
Social facts	Primary data	Secondary data
Negotiation	Common-sense knowledge	Comparative method
Lebenswelt	Sampling	Postmodernism
Objectivity	Subjectivity	Replication
Verstehen	Marxism	Functionalism
Interactionism	Qualitative methods	Positivism
Quantitative methods	Reliability	Experiment
Validity	Social policy	

- The ability of an experiment to be repeated exactly.
- The ability to remain aloof from what is being studied.
- Patterns of behaviour which show regularities over time, but which are also subject to change.
- The use of a smaller number to generate information about a larger number.
- A perspective which stresses the fracturing of social life.
- Information which is gathered by others but used by sociologists.
- A way of research which deduces information by looking for similarities or differences between two or more phenomena.
- A view of the social world which emphasises conflict and contradiction.
- The process whereby much of social life is the result of interaction between individuals.
- Collective phenomena expressed in statistical form.

- A way of researching social life which relies on the detailed description of phenomena.
- A way through which sociology may influence events in the real world.
- Looking at the social world from the position of individuals, rather than society as a whole.
- The quality whereby a research activity can be carried out again and the same results found.
- Where there is social agreement.
- The everyday experiences of people.
- What everybody knows.
- The view that the scientific method is the most appropriate form of studying phenomena.
- Sources of knowledge which are generated by sociologists themselves.
- The ability of a researcher to place her- or himself in the shoes of another.
- Where there is social disagreement.
- The way in which many social phenomena are created by the activities of individuals and groups rather than being *natural*.
- A way of carrying out research which follows a systematic and objective pattern.
- Patterns of behaviour which are governed by norms, values or rules and which often have an organisational form.
- Where personal opinion affects judgement.
- Where a method results in findings which are *true-to-life*.
- A perspective which focuses primarily on consensus and social order.
- Research methods whose end-results can be expressed numerically.
- A research design which seeks to establish maximum control over the subjects and minimum participation by the researcher.

COURSEWORK SUGGESTIONS

1.1

In the AEB syllabus you are allowed to do a piece of coursework entirely on secondary material. This can take the form of a content analysis or a literature search or a critique of an existing survey. Therefore, you could take one of the classical sociologists' work (or, more realistically, a part of it) and carry out an analysis of that. An interesting alternative might be to take one of the major A level textbooks – even this one! – and carry out a critical analysis of it. However, you need to consider the following issues:

1 How are you going to limit the secondary material you choose? By a theme? By using only one book? Or by tracing the development of a concept?
2 How are you going to get access to the appropriate texts? Are they easily available in the sociology library or will you have to go further afield?
3 Are there any other commentaries on your chosen writer which you might reference?
4 How are you going to organise your material so that the assessor can clearly see what you have done and why you have done it that way?
5 How are you going to fulfil the skills requirements of the syllabus, especially the need to interpret and apply, and evaluate? It is important that you do not just describe what your chosen writer has said but that you seek to provide a critical analysis of their work and evaluate its contribution to sociological understanding.

1.2

Statistics form much of the raw material of sociological analysis but have come under criticism for the way that they represent reality. Part of the argument against statistics is that they are capable of being manipulated by government, organisations, groups and individuals to give certain impressions rather than others. Collect as many different examples of published statistics as possible using official publications like *Social Trends*, as well as TV, newspapers and magazines. Analysing their sources, show how the statistics may be using different types of presentation and varying interpretations to create certain impressions. Classify the techniques used in some systematic way. You may need to consider the following points:

1 Are you going to collect any statistics or are you going to concentrate on one particular area of social life? If the latter, which area of social life would produce sufficient statistics in the media over a limited period of time?
2 How will you fulfil the evaluation skill requirement? You must come to a conclusion about how successful your coursework has been compared to your intention at the beginning.

K NOWLEDGE   U NDERSTANDING

Essential for any project is knowing where to find things out. So, make a list of the sources of sociology books which are going to be available to you. The obvious one to start with is your school/college library.

Make sure that when you have finished your coursework you go through it, satisfying yourself (and the assessor!) that you have shown the skills of interpretation, application and evaluation.

3 How are you going to familiarise yourself with the types of presentation of statistics that are possible? Do you know someone with information technology skills who could show you graphics packages on a computer? This would also be useful for other project activities you may be involved in.

4 How many examples will you need to carry out a thorough survey of the different types of presentation? What timescale will you allow yourself? You should begin collecting now.

5 Knowing where to get information from is an important part of the research process. *Social Trends* is an immense source of data for sociologists. Do you know where you can get hold of a copy?

CHAPTER 2

The family

In this chapter we will examine the arguments surrounding:

1 family breakdown;
2 functions of the family;
3 family roles;
4 family size and structure;
5 the inevitability of the family.

Before you begin any of the exercises you should have studied and should be familiar with at least one of the following texts:

Bilton, T., Bonnett, K., Jones, P., Stanworth, M., Sheard, K. and Webster, A. *Introductory Sociology*, 2nd edn (Macmillan 1987), chapter 7.

Elliot, F. R. *The Family: Change or Continuity?* (Macmillan 1986).

Giddens, A. *Sociology* (Polity 1989), chapter 12.

Haralambos, M. and Holborn, M. *Sociology: Themes and Perspectives*, 3rd edn (Collins Educational 1990), chapter 8, pp. 521–34.

O'Donnell, M. *A New Introduction to Sociology*, 3rd edn (Nelson 1992), chapter 3.

In addition, you should have your notes on the family in good order.

Introduction

The family is one of our most important social institutions because we spend so much of our time in it. Yet it is also the most private part of our lives and sociological knowledge about the family has had to deal with that fact. It is very difficult to enter the family to study it on a day-to-day basis, but sociologists have long been fascinated by the controversies and problems associated with family life. It highlights the connection between the structural level of society and individual lives. What seem to be personal troubles in the family can often have much wider causes and effects in the public world. Events in the wider world can lead to personal problems.

Often you will be asked to apply a particular concept to other issues. For example, what private or personal events in the family can contribute to public issues? Identify three.

Notice which way around you are asked the question. By carrying out exercises such as this, you will be developing your skill of application.

1 Family breakdown

Many commentators, religious leaders and politicians have expressed concern over the state of the family in modern societies. Because the family is often seen as the backbone of society, any threat to it is seen as pathological, that is, diseased or threatening to society as a whole. The focus of concern has been on several issues:

- the increase in divorce;
- the increase in illegitimacy;
- teenage marriages;
- violence in the family.

Divorce

It is well established that, since the Second World War, there has been an increase in divorce of quite dramatic proportions. The debate has mainly been between those who see the increase in divorce as an indication that people do not 'make a go of their marriages' or 'take marriage seriously', and those who argue that divorce rates tell us little about the state of marriage. A third position suggests that the increase in the divorce rate indicates a failure of married life to live up to increased expectations of it.

Those who see divorce as a threat to the structure of society suggest that the law on divorce is far too lenient, and that when it was difficult to get a divorce couples tended to stay together through any problems they experienced, and their marriages were the stronger for it. They believe that high rates of divorce create many social problems such as one-parent families, children without adequate supervision or lacking a role model, and a disproportionate amount of time in the courts being spent on divorce cases, etc.

The skill of application involves the provision of supporting evidence for particular points of view. Therefore, from your textbooks, provide supporting studies for all sides of the argument concerning the importance of rising divorce rates.

Produce an appropriate table to illustrate your results.

For this exercise you will need to read *Social Studies Review* vol. 5, no. 5, pp. 191–2. (See [5], p. 337.) To practise the skill of interpretation:

1 summarise the New Right argument about one-parent families.

To practise the skill of evaluation:

2 assess how 'true-to-life' (valid) the argument is.

Notice how evaluation can ask you to consider an argument's relevance to the 'real world'.

The second position argues that the rate of divorce is not an indicator of the number of unhappy marriages. When divorce was difficult to obtain, people with unhappy marriages remained together unhappily, separated legally or 'lived in sin' with someone else. Divorce is only the legal termination of a marriage. It is the last act of an unhappy private life, and becomes public only in the divorce figures. High divorce rates do not necessarily mean that people are turning away from marriage itself as divorcees have fairly high rates of re-marriage and entry into non-marital cohabitation arrangements with new partners.

The third attitude to the increase in the divorce rate suggests that it is a response to real changes in people's lives. Increased standards of living and a heightened emphasis on the ideology of romance mean that individuals now expect far more from their married lives than in the past. When the reality fails to live up to the expectation, divorce follows. Also, as people enjoy much longer lives, the experience of marriage also lasts longer with a greater likelihood that things will go wrong.

It might be, then, that changes in the divorce rate mean a change in our pattern of marriage. Instead of lifelong monogamy, we may be entering a stage where serial monogamy is the norm. This means that our society will be one in which people marry more than once during their lifetimes as they search for marital happiness.

You will need to know social facts before you can interpret them and apply them to particular issues. To practise this:

1 Find out in which years there were major changes in the divorce law.

2 Find out the divorce statistics for the subsequent years following changes in divorce legislation.

3 What does this knowledge suggest about the relationship between the law and divorce rates?

EXERCISE

Marriage and divorce

As with many statistics, you must be clear about the difference between the total number of marriages and the marriage rate.

K NOWLEDGE U NDERSTANDING

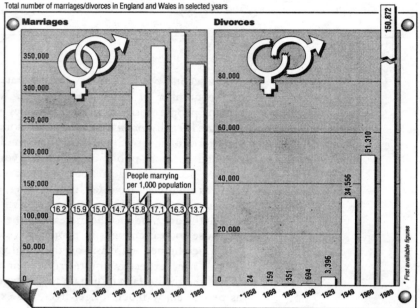

Total number of marriages/divorces in England and Wales in selected years

(Source: OPCS: Marriage and divorce statistics, Series FM2)

Answer these points:

1 Describe the changes in the patterns of marriage shown in the table, paying particular attention to the differences between the total number of marriages and the marriage rate.

2 Describe the changes in the number of divorces over the period in the table.

3 Using your textbook or your notes, list the reasons put forward by sociologists for the changes in patterns of marriage and divorce.

Sociology is about the real issues which affect people's lives in the most intimate ways. Social attitudes and behaviour are constantly changing. As a sociologist, you will be required to evaluate developments in social attitudes.

EVALUATION

1 Which do you think more accurately reflects public attitudes to illegitimacy: that it threatens the family or that it is no longer important as a stigma?

APPLICATION

2 What evidence can help you to decide?

Illegitimacy

The proportion of births to unmarried women has fluctuated since the Second World War although it has consistently been higher than before 1939. Again, the higher rates have been said to indicate a loss of respect for the sanctity of marriage – a weakening of the moral codes which encourage people to marry before having children. Children born outside marriage create both personal and public problems. Although the stigma of illegitimacy is not as strong as it used to be, it is still a mark which many children feel keenly. On the public level, lone-parent families may require state support in the form of additional benefit payments.

However, others have argued that the status of illegitimacy was made to protect the property of the father of a family, so that inheritance was passed on only to those sons who were born to his wife. In modern societies, with their greater tolerance and increasing numbers of one-parent families (brought about either by illegitimacy or divorce, plus the increase in the number of children born to cohabiting couples who choose not to marry), the stigma is no longer so important and, it is claimed, does not represent any threat to the family.

Teenage marriages

As the age at which people married fell in the period after the Second World War, there was a corresponding increase in the rate of teenage marriage. The problems associated with teenage marriages are, in fact, linked to the previous two issues we have looked at. It is argued that teenagers are not mature enough to marry and, therefore, many teenage spouses end up in the divorce courts during their twenties as they have grown up and grown apart from each other. Also, the major reason why so many teenage marriages occur is pregnancy. This in itself can create tensions in the marriage, which may then end in divorce. The figures show that those who married in their teens do appear in the divorce courts more frequently than most, but no more than some other categories do. For example, childless couples have a high frequency of

STRUCTURED QUESTION

Item A

Persons divorcing (per thousand married people), England and Wales

1979	1981	1983
6.0	11.9	12.2

(Source: adapted from *Social Trends*, 1986)

Item B

Percentage of women aged 18–49 cohabiting, Great Britain

Age group	1979	1981	1983
18–24	4.5	5.6	5.2
25–49	2.3	2.6	3.2

(Source: adapted from *Social Trends*, 1986)

Item C

In modern Britain, it is not the case that marriage is unpopular but only that being married to a particular partner is sometimes undesirable to a particular individual. People live together without being married for a whole variety of reasons: they are unable to marry because of a prior marital status or religious discord; they are unwilling to marry because of legal or financial difficulties; they may be engaging in *trial marriages*; they may want to marry but the law prevents them, as in the case of gay couples. But we have not yet reached the situation that exists in the United States where serial monogamy is increasingly the norm.

a) What is meant in Item C by the phrase 'serial monogamy is increasingly the norm'?   (2 marks)

b) What do the figures in Item B tell us about the rate of cohabitation in Great Britain?   (1 mark)

c) What have sociologists contributed to an understanding of the effects of changes in the divorce rate such as those shown in Item A?   (8 marks)

d) State one other reason why people may 'live together without being married', apart from those mentioned in Item C.   (1 mark)

e) Using evidence from all three items and from elsewhere, evaluate the argument that the modern family is a 'dying institution'.   (13 marks)

Look carefully at the mark allocations here. If you had an hour to answer this question, how much time would you spend on each part?

You will often be able to bring and apply your own knowledge of social life to sociological issues. For example, reviewing your own or your own family's acquaintances might help you to answer this question.

What reasons, other than those mentioned in Item C of the structured question above, can you think of that explain why people might live together in the same household without being married?

Notice that, before you answer this question, you have to interpret the reasons in the passage.

divorce. Couples who have been married for a long time and whose children have grown up and left home also have a high rate of divorce.

Violence in the family

The media often focus attention on cases of child battering and the impression is given that such cases are on the increase. This, along with wife battering, seems to indicate that the modern family is a destructive institution which is not only threatening society but is also dangerous for its members. However, there is no way sociologists can know how much battering occurred in the past and, therefore, whether there has been an increase. By its nature, violence in the family is a secretive thing and those cases which come to light do not tell the whole story of such violence.

You should have access to *Social Trends* which will give you information about social developments. You need to gain practice in interpreting the information in Social Trends. So, use an appropriate edition to check whether there has been an increase or decrease in teenage marriage divorces since the Second World War.

You may remember from your reading that there are many sociologists who are pessimistic about the family but that many others disagree with them. To begin to evaluate the pessimistic point of view, you need to establish the arguments for and against it.

1 In what ways did Laing, Leach and Cooper believe that the family is dysfunctional?

2 What counter-arguments can you provide?

2 Functions of the family

Loss of functions

The functions of the family are also linked to the idea that the family may be undergoing some sort of breakdown. The argument is that, at some time in the past, presumably when the family was extended, it carried out many functions, both for its members and for society as a whole. In modern societies, however, the family has *lost* many of its functions and has therefore declined in importance. Others have suggested that it is not so much a matter of functions being lost but of the family modifying itself to meet the changed circumstances of modern industrial society.

The functions that are said to be lost are those associated with health, recreation, economics, education, religion, etc. These have been taken over by outside bureaucracies, such as schools and hospitals. Others argue that, though there has been a shift towards specialised institutions, the movement has been exaggerated and there is still an enormous amount of activity on health and suchlike which is carried out in the family.

Socialisation

One of the major functions of the family is, of course, to produce and rear children. However, the socialisation process is never a simple one and its failure is often put forward as a reason why some people are deviant or criminal. 'Inadequate' socialisation is, however, a vague concept, inevitably involving value judgements since there is no agreement

INTERPRETATION APPLICATION

The application of relevant evidence is the first step in evaluation. In your reading you will have come across sociologists on both sides of the *loss of functions* debate. You need to interpret their studies correctly.

1 Which sociologists argue for the loss of functions and which against? Record your answer in the following table:

Loss of functions	
For	**Against**

EVALUATION

To evaluate, you need to be explicit about your assessment.

2 Which side of the argument convinces you and why?

Evaluate the argument that families are *factories which produce human personalities.*

For this exercise you will need to read Haralambos and Holborn, pp. 460–3 and interpret the material therein. But notice that you are asked to evaluate it, not just interpret it. To begin with summarise the argument and highlight the points you find most convincing. Then suggest some points against the argument. Finally, come to a conclusion in a separate paragraph which directly refers to the argument in the question.

on what constitutes effective socialisation. For example, some believe that children should never be physically controlled while others say that smacking is essential if children are to grow up with the appropriate amount of communality.

Another major function of the family that has been suggested is the stabilisation of adult personalities. This has many dimensions because the family provides identity and emotional support for its members in diverse ways. Attention has often focused on sexual satisfaction as this is claimed to be beneficial not only for husband and wife, but also for society as a whole, since the family channels and controls sexual desire which is often seen as a powerful, and potentially disruptive, force for society. Some commentators have, therefore, been critical of the *permissive* society where extra-marital relationships seem to be on the increase. Others have said that the permissive society is more imaginary than real, partly because extra-marital affairs have always gone on and partly because, in a post-AIDS, post-herpes society, people's sexual behaviour is likely to be modified in the direction of caution.

Negative aspects of the family

Some sociologists have looked more at the negative aspects of the family's functions, stressing the ways in which individual members may suf-

You will get some useful ideas for this exercise from *Social Studies Review* vol. 3, no. 3, pp. 84–8 (see [6], p. 337), but you will also need to apply your sociological knowledge and insight about the family.

1 Write a paragraph on the possible effects of AIDS on family structures.

However, you can also apply your knowledge of methodology to this issue.

2 What ethical issues might sociologists face when exploring these effects?

E VALUATION

In your reading you will have come across arguments concerning the negative effects of family life on members. You may be asked to evaluate these arguments. Therefore, assess the argument that the cost of family life to the child is low relative to the functional gains of having a whole family.

You should include concepts like stability, violence, psychological pressures and social reproduction. Be sure that your evaluation refers exactly to the argument in the question.

fer as they fulfil functions for society as a whole. Here the emphasis has been on the role the family needs to play to ensure that capitalism continues. So, the major function of the family is seen to be to produce the next generation of workers and to reproduce labour power daily. This, it is argued, is carried out at the expense of the mother of the family who not only bears the greater burden of housework but must also carry the next generation of labourers for the nine-months gestation period. The problem with this point of view is that members of the family do not see it that way. A woman bearing a child does not think that she is bearing a future labourer. Rather, she will bear her child whom she will love and cherish for itself.

Moreover, it is argued that the family exercises social control over and above the socialisation of children already referred to. The family, it is said, controls the work-force in two ways. Firstly, the traditional view that the husband is responsible for the material welfare of his family means that he is under strong pressure to take and keep a job, and not to withdraw his labour, either by refusing to work or by striking. Secondly, the family, usually in the person of the female partner, maintains the physical and emotional health of its members, particularly the father, keeping him in good order as a worker at no cost to the employer or to the system at large.

EXERCISE

Using Haralambos and Holborn, Bilton *et al.*, O'Donnell, Giddens plus any other suitable textbook, make a list of those studies which support the view that the family is, in essence, a happy institution, along with those studies which support the idea that the family is not always a positive experience for its members. You should try to cover as wide a range of issues as possible, including the effects on children, women and men, elderly people, unemployed people, etc.

Organise your list in whatever way you think appropriate but make a note of the main points of each study you mention.

The family and society

These issues raise fundamental problems about the relationship between the family and society. Clearly, the family stands between the individual and society. The family fulfils certain functions for society but is it at the expense of certain members? It is likely that the family has contradictory effects which are not the same for all of us. It gives identity and social location, but at what cost? On the one hand, it is the major way in which society is perpetuated and, on the other, it is responsible for many of our problems. Much energy, time and cost are expended in trying to resolve the problems of the family. It is not just a question of some families not performing their functions properly and, therefore, needing some sort of social-work help. The family is an intense and emotional unit which can raise passions and problems, even while performing its functions properly.

The individual's family circumstances must be a major influence on the happiness or sadness of that individual. The family can be a place of joy, responsibility, desire and fulfilment. But it can also be a source of despair, restriction and the most frightening cruelty. The State seeks to move the family in certain directions through the use of inducements, such as child benefit, but the family is also a main source of income for the State, both through income tax and duties on consumer goods. Without families buying goods, industry would suffer severe loss and, yet, millions of people remain unemployed and unable to purchase even basic items. It can thus be seen that the family is an essential part of modern society through the functions it performs. But it is not an unproblematic institution and some would see the family as the cause of all society's ills.

3 Family roles

Women and men

For many years, the role of women in society was seen as a product of their biological make-up. Many sociologists (but not all) have challenged

I NTERPRETATION

E VALUATION

To help you with this exercise you should read, if it is available to you, *Social Studies Review*, vol. 2, no. 5, pp. 36–40. (See [7], p. 337.)

1 Identify TWO contributions which feminists have made to the study of the family.

2 Which do you find the more important and why?

Note that you need to suggest reasons for your choice in order to carry out a full evaluation. For example, you could say that it was more convincing, had more evidence to support it, dealt more with the central issues, was more *true-to-life*, etc.

Evaluation is about making choices and giving reasons why you have chosen as you have. Often these choices will be about real social issues. For example, which do think is the more effective form of child-rearing, individual or collective?

Give reasons for your choice.

An important issue you might raise in thinking about your choice is, *effective for whom?*

this idea and argued that female roles are the product of social pressures and influence, that they are *socially constructed*. Much research has gone into examining male and female roles in many different societies in an attempt to assess how widespread male dominance is. Some argue that female subordination is so common as to be universal. Others argue that male and female roles were much more equal in pre-industrial societies, and that some societies were matriarchal in their power arrangements. Many sociologists now argue that both sexes exercise various sorts of power in different ways and that different societies will display various combinations of these types of power.

For example, the role of women within the family has been considered by many traditional observers as *natural* or *inevitable*. After all, women are the bearers of children and, therefore, they must instinctively be responsible for their children's physical and emotional well-being, as

One of the more important arguments in the sociology of the family concerns relationships between husband and wife. You will have read about this. However, you will need to apply studies and arguments to this debate. To start, list the sociologists who support the idea of growing equality in marriage and those who criticise it. For each sociologist you mention, identify one major argument put forward.

For this exercise you will need to read *Sociology Review*, vol. 1, no. 1, pp. 31–2. (See [8], p. 337.)

List the main arguments which sociologists have put forward in attacking sociobiology.

Note that, by extracting the arguments, you are interpreting the material.

There are many different types of feminist sociologist. You may interpret some of their arguments from *Social Studies Review*, vol. 2, no. 3, pp. 23–6, vol. 3, no. 4, pp. 139–41 or vol. 6, no. 1, pp. 16–19. (See [9], [10], [11], p. 337.)

By comparing them you will begin to evaluate them.

1 Identify different strands of feminist thought.
2 Which do you find the most realistic view of the family and why?

Here, your evaluation must be in terms of how close to real life you find each of the strands of feminist thought.

well as for the running of the household, the housework and the care of their husbands. As men are the bread-winners, they also fulfil their *natural* function as providers. Housework and child-care are seen as somehow alien to men. These role models are passed on to the next generation through socialisation, thereby ensuring the stability of the family.

Some women have challenged this state of affairs and forced many married couples to reconsider the *natural* division of labour within the family. It is argued that men now take on a greater share of household duties and child-care, and that, generally, the conjugal relationship is becoming egalitarian. Decisions are made jointly; financial affairs are discussed; the welfare of the child (or children) is of equal importance to both partners; and housework, cooking, etc. are shared. The emergence of the *New Man* is said to be the product of a long process of change, linked to the needs of industry for female workers.

However, it could be argued that this view is an idealised, middle-class version of family life which may not even correspond to middle-class family reality. It is certainly not true of all middle-class couples. Some sociologists argue that men do not have an equal share of housework, nor do middle-class men make better houseworkers than working-class men. While there may have been marginal changes in the way husbands and wives organise their domestic affairs, women retain the major burden of housework.

The issue of housework needs to be discussed in the light of the changing status of men and women as bread-winners. Women constitute over 40 per cent of the work-force and, clearly, their income is as important to the living standards of the family as that of the husband. Most women are in employment because it is financially necessary. Only a minority of mainly middle-class women *choose* to stay at home with children rather than work outside the home. Women who are at home are usually forced into this position because they are unable to find work that will fit in with their domestic arrangements and child-care.

Some sociologists believe that most of the women in this position are unhappy with their situation and would work outside the home if able to. Few women claim to be content with the *housewife* role. Men who have given up employment to look after their children, because their

Housework is a crucial area of sociological interest in the family and an important part of domestic life. From your reading:

1 choose one feminist writer on housework and describe the main features of her or his views on housework;

2 state one advantage of this view and one disadvantage;

3 how far do you agree that this view is an accurate account of modern housework?

4 What evidence can you find for your answer to 3?

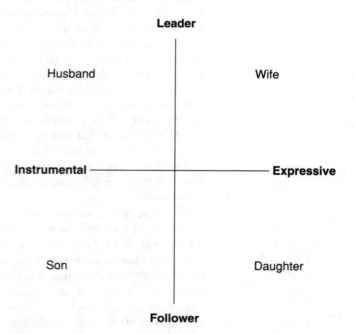

Sociologists often use diagrams to express their viewpoints. For example:

Leader

Husband   Wife

Instrumental ———————————— **Expressive**

Son   Daughter

Follower

You need to interpret the diagram to answer the following question.

Which sociological perspective views family roles in this way?

To begin an assessment of which of the two methods above would be the more appropriate in researching domestic labour, make a list of the advantages and disadvantages of each, in the following format:

Participant observation		Surveys	
Advantages	**Disadvantages**	**Advantages**	**Disadvantages**
	1 Probably limited to your own home	1 Can gain information about a large number of homes	

partners have either died or left home, are often given much publicity. Sympathy is felt for their plight, accompanied by a sense of admiration at their ability to cope with the running of a household single-handedly. Women on their own as single parents, however, which is the norm, receive no such admiration. The fact that these male-headed one-parent families are a minority of one-parent families in Britain is significant. (See Coursework Suggestion 2.1 on p. 65.)

Other aspects of male and female relationships in the family which have attracted sociological attention have been the issues of sex and sexuality. While some sociologists argue that the family is the natural unit for the expression of sexual feelings, others have suggested that sexuality is influenced much more by society than is commonly supposed. These latter sociologists argue that the proper exercise of sexuality is channelled and controlled by social forces that seek to impose definitions of normality onto individuals. Against this social construction of sexuality, other sociologists have argued for the growing privatisation of sexuality, pointing to laws which protect individuals from interference in their private sexual practices.

For this exercise you need to read *Social Studies Review*, vol. 2, no. 3, pp. 26–7. (See [12], p. 337.) Imagine you are faced with the following question: To what extent do you support the radical feminist view of rape?

In answering, you would be required to interpret what the view was and apply evidence to the view in order to evaluate it.

In your reading about gender you will have come across the concept of patriarchy. To practise interpretation:

1 summarise the meaning of patriarchy in one paragraph.

To practise evaluation:

2 What criticisms have been made of this concept and, in your opinion, do they make the concept useless?

Elderly people

Some sociologists suggest that old age is socially constructed as well as being a biological fact. For example, where life expectancy is low, the *old* are people of an age which would be considered relatively young in societies with longer life expectancies. Others would argue that capitalism shapes or *structures* the way that old age is seen and treated, so that the old of different classes have different experiences in society. Some others have stressed the gender inequalities which occur among old people.

The role of elderly people in the family and within society differs from society to society. The status of the old, for example, tends to be low in industrial societies and high in non-industrial societies. In industrial society, the elderly tend to be seen as dependent or burdensome, since they do not contribute to production and a minority may have to be looked after. Provision of care for the minority of the elderly who need support has, until recently, been provided increasingly by the state in the form of pensions, old people's accommodation, day-care centres and health care. This is a clear example of social policies impinging on an area of family responsibility. Hence, the contribution of elderly people to family life, it has been argued, has declined. The grandmother or grandfather is no longer always seen as an integral or even central part of family decision-making or family life.

In recent years, government policy in Britain has advocated the *move back* to looking after the elderly in the family. The argument is that the old can be more comfortable, are more useful and feel safer if looked after within the family. Care within the family also has the effect of saving public money. On the other hand, many families have suffered enormous strain in looking after an aged relative, especially where they may be infirm or senile. Indeed, most of the responsibility for the care of old

Old people are often presented, in stereotypical ways, as being a *social problem*. In order to challenge this stereotype, you should apply your knowledge of old people (including your own experiences) to see if it confirms or undermines the stereotype.

Many of the questions you will be asked will have political and social policy aspects to them. You will usually be asked to evaluate these in some way. You should always try to apply evidence in your evaluations, especially if you are told to do so in the question. Look at the following example:

Using any newspaper reports or sociological study, assess the effects of *community care of the elderly* on society and the family.

people has fallen in the past on married daughters who found, until a 1986 European Court decision, that they had been denied the right to claim allowances from the state to help pay for the care of the elderly, unlike their unmarried female counterparts. So, families have not only suffered the material and physical strain of caring for infirm relatives, but have also suffered financial hardship as a result of the carer being forced to give up paid work while simultaneously being unable to claim state cash benefits. This is another example of state policies affecting personal life.

Children

The role of children in the family has changed enormously as their ability to contribute to the household economy has diminished. This is mainly the result of successive legal restrictions on the age at which the young may work for payment, and where they may work. Moreover, the family itself has become much more child-centred as families have turned in on themselves. The consequences of this are varied. Certainly, the lives of young children are different from the past, if only in material terms.

To carry out this interpretation exercise you should read *Social Studies Review*, vol. 3, no. 4, pp. 126–31. (See [13], p. 337.)

List the sociologists who have contributed to the debate about childhood and attribute one major point to each of them in the following format:

Childhood		
Aries	Argues that	Childhood is Socially constructed

Child abuse has only recently been a focus of sociological research. You are likely to find information about it in magazines like *Sociology Review*. When you have an article of interest in front of you, you should try to use your skills to make it relevant to the examination.

For example, if you read *Social Studies Review*, vol. 2, no. 1, pp. 23–8 (see [14], p.337), you could:

INTERPRETATION

1 interpret the major approaches to child abuse that have been adopted;

APPLICATION

2 apply this information to the argument that the family is dysfunctional for children;

EVALUATION

3 choose which approach is the most realistic, giving reasons for your choice.

Generally speaking, they are better fed, clothed and sheltered than they were. Some families in poverty, however, still cannot provide a decent standard of living for their children. In the family, they are more likely to be consulted in decision-making although they may not have any final say.

Some sociologists have, therefore, argued that childhood is socially constructed and is the product of changing social forces, not a *natural* state at all. Thus, in the past, children were treated as *little adults* and have only recently come to be seen, without question, as children. Others have argued that this view is based on suspect evidence such as official reports and that, when the personal accounts of parents in the past are examined, a much more child-centred view of parenthood emerges.

However, not all children find the family a safe and attractive place. There is increasing evidence that many children suffer from battering and sexual abuse by close members of the family. Many may suffer from psychological disturbance because of the intensity of family life and the demands it makes on them. There is evidence that structural phenomena such as rising unemployment can increase the tensions of family life.

APPLICATION

You should draw upon different sources of evidence in order to apply such evidence to sociological debates. For example, newspaper accounts of family violence are commonplace. However, different types of account tell us different things. So, statistical accounts tell us about the extent of violence, while descriptive accounts tell us about its nature. Always be careful to be critical of these accounts, as you should be assessing their worth as evidence.

You can use *Social Studies Review*, vol. 4, no. 2, pp. 44–6, (see [15], p. 337), for this exercise, but any textbook should describe the variety of family forms in Britain.

1 What are these forms?

You should also apply your knowledge to a sociological problem by answering this question:

2 How far do these forms differ from the past?

Be careful to show similarities as well as differences.

Arguing and divorcing parents may produce strain on the children as they try to cope with the conflicting demands on their affections. In the United States, thousands of children disappear from the family each year. Not all are abducted; many leave voluntarily and gladly suggesting that all is not rosy in the modern nuclear family.

Sociologists often find it difficult to investigate these problems precisely because they are so personal. Moreover, these sorts of issue arouse much emotion, and it is a problem for investigators to divorce themselves from the passions that may be present during the investigations. By their nature, many of the issues are hidden from view and family members may be reluctant, or even frightened, to talk about them. Yet sociologists continue, by a variety of methods, to look at these personal problems.

4 Family size and structure

Families in modern Britain are, in one indisputable way, fundamentally different from those of the past: they are smaller. This does not mean just that average family size has fallen, although it has, from having around seven or eight children in the mid-nineteenth century to having around two children in the 1980s and 1990s. It also means that the number of children born into families has fallen. Owing to the decline in infant mortality, achieved through improvements in hygiene and midwifery, the large majority of children born now survive into adulthood. This was not true of the nineteenth century, when a large percentage of babies born were likely to fall victim to the diseases carried in bad water and sewerage.

In your reading you may have come across the work of Angela McRobbie. Whenever you read about a sociologist's findings you should try to be evaluative about them. Ask yourself the following:

1 What criticisms can I make about this study?
2 How do these criticisms affect my view of the study?
3 Does the study still tell me something valid about this issue?

Women and child-bearing

The decline in infant mortality suggests a change in the way people have thought of child-bearing over the last century. From holding a position where children were seen as an advantage to the family, and a large number of births was needed to ensure a supply of children, people can now make the decision to limit the number of pregnancies that they will have through the use of contraception; or they can make the decision to terminate pregnancies through the use of abortion.

It is, therefore, not just the availability of efficient contraceptive techniques that is important. Equally important in explaining this change is the fact that thousands of individual decisions have been made by potential parents to use these techniques in order to limit the number of children that they have. There has thus been a shift in the ideological conception of the family as to what is seen as the ideal family size. In short, big families are no longer the norm in modern industrial societies.

This also implies a massive change in the way women view themselves and the way they may live their lives. For nineteenth-century wives, children were the focal point of their physical existence. As the number of pregnancies, especially among the working-class, was large, the ordinary wife could face a life of fairly continuous pregnancy and the real dangers that faced them during child-birth. Limiting families removed, to an extent, the threat of death which hung over many women then as they went from one pregnancy to the next.

Contraception brought about possibilities for women also. To control your own fertility is to have greater power over your own body and to introduce choices into your life. Women can now choose to enter the labour market (if they can get a job), delay motherhood or reject the idea of having children altogether. They may no longer see their main role in life as child-bearers and child-rearers. Rather, they may see themselves primarily as workers, who may or may not also have children.

The family in history

However, the relationship between size and structure of the family is a complicated one. While the large families of the nineteenth century are associated with the idea of the extended family, and smaller families with the nuclear, they are not always the same things. Not all big families are extended and nor are small households necessarily nuclear families. One sociological argument suggests that agricultural societies, now and in the past, are characterised by extended families and/or households, while industrial societies have nuclear families which are better suited to the needs of those societies.

This over-simplifies the range of household formations that exist in all societies and circumstances. For example, historical research has shown that, while households in agricultural Britain of the eighteenth century may have been large, they were not necessarily composed of the extended family. Lodgers and servants were a main component of what was counted as a large household. While families may have been close in the

You should always try to apply historical knowledge or contemporary events to points made by you in order to support your case. For example, you may know of other information which is relevant to a particular issue, as in the following question.

What other social developments may have changed the way women see themselves?

agricultural past, the poor hardly had the material conditions in which to live happy, extended-family existences. The extended household may have been more prominent during the early part of the industrial revolution, not because it was the preferred way of life for the workers who were forced into the towns, but because it was a sensible financial arrangement under conditions of squalor and uncertain income.

The contemporary family

In industrial Britain, it is often assumed by government agencies and the like that the typical family form is the nuclear family – the close, warm mother-father-and-two-children set-up. But it is by no means clear that this is typical at all. If we examine the percentage of households which comply with this arrangement, we find that it is, in fact, a minority of households in Britain at any one time. However, we must recognise that many living arrangements which are not nuclear in form are either potentially nuclear (student houses, for example, contain many people who will go on to form nuclear families) or are the remnants of nuclear families (old couples living alone).

There are still many people who do not conform to this ideal type, either through choice or because they do not have the opportunity to do so. Firstly, there are examples of extended family arrangements still in existence in traditional working-class areas of the country and among some of the ethnic minorities in the larger cities. Also, modern communication systems allow the various parts of the extended family to keep in

From your reading you will know that some sociologists and historians have argued for the extended family being dominant in the past, and others against:

1 In two columns, list the sociologists and historians under titles *For* and *Against*.

When evaluating the idea that the extended family was dominant in the past, you should refer to evidence for and against, in answering this question.

2 Referring to the evidence, assess the idea that the extended family was the dominant family structure in the past.

Application may involve using your knowledge to solve particular problems set for you. For example, you are asked to match text to diagram in the following exercise.

Connect up the representation on the left with the appropriate concept on the right.

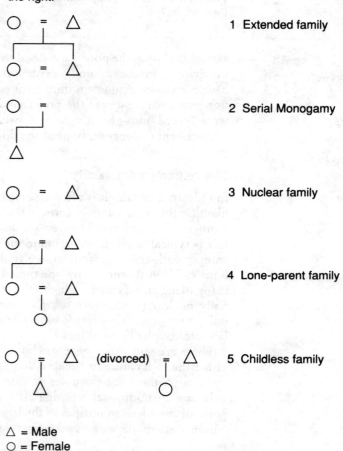

1 Extended family

2 Serial Monogamy

3 Nuclear family

4 Lone-parent family

5 Childless family

△ = Male
○ = Female

touch with each other, to arrange participation in family ceremonies, etc. in what is called the modified extended family.

For many people in institutions there is no choice about which family structure they will live in. For people with mental or physical disabilities who are confined in institutions, the only *family life* they will experience is what the staff of the organisation can offer them. For old and infirm people, hospitalisation or some sort of sheltered accommodation is likely to be an option.

But it is also the case that more and more people choose not to live in circumstances which are seen as the typical family form. Couples may choose not to have children for many reasons. It is, of course, difficult to classify a family as childless until the female has reached past child-bearing age but there is no doubt that this is an option which some couples will have chosen. For others, childlessness is a result of circumstances beyond their control and a source of much pain and anguish. (See Coursework Suggestion 2.2 on p. 65)

Non-family households

There are still many people for whom we have not yet accounted because there is still an enormous variety possible. Many people choose to live alone or as a lodger somewhere for private reasons or because they have little choice. There are the homeless and the tramps who have taken up a lifestyle very different from that which most people would see as normal. Student houses or shared accommodation of various types are other options. Gay couples represent one form of household which is unlikely to have children attached, although it is not unknown for gay parenting to exist, for instance, through artificial insemination by donor.

This great variety of family forms provides problems for the social policy makers who have to try to fulfil the needs of those who pay them. The ideology of the nuclear family is so strong that policy tends to be made on the assumption that the nuclear family is dominant. Thus, it may miss many people (some would argue the majority) who live outside this form.

5 The inevitability of the family

Experiments in family life

The debate about the universality of the family has been a recurring one in sociology. Some have argued that the biological imperative is so strong that the family appears in all societies in a fairly similar form. Others have suggested that that which is seen as a family in any society is socially constructed, i.e. subject to social and moral influences. While the family is, undoubtedly, the major social unit in most societies, it has taken so many forms that it is hard to talk about it as a single institution at all. Attempts to organise social life without a recognised family unit have occurred, but people have a habit of adapting social experiments to meet their own needs and to suit their own desires. But this does not mean that one family form is somehow natural and others are perverse.

EVALUATION One of the necessities of evaluation is that you are aware of any methodological problems that may influence the evidence. For example, what difficulties might sociologists face in investigating the types of household identified in the paragraph above?

INTERPRETATION Notice that you have first to interpret the main text in order to identify the types of household.

Children are brought up in many different ways, both inside and outside some family arrangement. Love can be, and is, found among people who are not part of the family. Sexual satisfaction is not to be found only between husband and wife. Warmth and security are available in many different relationships. It is, therefore, mistaken to make judgements about people's private lives or base policies on whether they live in one type of family or another. For example, to see the children of lone parents as being from broken homes may be to impose inappropriate stereotypes on them.

The individual, the family and society

There are strong ideological and material forces which both project and protect the nuclear form as the *typical* family in modern industrial societies. Many tax and benefit policies of the State are based on the assumption that most people live now or will live in a nuclear unit. Advertising portrays the family in a stereotyped way, with women carrying out *female* roles, children playing other roles, depending on their gender, and men still others.

There is no logical reason why people must marry – reproduction can be achieved quite easily without it! Children can be reared by anyone – not necessarily the natural father or mother. Yet most people do marry and have their children within marriage. And most people are brought up in families of one type or another. So there are strong cultural imperatives that favour the formation of family units and these must, in some way, satisfy the needs of individuals to a large extent. Where they do not, change in the family is likely to occur, either on an individual basis

---

You will remember that George Murdock is an important sociologist in the field of the universality of the family. Answer this question.

Using any evidence you may know of, assess the validity of Murdock's work.

In evaluating a proposition you can draw on many types of evidence as, for example, in this exercise.

1 To what extent would you agree that the one-parent family is stereotyped?

2 Can you provide any examples from television to support your argument?

STRUCTURED QUESTION

You do not have to answer questions to practise your skills. For example, underline any sociological concepts you can find in these items and provide a definition for each of them. This will help you to make use of your skills.

INTERPRETATION

KNOWLEDGE   UNDERSTANDING

Item A

The State played an increasingly authoritarian role as it took over governmental functions and the Church's religious concerns. These undoubtedly had a significant impact on the family. Education became formalised under a relatively central system. Three essential tasks remained the prerogative of the nuclear family – satisfaction of emotional and sexual needs, child-rearing and the provision of a satisfactory home life. These have developed in a growing, media-led culture which appears to be supportive of romantic notions.

Item B

Advertisers present the family in a stereotypical way. The *Oxo cube* family has been identified as the prime example of the way in which family structure and family relationships are represented in the advertising media. However, these *representations* have very real effects. Those citizens who do not conform to the image may be seen in some way as *social problems* and many items of government propaganda and policies are produced with the stereotype in mind.

Item C

Men tend to steer clear of day-to-day family budgeting decisions but take a far more active role when larger amounts of cash are involved. That's the verdict of research commissioned by the Leeds Permanent Building Society...

"We found the results surprising," said a society spokesman. "Given the results of previous studies and the fact that our branches tend to have more women than men coming in to open family accounts, we had expected more women to be the dominant financial decision-makers in families than proved to be the case."

In fact, this assumption is true for the handling of everyday household finances . . . But when it comes to making long-term savings and investment decisions, men take the lead in nearly three times as many households as women.

(Source: adapted from Jill Papworth, "Who pulls the purse strings?", the *Guardian*, 16 March 1991)

Notice, in (b), the skills that you have to perform. You need to interpret the functions in Item A, know some other functions and apply some examples in support.

a) According to Item B, what is the consequence of the presentation of the family in a stereotyped way by the advertising industry? (1 mark)
b) Apart from those identified in Item A, what other functions does nuclear family perform in modern society? Give examples in support of your answer. (5 marks)

c) Assess the extent to which the stereotyped view of the family, suggested in Items A and B, is an accurate description of the distribution of households in modern Britain. (7 marks)

d) To what extent do sociologists agree with the idea that citizens who do not conform to the image may be seen in some way as *social problems* (Item B)? (4 marks)

e) Using evidence from Item C and elsewhere, assess the argument that husbands and wives have come to share responsibility for family affairs. (8 marks)

(divorce, separation, infidelity, etc.) or on the institutional level (changes in family forms, size, and so on).

Conclusion

The family is, therefore, a dynamic institution, responding to changes in personal and social circumstances. As the social institution which individuals are most concerned with, the family represents a *central life interest* for most people. To most it is the source of many problems and satisfaction but, for the sociologist, it is more than this. The family also represents a crucial intermediate grouping between the individual and larger social formations such as the State, and, therefore, forms a crucial, mediating structure in society.

To help you understand that the family is dynamic , look at this:

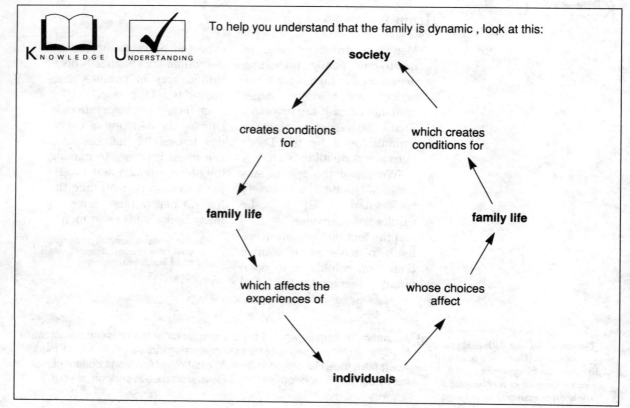

society

creates conditions for

which creates conditions for

family life

family life

which affects the experiences of

whose choices affect

individuals

Important points to bear in mind

1 The family as a social institution is the locus of both much satisfaction and many problems.
2 The family stands between the individual and society, performing functions for society and providing a haven for individuals from society.
3 Relationships within the family are constantly changing and developing in response to many external and internal factors.
4 The variety of family forms in any age is much larger than the stereotypes of family life suggest.
5 The family is a central institution in most societies and is often, therefore, the object of social policy developed by the state.

APPLICATION

Is there such a thing as a *normal family unit*?

In answering this question you need to think of which parts of your course you should apply to the issue. For example, you could refer to any of the following: households and family; the history of the family; family diversity; domestic labour.

KEY CONCEPTS

It is important that you are familiar with and are able to use the concepts in this section in appropriate ways if you are to apply them effectively in the examination. Check your understanding of the concepts by carrying out this exercise. From the following list of concepts, choose the ones which most closely answer the questions below.

Death of the family	Serial monogamy	Social control
Divorce	Primary socialisation	Social reproduction
Role models	Patriarchy	Matriarchy
Domestic labour	Conjugal roles	New Man
Sex	Childhood	Old age
Gender	Household	Ideology
Nuclear family	Extended family	

1 What can be said to be an adult, generational phenomenon which can be socially constructed?
2 What do sociologists call a situation where one person marries a succession of people throughout his or her life?
3 What do we call a family with only two generations in it?
4 What is the concept sociologists use to describe the process whereby the same features appear across generations?

5   What are ideas which serve the interests of particular social groups?
6   What is the technical term for the people living under the same roof?
7   What is the phenomenon said to be created, in part, by the extension of schooling and the decline in young people's labour?
8   What do sociologists call the full range of individuals to whom a person is related?
9   What is the legal termination of a marriage called?
10   What is the process called whereby constraints are imposed to create social order?
11   What do we call a husband who takes an active role in domestic labour?
12   What are the relationships between husband and wife called?
13   What do we call a system where males hold power?
14   What are the people whom we imitate called?
15   What is the process whereby children receive the norms, values, attitudes and behaviour patterns from their parents?
16   What do sociologists call the biological differentiation between the sexes?
17   What is a situation called where the female partner dominates in marriage and society?
18   What are the behavioural differences between the sexes usually called?
19   What do sociologists call the idea that, in modern societies, the family is breaking up?
20   What is the technical name which sociologists apply to housework?

COURSEWORK SUGGESTIONS

2.1

The issue of conjugal-role relationships is likely to be a popular subject for an A level project. The reasons for this are clear. It is an issue which concerns most people as most have had some personal contact with the demands of domestic labour. Therefore, it is a topic with easy access for most individuals and an area where most aspiring sociologists could gain some useful information.

However, because of its very popularity there are some important questions to be addressed.

1   You will need to be strict in limiting the scope of your project. A vague, all-encompassing project which tries to deal with every aspect of the domestic labour debate is likely to work less well than one which is tightly focused on one aspect of the controversy.
2   You will need to have your chosen aspect well contextualised in the available literature. It is not enough just to reproduce the Young and Willmott/Oakley debate, without relating it to your specific interest.
3   You will need to consider carefully what method you are going to use. This is most likely to be a participant observation on your own family or a more general survey using questionnaires or interviews.
4   If you choose to carry out a participant observation exercise on your own family, you will need to consider very carefully the problems of objectivity and ethics which will arise.
5   If you choose to carry out a survey, you must ask clear, precise questions that will enable you to gain the information you need. General questions about housework do not tell you very much.

2.2

The comparative method is at the heart of sociological research and a useful project might be to carry out a statistical analysis of the household composition of a specific area of your city, town or village and compare it to the *national averages* for types of household.

The difference from, or similarity to, the statistical average could then be related to the types of social problem you may or may not find in your chosen area, and to where social policy might be directed.

You will need to consider the following points.

Consider which is the best way to present your comparisons: diagram, charts, tables, text, etc.

1 How are you going to find out up-to-date figures for national household compositions?
2 Which area of your locality are you going to investigate and compare to the national figures?
3 How are you going to find out the composition of households in your chosen area? If it is small enough, could you conduct your own survey? You will need to consider how much time is available to you.
4 If your area is large, is there any way you can find out the figures without primary research? Could any other departments in your school or college be able to help you? What implications do the figures already being collected have for your original intentions?
5 How far can you legitimately generalise about the social problems likely to be found in your area? What other factors might you need to know?

CHAPTER 3

Education

In this chapter we will examine the arguments surrounding:

1 what is meant by education;
2 educational under-achievement;
3 knowledge in schools;
4 education and work;
5 the experience of education.

Before you begin any of the exercises you should have studied and should be familiar with at least one of the following texts:

Ball, S. *Education* (Longman 1986).
Bilton, T., Bonnett, K., Jones, P., Stanworth, M., Sheard, K. and Webster, A. *Introductory Sociology*, 2nd edn (Macmillan 1987), chapter 8.
Giddens, A. *Sociology* (Polity 1989), pp. 416–39.
Haralambos, M. and Holborn, M. *Sociology: Themes and Perspectives*, 3rd edn (Collins Educational 1990).
O'Donnell, M. *A New Introduction to Sociology*, 3rd edn (Nelson 1992), chapter 4.

In addition, you should have your notes on education in good order.

Introduction

After the family, schools are probably the most important social institutions we come into contact with, in terms of influencing our life chances. We spend a great deal of our early lives in educational institutions of one sort or another, from nursery schools to universities. But it is not just the amount of time we spend in them that makes schools important. The education we receive and the qualifications we obtain as children and teenagers will all affect our life chances – what sort of job we will obtain, our lifetime earnings, even our hobbies and interests. Education is not the only determinant of our life chances as social background, inheritance and chance will also play their part. But it is claimed that, in modern industrial societies, our educational qualifications are a crucial

What do sociologists mean by the following concepts:

- socialisation;
- certification;
- public schools;
- formal institutions?

element in determining where we will eventually find ourselves in the occupational structure.

1 What is meant by education?

It is often assumed that what we learn in schools makes up our *education*, but the term is actually more difficult to define than this. Modern educational systems are a relatively recent development (only about 120-years-old in the case of Britain) but this does not mean that education did not occur before state schools were developed. Children have always had to learn things to prepare for adult roles. In the past the family had prime responsibility for teaching the young but, in modern societies, this function has been largely taken over by formal institutions. The implication of this for individuals is that we are no longer judged on abilities by our family and friends alone but in a formal way too, often by strangers and in comparison to many other people.

IQ

The education system, therefore, claims to make judgements about pupils and students in an objective way (without favouring any particular child just because he or she is a certain person's son or daughter) and so provides a measurement of each child's abilities, qualities, attainments, skills, etc. To do this, the education system has traditionally relied on the concept of IQ (Intelligence Quotient). Through the use of tests, each child could be given a measure of intelligence compared to all other children in the same age-group. On the basis of IQ scores, children were divided into ability ranges which acted as a guide for parents and employers as to their potential achievements in the future.

Many psychologists and biologists have argued that intelligence, as measured by IQ tests, is inherited rather than learned. Sociologists have often challenged this.

How far do you agree that IQ is a major determinant of educational success? Examine both sides of the argument before you come to a conclusion.

From your reading, what evidence can you apply to the issues of banding and streaming in schools?

This division of children could be carried out formally, for example, by streaming, setting, banding or even by allocating children of different abilities (IQ scores) to different types of school. Or the separation could be done informally, for example, through the way teachers treated children with different IQ scores. IQ is thus a central concept in the sifting and sorting of children and it has a powerful influence on the way we think about education. Even MENSA – the organisation for highly intelligent people – uses a type of IQ test for prospective members.

However, the concept of IQ is not universally accepted as an objective measurement of intelligence. On the contrary, some would argue that all IQ tests measure is the ability to complete IQ tests. The argument is that intelligence is actually a very complex concept which is much wider than can be tested by a written examination of a particular type. Moreover, children can quickly be trained to do these tests so that those children with more practice will do better than those with little familiarity with the tests. And the content of IQ tests is often biased, using contexts and situations familiar to white, middle-class boys and creating a less favourable environment for ethnic minorities, children from the working-class and girls.

Nevertheless, the supporters of the idea of IQ have used it to demonstrate not just individual differences but also social differences. For example, some psychologists have argued that, as they have found that the average IQ test scores in America for black children are lower than the average scores for white children, then blacks, as a race, are genetically different from (and, by inference, inferior to) whites. This claim has aroused immense controversy and debate.

Opponents of this claim point out that the methodology of such studies is suspect. There is no direct, proven link between genes and intelli-

IQ tests have often been criticised as unfair.
Answer the following question:

1 To what extent do you agree that IQ tests are culturally biased?

Whatever conclusion you reach, you need to supply evidence to support your arguments.

Your own situation can often be a good starting-point for asking sociological questions.

1 List the ethnic groups present in your school or college, remembering to include white as well as non-white groups.

2 How typical of the ethnic make-up of the country as a whole do you think your school/college is?

the qualifications needed to enter further education courses, including A level. Though all social groups showed some advance, the improved standards were not equally spread out across all social groups.

Social groups and educational attainment

The three groups most often looked at in this context are girls, ethnic minorities, and the working-class. However, it should be remembered that these categories are not mutually exclusive and some groups suffer double or even treble disadvantage in schools. This does not mean that every male, white, middle-class person performs better than every female, black, working-class person. The statistics are averages for groups and cannot predict what any single individual will attain.

There are other problems with comparing these large groups in terms of their educational qualifications. The categories working-class and ethnic minority are so large that they conceal many differences within the group. For example, there are differences in attainment between the children of Afro-Caribbeans and those of South-Asian origin. But even this division does not tell the whole story of differential achievement as Bangladeshis, for instance, tend to gain fewer qualifications than other South-Asian students. Also, other ethnic groups – minorities within the minority – such as the Chinese, Vietnamese, Travellers, Cypriots, etc.,

You will have to know many sociological reasons for a specific phenomenon.

1 What do sociologists argue are the main reasons for female under-achievement in schools?

Reading *Social Studies Review*, vol. 6, no. 4, pp. 156–9 (see [17], p. 337), will help you here. But you also need to assess the validity of these arguments. So,

2 how convinced are you by each of these reasons?

The rise of the three Es

Up until fairly recently it was not uncommon for educationalists – especially feminists – to advocate single-sex secondary schooling on the basis that overly aggressive boys tend to dominate in the classroom, and their influence is also instrumental in gendering school subjects effectively. However, the proposal for single-sex state schools for Muslim girls brings into sharp focus demands both for an authentic multiculturalism in British schools and for equality of educational opportunity, particularly for female students.

Those in favour of the proposal argue that, far from being anti-women as some critics would have it, Islam gives women a central role in its theology and history. Opponents described it as paving the way for apartheid in British education and one which would set back the struggle of British Muslim women for equal rights and fair treatment under the law.

(Source: adapted from *Social Studies Review*, vol. 6, no. 2)

KNOWLEDGE **U**NDERSTANDING

Which newspapers and which texts are likely to be the most appropriate sources for your research?

The debate highlighted above is a continuing one. Make a list of the arguments both for and against single-sex state schools for Muslim girls. You may use the material above, any that you can think up, or any you can find in your textbook. As a start, you might be able to find the article cited in *Social Studies Review* in your sociology department or school or college library.

However, you should then provide any empirical evidence that you can find about this issue, either from sociology texts or perhaps even from the newspapers, remembering that newspaper articles are not usually produced by sociologists!

Finally, come to an evaluation of both sides of the argument, stating which you find more compelling and why.

tend to be invisible in discussions of ethnic minority educational achievement.

There are similar problems with the category, working-class. In the area of gender, however, the issue is slightly different. Female students have increasingly improved their pre-18 performance in exams so that they now achieve more at school, in terms of qualifications, than boys. However, in higher education, differences in attainment begin to appear so that males dominate the ranks of post-graduates. But it is in the area of subject choice that gender differences in attainment are more apparent. Boys predominate in the *high status* subjects of science and technology and girls in the arts and social sciences. This is not just a question of prestige, but has important implications for careers, lifetime earnings and power.

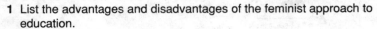

In assessing an approach to an issue you should think about the arguments and the evidence about it. For example:

1 List the advantages and disadvantages of the feminist approach to education.

2 Attach appropriate studies to any of the points you make.

Explanations

Different sociologists have looked to various areas of social life to try to explain these variations in achievement. Depending on sociological perspective, they have tended to emphasise home background, the situation of schools or larger social factors as the main reason for educational under-achievement.

The range of factors put forward in studies of educational under-achievement is bewildering. In terms of home background, for example, issues such as child-rearing practices, parental attitudes, language spoken, material provisions, the toys children are given, etc. have been cited as influences on children's performance at school. At school, teachers' expectations, who students mix with, the organisation of the school, ethnocentric curricula, etc. have been cited. In the case of societal factors, items such as government policy, the ideology of domesticity, racism and the needs of industry among others have all been put forward.

Many questions in the examination require you to make judgements about competing explanations. In terms of educational under-achievement, sociologists have put forward the three factors cited in the preceding paragraph. For each of these address the following:

1 List the main reasons put forward within the factor. For example, for home background, you might begin with parental interest.

2 Provide supporting studies for each factor where you can.

3 Assess the relative power of each factor to explain under-achievement.

Note that *relative* means that you have to decide which is/are more or less powerful in explaining under-achievement.

Making decisions is a good way of practising your skill of application.

From the following list take each item and place it in the appropriate cell of the table:

- Marxism
- interactionism
- cultural deprivation
- cultural reproduction

		Explanation of under-achievement		
		Home	**School**	**Society**
Perspective which looks to this for an explanation		Functionalism		
Explanation is called			Clash of cultures	

Gender and ethnicity are important themes which run throughout sociology.

For gender you will have come across Dale Spender's work on education in your reading. See, for example, Haralambos and Holborn, pp. 283–90.

1 Assess Spender's work, stating what it explains convincingly and what it might lack.

2 Use any information from your reading to support points made.

For ethnicity:

1 evaluate the relative importance of racism as an explanation for ethnic-minority under-achievement by comparing the effects of racism with reasons such as English-as-a-second-language, lack of motivation, etc.

STRUCTURED QUESTION

Item A

Figures show a 10 per cent increase this academic year in the number of new entrants on first degree courses, with a leap in the number of female students. There are now more than 382,000 students – three-quarters of whom are undergraduates.

The figures show the continuing popularity of social sciences, leading other courses with more than 39,000 undergraduates, 5,000 more than on engineering and technology courses. The least popular courses are in librarianship and information science, with about 300 students.

There are over 4,000 more female undergraduates this year than last, a much greater rate of increase than for men who increased their number by 2,800. Only 11 per cent of engineering students are female, although this is the one field with guaranteed job opportunities for graduates. Women are massively over-represented on modern languages and education courses.

(Source: adapted from Barry Hugill, © the *Observer*, 24 February 1991, p. 9)

Item B

Staying-on rates

| | Age 16 | | Age 16–18 | |
	FT	PT	FT	PT*
UK (1988)	50	41	35	34
Germany (1987)	69	31	47	43
Japan (1988)	92	3	77	3
France (1986)	78	3	66	8

*FT = Full Time   PT = Part Time
Figures are for the participation by percentage of age group
(Source: adapted from DES. Reproduced with the permission of the Controller of Her Majesty's Stationery Office.)

Your knowledge of the wider world can often be applied to questions. For example, why do you think these countries were chosen for comparison?

APPLICATION

Item C

Blacks and Asians 'losing out in university stakes'

Asian and black applicants for university places are less successful than whites, according to figures released ... by the Universities Central Council for Admissions.

Fewer than half the candidates from ethnic minorities in Britain are gaining admission to universities, compared with 53 per cent of white applicants.

The UCCA figures show that 44.7 per cent of all Asian applicants were accepted by universities. Just under 50 per cent of Chinese applicants were successful, while fewer than 39 per cent of Pakistani applicants won a place. But fewer than one in three blacks were accepted.

Nearly eight per cent of new university students last year were from non-white families, higher than the estimated percentage of the overall population, but only half the 16 per cent non-white admissions reported by polytechnics and colleges.

(Source: adapted from James Meikle, the *Guardian*, Saturday 13 July 1991)

a) With reference to Item A, how many students were on engineering and technology courses?   (1 mark)
b) Look at Item B. Describe the patterns of staying-on rates shown there.
                                                                                   (3 marks)
c) In what ways has the government tried to increase the staying-on rate in the UK?   (5 marks)
d) Assess sociological explanations for the choices of subject made by men and women shown in Item A.   (8 marks)
e) Evaluate sociological contributions to an understanding of the differential acceptance rate to universities, described in Item C.
                                                                                   (8 marks)

You need to apply your knowledge of government policy on education to the particular issue of the staying-on rates.

APPLICATION

The problem with all these influences is how to combine them to provide a comprehensive and convincing explanation of under-achievement. It is not likely that any one factor is going to be decisive. Even if all the factors in one of the three main areas of social life that we have explored could be said to apply, this could not provide a complete account of educational *failure*. It is likely that some combination of home, school and societal factors will begin to offer an understanding of the reasons why some groups do less well than others. But even here we should be careful not to attempt to explain all under-achievement by the same combination of factors. Individuals are likely to be affected by different factors depending upon which part of the working-class they come from, which ethnic group they belong to, whether they are middle-class or working-class, girls or boys etc. However, sociologists are generally agreed that the interaction between experiences at home, at school and in society at large explains why some types of individual do less well in the education system than others.

Methodological awareness also needs to be applied wherever it can. For example, when you see extracts such as Item C above, you should be asking yourself questions such as the following:

What problems might be encountered by having both Asian and Pakistani categories in this passage?

APPLICATION

These differences in achievement obviously have individual effects in that those who do less well at school are more likely to end up in the less well-paid jobs. However, this is not inevitable. Individuals do get on in the world without having formal educational qualifications. There are many skills which can earn someone a living that are not learned in schools. People may achieve occupational success through luck, raw talent or flair without necessarily having any formal qualifications. However, there are also social effects, such as the concentration of ethnic minorities and women in the worst-paid jobs requiring fewer qualifications. But the appearance of the children of the working class, women and ethnic minorities in the *under-class* or the *reserve army of labour* is a vivid consequence of the result of their schooling.

3 Knowledge in schools

It might be supposed that what children learn in schools may be found on their timetables but sociologists make a distinction between the formal curriculum, which is the list of subjects that a school offers its students (maths, chemistry, French, etc.), and the hidden curriculum, which is all the other things a student learns in school, both intentionally and unintentionally, inside and outside of lessons.

The formal curriculum

In the last few years, there have been major changes in the content of the formal curriculum in schools in England and Wales. For the first time, a national curriculum has been introduced and, by the end of 1995, it will control with the force of law the great majority of what is taught and learned in schools in England and Wales. Schools in the private fee-paying sector do not have to follow the national curriculum, but it is expected that most of them will do so.

In the primary sector, now identified with key stages 1 and 2 of the National Curriculum, the central importance of the three Rs – reading, writing and arithmetic – is maintained. These are the basic skills which children need in order to live successfully in the modern world. Indeed, some sociologists argue that the need to equip workers with these basic skills was the main reason why a state education system was first set up at the end of the nineteenth century. However, to these basic skills have now been added a knowledge of science and of a foreign language, together with Information Technology in the secondary sector (key stages 3 and 4).

INTERPRETATION

For some sociological issues there is a central piece of work which you should know about. For example, Karabel and Halsey are very important in the field of educational knowledge. You need to draw out the main points of their work from your reading.

For this exercise you should read *Social Studies Review*, vol. 6, no. 3, pp. 108–11. (See [18], p. 337.)

List the studies Buswell uses in supporting her arguments, noting the major points in each study. This will develop your skill of interpretation.

Before the National Curriculum was introduced, the secondary curriculum was much more diverse. Students were given more choice about which subjects they could take and there were marked differences between the choices of different social groups. Girls tended to go for the Arts, languages and some social sciences, while boys tended to go for mathematics and the sciences. But there was also a class difference at this point, with the children of the working class tending to dominate vocational subjects like technical studies, while the children of the middle class tended to be concentrated in the more 'academic' subjects.

The results of these subject choices were not just that students followed their interests. The qualifications that people obtain have a value in the labour market and help them to 'buy' a position in the work-force. But certain subjects are seen as more valuable currency than others. This 'hierarchy of subjects' usually places the sciences as the most valuable, with craft or practical subjects least important. This means that the subjects that students choose or are allowed to take are important for their future careers.

Some sociologists argued that students' choices of subject were free, with everyone having the opportunity to perform to his or her best ability in the subjects desired. Where restrictions on choice were made, they were on the basis of objective criteria, such as test scores, past performances, etc. Other sociologists argued that the system operated to discriminate against certain groups, so that girls were channelled into 'domestic' subjects and the working class into less academic areas. This was achieved through teacher expectations, peer-group pressure, the 'blocking' of options against one another, and the middle-class, male bias of many examinations. Thus, 'educational failure' was not just a matter of individuals not passing exams; it was 'socially constructed' by the way in which some social groups were channelled into lower-status subjects.

Your reading will have acquainted you with the concept of cultural reproduction.

1 How convinced are you that cultural reproduction does, in fact, take place?

2 What evidence has influenced your decision?

Using any text or your notes, search for studies which have included analysis of the factors indicated in the paragraph above. By taking each factor separately and listing the studies about it, you will be applying evidence to these factors.

The impact of the National Curriculum

With the introduction of the National Curriculum students are no longer able to choose their subjects to the same extent. In addition, there are standard assessments for different ages which test the achievement of each student.

The claim for the National Curriculum is that, by being given a clear set of aims, students know exactly what is expected at various stages in their educational lives. This has the effect of giving all children, regardless of gender, class or ethnic origin, the chance to maximise their achievements and, thus, raise educational standards overall. It also allows parents to make judgements about the success or failure of different schools by providing a national measure by which schools can be compared. This enables parental choice to be exercised on the basis of a rational decision and helps to reduce various kinds of bias in subject choice.

The National Curriculum represents a return to a more traditional curriculum which tends to squeeze out subjects like the humanities and peace studies but also introduces more modern skills like information technology.

However, some sociologists have argued that the introduction of the National Curriculum represents an increase in central control over the curriculum and imposes on every student a set of subjects which might not be appropriate for everybody. The amount of free choice is so small that individual needs are ignored. Moreover, the extra resources needed to introduce the National Curriculum have not been made available so that its introduction has not been as thorough as it should have been. The fact that the private schools do not have to follow the National

Apart from the National Curriculum, sociologists have commented on other changes to the education system which have occurred during the 1970s and 1980s.

1 Choose THREE changes and list the main sociological points which have been made about them.

2 Take note of any studies mentioned as evidence.

Sociologists are often critical of themselves and their subject. They *can* also be defensive about sociology.

1 What are the subjects of the National Curriculum?

2 Where do the social sciences fit in?

3 What implications do your answers have for sociology as a school subject?

Curriculum means that it is not, in fact, national at all. This has the effect of introducing a fundamental division in the type of education that British children receive.

The hidden curriculum

Schools also teach lessons which are beyond the realm of academic subjects, in what is known as the *hidden curriculum*. For the individual student this means learning certain ways of behaving and thinking which will be important for the conduct of their adult lives. In school, it is argued, we learn to obey authority, and learn about work and discipline, social and political values.

Certainly, for most individuals, schools are the first formal organisation they experience and the first place in which they are likely to meet large numbers of non-family members at the same time. Our first few weeks at school are, therefore, often very frightening, but can also be exciting as we learn to mix with other people and become *sociable*. Many children now have earlier experience of schooling from their attendance

Sometimes sociology students give a description when a question asks for analysis. Description involves your knowledge of something while analysis often involves an evaluation of it. For example:

1 Identify the major features of the hidden curriculum;

2 How important is it in relation to the formal curriculum?

The first task is description, the second combines analysis and evaluation.

You will need to know the sociological concepts which are used in a particular area.

What do sociologists mean by:

- conformity;
- social order;
- legitimacy;
- teaching styles;
- authority?

at play-groups, crèches, nurseries and pre-school groups, and this eases their transition into formal education.

Some sociologists argue that the hidden curriculum is the real reason why schools were set up, rather than for the teaching of academic subjects. The argument takes several forms but the basic idea is that society needs citizens who accept the fundamental arrangements of society so that social order or social stability is achieved. This would include, for example, accepting that those in power in society have a right to be in control. Accepting the legitimacy of those in power is not a natural event; it has to be learned.

It is in schools that we learn to conform to the way things are, through such phenomena as teaching styles. In the traditional method, the teacher holds authority and acts as a deliverer of knowledge to the subservient masses. Some argue that, in the postmodern world, as certainty of knowledge collapses, teaching styles will change so that the teacher becomes more of a facilitator, drawing upon the students' own experiences. However, others argue that the lesson of obedience is the most important and it is this which is the main function of schools.

But there are other hidden lessons in school. For example, gender differences are said to be reinforced by the way schools operate. This issue illustrates the many different ways in which the hidden curriculum is said to work. The process of reinforcing gender differentiation is a subtle and complex one involving, among other factors, the way teachers and careers advisers interact with boys and girls, the channelling of girls and

This exercise is quite long because it involves a great deal of skilled performance from you.

1 Find TWO studies of gender and the hidden curriculum.

2 Describe the major findings of each.

3 Assess the contribution of each one to an understanding of this issue. Begin by listing the strengths and weaknesses of each.

You should be able to apply your knowledge about one aspect of sociology to other issues by thinking about how your knowledge can be transferred to a different context. Consider, for example, the following:

In the context of Coursework Suggestion, on p. 96, why might a positivist prefer to use a stopwatch?

boys into different subjects through tradition and pressure from peers, parents and teachers, and the domination of men in the teaching hierarchy, providing role models for boys but not girls.

However, some sociologists have challenged whether the hidden curriculum is as important as it is made out to be or, indeed, whether it is important at all. They argue that schoolchildren themselves see the formal curriculum as more likely to affect their lives than the hidden curriculum. If it is hidden, how do we know it exists? If it is so important, all students should be affected by it yet many girls reject the stereotypes which the hidden curriculum is supposed to teach them. So, why does it seem to affect some and not others? If sociologists can spot the workings of the hidden curriculum, why do only some students reject dominant values and end up as critics of those in power? (See Coursework Suggestion 3.2 on p. 96.)

4 Education and work

Right from the beginning of the state education system in 1870, the connection between education and work has been recognised. It was argued at the beginning that there was a need for schooling to teach young people the basic skills needed by industry. This was necessary because our major industrial competitors invested in the 'human capital' of their chil-

Often it is possible to take old sociological theories and apply them to contemporary issues. For example, human capital theory was developed in the 1950s.

1 Find out its main points.

2 Discuss, in a paragraph, its relevance for education in the 1990s. You might find the concept of vocationalism useful here.

Social mobility studies often have many statistics in them. You need to be confident in interpreting them and so you should practise doing this. Look at Haralambos and Holborn, pp. 295–304, tables 10–12.

What are the implications for the amount of social mobility in society in these tables?

dren to a much greater extent. As technology advanced it was argued that workers needed to enter industry with at least basic numeracy and literacy skills so that they could follow written orders.

Education and social mobility

But the relationship between education and work is more complicated in modern Britain. As the occupational structure has grown more complex, producing more and more levels in the occupational and technological hierarchies, the education system becomes seen as the most important way in which individuals can climb the social hierarchy. The reason for this is that entry to higher status jobs has increasingly become dependent on formal educational qualifications. More jobs now demand basic qualifications before an individual can be employed, but many jobs have also increased the level of qualifications which are requested. Thus, the type of education which an individual receives will influence the extent to which he or she is socially mobile.

The way that social mobility is viewed, however, depends on whether the sociologist sees the education system as a meritocracy or as a means of cultural reproduction. In the former case, everyone is seen to have an

Another aspect of interpretation is to work out correctly what position a sociologist is taking. For example, in Haralambos and Holborn, pp. 229–53, which sociologists do you think would tend to see society as a meritocracy and which as a system of cultural reproduction?

By listing them in two columns you will have a clearer view of the evidence.

Sociologists' positions on:	
Meritocracy	**Cultural reproductions**

Thinking about events in your own experience is an important part of applying sociological knowledge.

1 How has the New Vocationalism appeared in your school or institution?

2 What do your teachers think about it? Are their opinions enough for a valid assessment of the success or failure of the New Vocationalism?

equal chance of maximising their educational potential. The education system is seen as a neutral device that sifts and selects individuals on the basis of their ability alone. In the case of cultural reproduction, individuals are selected to be upwardly mobile, not on the basis of abilities, but according to their social characteristics – their class, gender and ethnic group.

The likelihood is that some individuals will find the education system offers them a chance to obtain qualifications and 'move up in the world', but that some social groups will find the education system disadvantages them in relation to other social groups. Of course, individuals within the disadvantaged social groups will also find the education system does not provide them with enough qualifications to obtain good jobs and that they will have to follow their father, mother or guardian into the same type of occupation and, therefore, roughly the same social class. It was this idea that the education system is 'failing' British industry in some way which provided the impetus for the development of the *New Vocationalism* whose origins can be traced to a speech made by Labour Prime Minister James Callaghan at Ruskin College, Oxford in 1976.

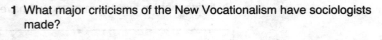

Though sociologists may seem overcritical at times, it is through criticism that an assessment is arrived at.

1 What major criticisms of the New Vocationalism have sociologists made?

2 How convincing do you find these criticisms and why?

3 Are any studies more convincing than others and, if so, why are they?

Education and industry

Politicians saw the failure of the education system less in terms of disadvantaging individuals and more as failing to provide industry with enough recruits of the right calibre and with useful skills. The argument was that Britain's continuing failure in world economic markets was at least partly the result of a skills shortage in industry as teachers failed to equip their students with the appropriate competences for the modern, technological world. This could be shown by the way that Britain failed to capitalise on its discoveries in the field of computer technologies.

Both Labour and Conservative governments maintained that schools had become divorced from industry and that the curriculum was dominated by the academic concerns of the universities, rather than the needs of industry. This meant that individuals who left school at 16 or 18 to enter the world of work were ill-equipped to deal with the challenges of modern industry. Even those who left education with higher qualifications tended to prefer to enter the professions, such as law or medicine, rather than engineering or manufacturing industry.

Education and training

Therefore, the education system had to adapt itself to more of a training approach than the traditional academic subject emphasis. Throughout the 1980s, the Conservative Governments developed the idea that all 16–19 year olds should be involved in further education or training for at least two years. They introduced the Youth Training Scheme (YTS), now Employment Training (ET), for those young people who wanted to leave full-time education, and altered the social security arrangements to make it financially difficult for them to refuse an ET place without making themselves effectively homeless.

In schools, the curriculum was changed to reflect the need for more training opportunities for all children. This took the form of many new initiatives. GCSEs were developed which laid down the precise levels of ability that students could obtain. GCSEs feature a more practical emphasis so that employers might find them more useful as indicators of the applicants' abilities. The Certificate of Pre-Vocational Education

E VALUATION

To develop the skill of evaluation you need to practise your critical ability. Often criticisms emerge from your own or your peers' experiences. For this exercise, for example, you might draw on the experiences of someone who has done Employment Training.

Suggest TWO sociological criticisms of Employment Training.

If they are to be sociological, you need to apply evidence other than a personal opinion. But, if you have asked someone about ET, this could be a starting point.

One of the more difficult questions that crops up in sociology examinations is the one which asks you to compare and contrast two things. You can familiarise yourself with this process by carrying out this interpretation exercise:

Read *Social Studies Review*, vol. 6, no. 4, pp. 143–7. (See [19], p. 337.)

What does the article suggest is (a) the main similarity and (b) the main difference between the training systems of Germany and Britain?

(CPVE) was an alternative curriculum for students of all abilities. Its aim was to prepare them more directly for the world of work. In the event, it tended to be only the students of lower ability who found themselves on CPVE courses. More recent vocational initiatives include the Diploma of Vocational Education and the specific and general National Vocational Qualifications. The Training and Vocational Education Initiative (TVEI) was a large-scale experiment in many areas of the country which tried to introduce a whole number of developments that would be useful to industry, such as information technology, records of achievement, work experience, and so on.

All students were to receive teaching in enterprise culture, economic awareness and other social skills which an employer might find useful. For example, social- and life-skills education was suggested as a way in which students could develop a sense of teamwork, individual initiative, responsibility, etc. It is also argued that A levels and AS levels will have to change to meet the challenge of this new approach. Some educationalists argue that coursework should become an important component of the A level, as well as core skills, for all 16–19 year olds. Others, notably the present Government, are less keen to make changes to the 'gold standard' of A level. Nevertheless, the effect of all these changes, it is argued, is to give school-leavers *transferable skills* which will make them attractive to employers, because they will be able to use these skills in the new contexts which employers will set for them.

Many educationalists and sociologists are sceptical of the claims for the New Vocationalism. They argue that the central idea of giving students transferable skills is fine in theory but difficult in practice. Much of the educational content of vocational courses is lost and, instead,

What do you think are the *core* or *transferable* skills which every young worker should have?

When you have made your list, look up any text and compare your ideas with the skills identified in ideas of the New Vocationalism.

For this exercise, you will be interpreting and applying evidence from *Social Studies Review*, vol. 2, no. 2, pp. 21–5. (See [20], p. 337.)

1 Write a paragraph on how the preparation of females for work differs from that of males.

2 Use evidence from the article to support your points.

students are taught the obvious. Moreover, it is lower-ability students who tend to be channelled into vocational courses and, therefore, the New Vocationalism introduces another form of selection, or cultural reproduction, with working-class and ethnic-minority children disproportionately represented on these courses, while middle-class and white children continue to predominate on the higher status, academic A level courses.

While acknowledging that there have been many beneficial developments from the new initiatives, sociologists argue that these have been the result of teachers using the opportunities which are presented, by the offer of extra resources and money through the initiatives to develop educational programmes, but not necessarily envisaged by the Government. For example, the TVEI has laid great stress on equal opportunities for women and ethnic minorities. While the Government sees this as necessary to ensure that the most effective use is made of all the human resources of the population for the needs of industry, opponents argue that this policy is often at odds with the Government's own family policy which stresses the role of the woman as homemaker. Nevertheless, teachers have used the policy to put forward claims for equality of treatment for boys, girls and all ethnic groups, and these claims go beyond the strictly vocational nature of education.

5 The experience of education

All children in Britain have experienced the classroom at one time or another, and have found it to be a place that can be absorbing and interesting or boring and routine. But experiences in the classroom are not the same for everybody all the time. Indeed, pupils have systematically different experiences along many dimensions.

Teaching styles and individual experience

The teaching and learning styles of different schools vary so that even the minute-to-minute experiences of schoolchildren differ. For example, some schools rely on traditional *chalk-and-talk* methods where the

EXERCISE

The phrase 'hidden curriculum' was first used by Jackson in *Life in Classrooms* (Holt, Rinehart & Winston 1964) and refers to all those things pupils learn in schools that are not overtly taught. These are mainly attitudes, values and principles of behaviour which, though not explicitly spelled out by teachers, are rewarded when pupils display them through their actions.

The hidden curriculum can be found in the way that a school is organised, in the way that pupils and teachers interact and in the content of the subjects taught. Most schools are organised in a hierarchy of authority. There is not much doubt about who is in charge or about how decisions are made. Even the physical layout of the traditional classroom, with the teacher dominant at the front of the room, controlling the blackboard and able to see all that happens, encourages pupils to internalise a view of themselves as inferior and subject to those more powerful. School uniforms can be interpreted in the same way. Those who support the wearing of uniform, usually adults, stress that it encourages pupils to develop loyalty to the group . . . The hidden curriculum is also traceable within the mainstream curriculum which reflects an elitist, male and ethnocentric view of what is worthwhile knowledge.

(Source: adapted from Patrick McNeill, *Society Today 2* Macmillan 1991)

E VALUATION

Make sure that your conclusion emerges directly from your arguments and is not unconnected.

The passage outlines elements of the hidden curriculum. Searching the literature, find other features of schools which may be part of the hidden curriculum. Identify also the arguments against the effects of the hidden curriculum. From your reading come to a conclusion as to whether the hidden curriculum is an effective influence on schoolchildren, looking at the balance of evidence you have collected.

I NTERPRETATION

You may be asked to interpret diagrams to explain concepts. Practise this with the following exercise:

Schools are said by sociologists to have *echelon authority*, which can be represented by:

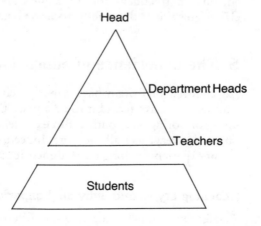

Head

Department Heads

Teachers

Students

What do you think is meant by echelon authority?

INTERPRETATION

Evaluation can be carried out not just on sociological arguments but also on personal experience. Look, for example, at the following questions:

1 From your own experience, list the teaching styles you have had.

EVALUATION

2 Which was the most effective for you and why?

pupils tend to be passive recipients of teachers' talk. On the other hand, some pupils experience only *progressive* education methods, with an emphasis on discovery learning and the pupils following their own interests. Traditional methods have been accused of being tedious and of ignoring pupil involvement. Although it seems obvious that progressive education should be more enjoyable than traditional teaching styles, it has come in for much criticism. It is claimed to have brought educational standards down because pupils lack teacher-direction and individuals may become lost within a class of individually learning pupils.

But the attitude of pupils towards school also varies according to their overall experience of education. For many students, education can be a liberating experience, introducing them to new worlds and subjects, and broadening their horizons beyond their home background. Moreover, by providing individuals with qualifications, education can empower them, enabling them to have lifestyles which they would otherwise be denied. On the other hand, other pupils' educational experiences are composed of frustration and a sense of failure as they do not achieve the qualifications they desire. Indeed, it has been argued that this sense of failure is important to society as a whole, as individuals who do not achieve in schools blame themselves rather than society for their lack of achievement and, thus, accept their lower-status position in society.

Also, for large numbers of pupils, school is a place that they *have* to

EVALUATION

When evaluating, it is essential that you have decided on some criteria against which you are going to measure what is to be assessed. With this in mind, assess the concept of *de-schooling*, concentrating on its practicality or otherwise.

APPLICATION

You will need to practise applying your knowledge of society at large to issues. Therefore, answer these questions:

1 Place the following in order of the status generally attached to them, with the high-status type at the top of your list:
   • comprehensive school;
   • grammar school;
   • private tutorial college;
   • secondary modern school;
   • city technology college;
   • private boarding school.

EVALUATION

2 Are any particularly difficult to place and, if so, why?

go to and they experience it as social control or social constraint. They cannot wait to get out into the adult world (and many of their teachers cannot wait either!) since, for these students, school is a place of containment. Teachers struggle to keep them occupied but, usually, with limited success. It is these students who form the major control problems in schools.

Types of school

The experience of pupils in schools will also vary according to the type of school that they attend. For example, those educated privately are likely to be in a more privileged position than most of those in state comprehensive schools. This is true especially of those in high-status public schools, such as Eton, Harrow or Benenden. The private sector does not have to follow the National Curriculum, or set students the standard

INTERPRETATION

To practise a range of skills in this exercise you need to read *Social Studies Review*, vol. 3, no. 1, pp. 11–14. (See [21], p. 337.)

1 What are the two positions regarding the 'problem with schools'?

EVALUATION

2 Which do you find more convincing?

APPLICATION

3 Provide arguments to support your choice.

assessment tasks. In the past, and even in some counties today, the experience of those in grammar schools differed significantly from that of those in secondary modern schools. Selective systems are designed to provide a different set of experiences for pupils who are perceived to have different needs.

These are not the only divisions in the school system. In the 1980s, the Conservative Government introduced a number of city technology colleges (CTCs) which were to be funded primarily by private industry and would be situated in the inner cities. The curriculum for such schools would, as the name suggests, be weighted towards technology across the full range of ability. However, critics of CTCs argue that the amount of private funding is limited and money which would otherwise go to state schools has been diverted to fund the 20 proposed colleges. Moreover, they are not all situated in the inner cities and have variable curricula, some concentrating on the performing arts, others on a Christian basis, depending on who provides the limited amount of private funding. It is argued that such colleges re-introduce selection in areas which had eliminated it and have done so in a time of declining rolls so that other state schools will have to close to accommodate the new provision.

A further type of school – the grant-maintained – has been introduced for those educational institutions which wish to 'opt out' of local authority control and be funded directly by the Department for Education (DFE). The schools which initially opted out were largely those which had been under threat of re-organisation or closure. Therefore, they appealed to the DFE and were granted 'opt-out' status bringing about changes in the type of education which their students will receive.

Although they do have to follow the National Curriculum, they need

It is important to use your sociological skills when looking at recent developments in society.

APPLICATION

1 List, in two columns, the advantages and disadvantages of 'opted-out' schools.

Opted-out schools	
Advantages	**Disadvantages**

INTERPRETATION

2 Search the newspapers for articles about them. Are any comments positive or negative? Does the newspaper itself make a difference?

STRUCTURED QUESTION

Item A

One of the aspects I find most worrying is competition between types of school. We now have three groups in supposedly fair competition with each other – the maintained schools, the independents and the newly created semi-independent sector consisting of the city technology colleges and the grant-maintained schools which have opted out of local authority control. Anyone who believes that this is truly a competition should think again . . .

What dismays me, however, is first of all the claim that, because children in independent schools sometimes do better at exams than those in maintained schools, this is evidence of superior teaching. In fact, it is often merely a reflection of smaller classes and the fact that independent schools deal mainly with some of the most socially privileged children, while maintained schools must teach everyone irrespective of wealth . . .

Most worrying of all is the rigged competition between the semi-independent sector and the maintained schools. The millions of pounds of public money given to the CTCs is an utter disgrace. The Nottingham CTC alone received more money for buildings than all the schools in Leeds and Sheffield put together.

(Source: adapted from Ted Wragg, *Times Educational Supplement*, Friday 2 March 1990, no. 3844, © Times Supplements Ltd, 1990.)

Item B

The attraction of policies like the National Curriculum, devolving school budgets, CTCs, opting out and open enrolment, according to Conservatives, lies in the manner in which they extend parental choice. Unfettered by the demands and constraints of LEAs, for example, the 'state independent schools' and CTCs are claimed to offer parents greater control over what kind of education their children receive and how their chosen school develops. The Conservative view is that, by allowing schools to compete more openly with each other for pupils and for funds, and by not having 'popular' schools subsidising those which are 'less popular', the overall standard of education on offer will be improved. In short, the freer operation of market forces within the reformed state sector will allow for a wider range of schools, offering different subject strengths to the consumer (in this case, the parent). It will also, according to this view, force the least popular schools to increase their attractiveness to potential recruits by improving their educational performance.

(Source: adapted from 'Research Roundup', *Social Studies Review*, vol. 3, no. 1)

Item C

What do sociologists mean by a 'selective system of education'?

Though the debate between those who argue for a selective system of education and those who argue for a comprehensive model seems to have died away, the issue is still very much a live one. The reforms of the 1980s threaten to undermine the principle of comprehensive education and introduce selection by the back door. Comprehensive education therefore needs to be defended all over again.

a) According to Item A, what are the three types of school in Britain today?

(1 mark)

b) Why, according Item B, will schools be forced to 'increase their attractiveness to potential recruits'?

(1 mark)

c) Evaluate the relative merits of the arguments put forward in Items A and B.

(5 marks)

d) Assess sociological contributions to an understanding of the impact of the reforms identified in the items.

(9 marks)

e) Assess the sociological arguments for and against comprehensive education (Item C).

(9 marks)

You need to interpret the differences in the two items and then directly compare their strenghts and weaknesses.

INTERPRETATION

EVALUATION

APPLICATION

Item B in the above question claimed that educational changes increased parental choice.

What *limits* to parental choice can you suggest?

By doing this exercise you will be applying your political and sociological sense to a controversial issue.

---

not follow the plans of the Local Education Authority and, so, may ignore such developments as equal opportunities policies, records of achievement, work-experience placements, etc. Critics of the 'opt-out' schemes argue that these prevent the rational planning of educational provision in a time of falling rolls, especially as the number of grant-maintained schools increases.

The powers of individual schools have been both enhanced and restricted under the 1987 Education Reform Act, so that the experiences of individual students are likely to become similar and different at the same time. The imposition of the National Curriculum means that most students in the state sector will be following similar schemes of education throughout their time in schools. But as schools gain control over their own budgets, and governors and parents are given more powers, individual schools may develop greater differences from one another. It is one of many paradoxes or contradictions in human existence that freedom and constraint, similarity and diversification can occur simultaneously.

APPLICATION

Educational issues raise larger sociological ones. You should apply your knowledge across topic boundaries. Consider, for instance, how the last sentence in the paragraph above relates to the issues of structure and action.

Conclusion

The importance of education to the individual is beyond doubt. It is a major determinant of experiences in later life, and life chances. As such, it is the object of much social policy and social engineering. Politicians have looked to education to solve some of society's problems, ranging from industrial failure to racial discrimination. Therefore, any government seeks to influence what goes on in education through social policy, from the compensatory education programmes in the 1960s to proposed vouchers schemes in the 1990s. The education system is, thus, a fascinating arena for sociological study as it is constantly in a state of change, mostly in response to social or governmental pressures to perform in certain ways. But most of all, it is the fact that nearly everyone goes to school at some time in their lives which makes everybody an 'expert' on education. The sociological task is to explore the social implications of education and gather evidence about schools' performances so that supported statements about education can be made and not just the evidence of common-sense experiences put forward.

Important points to bear in mind

1 Education is the single most important avenue for social mobility but it is not the only one.
2 The social characteristics of an individual will affect the education he or she receives but natural ability will also be a factor.
3 Not every black or female under-achieves.
4 What counts as educational knowledge will vary from time to time and from society to society.
5 Schools are not just state controlled; the private sector is a small but crucial part of the system.

There are three perspectives that are usually identified in education – functionalism, Marxism and interactionism. You should practise assessing these like this:

1 which perspective most closely reflects the reality of the contemporary education system, and;
2 what has persuaded you that your choice is the correct one?   .

EVALUATION

KEY CONCEPTS

It is important that you are familiar with and are able to use the concepts in this section in appropriate ways if you are to apply them effectively in the examination. Check your understanding of the concepts by carrying out this exercise.

For each of the following paragraphs, fill in the missing blanks with the most likely concept from the subsequent list.

The causes of _____ are among the most discussed in the sociology of education. Sociologists have tended to focus on _____ factors, _____ factors or _____ factors. Psychologists and biologists have tended to focus on _____ and _____.

IQ	Societal	Home
Educational 'failure'	Genetics	School

Education is one form of _____ but the form which this takes is disputed. Some sociologists argue that the main function of education is to justify the status quo through a process of _____. Others argue that the main task of education is to provide differential qualifications or _____ for social groups, providing them with different types of _____. Still others suggest that the main function of education is to ensure that middle-class children end up in middle-class jobs and working-class children end up in working-class jobs – a process known as

_____.

Cultural capital	Certification	Secondary socialisation
Cultural reproduction	Legitimation	

During the 1980s, the Government sought to mould education to fit the needs of business through the introduction of the _____. Their aim was to encourage a climate of entrepreneurial endeavour which they called the _____. The Government was also concerned with extending parental choice by providing assistance for some children to attend the _____ and allowing some schools to _____ of Local Education Authority control. At the same time, the Government introduced the _____ which determined what should be taught in the state sector.

New Vocationalism	Opt out	Private sector
National curriculum	Enterprise culture	

While _____ was seen as mainly the result of the child's background, _____ were the ways in which it was dealt with. Nor was it just those in the working class who were seen as having inadequate backgrounds but _____ was also seen as a factor. However, as attention switched to the schools, explanations began to focus on issues such the _____. Nevertheless, it is important to recognise that many people see education as providing equal opportunities for all, regardless of social background – a system of _____.

Compensatory education programmes		Under-achievement
Ethnicity	Hidden curriculum	Meritocracy

COURSEWORK SUGGESTIONS

3.1

Comparisons of the educational qualifications of different social groups, for example, males and females, are likely to prove a popular choice for A level projects. This is because the target audience for this type of research is accessible and likely to co-operate. It is, therefore, important that, if you choose to do this sort of research, you pay attention to the methodological problems that might result. You must also ensure that you provide a proper analysis of your results which relates to the hypothesis you set yourself and does not just describe in words what your statistics show. One variation which you might try is to compare the educational qualifications of your peers and their parents. This would set you another methodological problem of how to find out the appropriate information from the parent group.

You will need to consider the following points:

You can use the brainstorming technique to develop an appropriate hypothesis. How can you find out about this technique?

1　How are you going to sample your chosen groups? What alternative sampling techniques are available to you? It is not enough just to choose your friends.
2　What hypothesis or hypotheses will you choose and how will the questions you ask relate to it or them?
3　How will you present your findings? Can you use a graphics package to produce first-rate statistical representations? If not, where can you learn to do so?
4　What checks on your questions will you introduce to ensure that you gain the information you require?
5　How large would your sample have to be before your statistics can be said to be significant?

3.2

Classroom observation could be an interesting area for your coursework project. However, it is important that you know precisely what you are going to be looking for before you begin to observe, and what you will accept as a 'successful' observation of the phenomenon that you are interested in. For example, if you are examining the time the teacher gives to girls and boys in the class, how are you going to measure it? While you may choose just to observe without imposing any system, you need to know the justification for this type of observation and refer to it in your report. An alternative might be to introduce a time element into your observations and check what is happening every minute. You will need a stopwatch for this sort of approach. Or you may seek to video a classroom and use this, together with a commentary, as your evidence.

You need to consider the following points:

1　If you are observing covertly, what are the ethical problems connected with not telling the members of the class that they are being observed?
2　If you use a video recorder, what are the limitations of the tape as evidence? You will need to refer to these in your final text.
3　Your observations need to be *directly* connected to your aim or hypothesis, and not just general.

This question raises important ethical issues which you must address in your project.

4 How many classes are you going to observe and when? Will you seek their permission beforehand? What if the teacher does not want you to do it?
5 You will need to consider how representative your chosen classes are.

CHAPTER 4

Work and leisure

In this chapter we will examine the arguments surrounding:

1 work, leisure and unemployment;
2 work satisfaction and alienation;
3 technology and automation;
4 industrial conflict;
5 industrialisation and industrialism.

Before you begin any of the exercises you should have studied and should be familiar with at least one of the following texts:

Bilton, T., Bonnett, K., Jones, P., Stanworth, M., Sheard, K. and Webster, A. *Introductory Sociology*, 2nd edn (Macmillan 1987), chapter 9.
Deem, R. *Work, Unemployment and Leisure* (Routledge 1988).
Giddens, A. *Sociology* (Polity 1989), chapter 15.
Haralambos, M. and Holborn, M. *Sociology: Themes and Perspectives* 3rd edn (Collins Educational 1990), chapter 6.
O'Donnell, M. *A New Introduction to Sociology*, 3rd edn, (Nelson 1992), chapter 11.

In addition, you should have your notes on work and leisure in good order.

Introduction

The categories *work* and *leisure* account for how most of the time in our adult lives is taken up. Even when people are out of work, they spend a great deal of time in enforced leisure, thinking about or seeking paid employment. Paid labour is obviously important because it provides individuals with the income through which they are able to consume the good things of life. Among the good things are the leisure activities which people follow and the opportunities for leisure which modern societies provide for the majority of the population. But work and leisure have more importance than this alone for they also provide us with a source of status and identity as individuals and they shape the social arrangements within which we spend a great deal of our lives.

In approaching any sociological topic, you should be familiar with the basic concepts in the area.

For each of the following, provide a definition:
• paid employment;
• enforced leisure;
• non-work obligations;
• work-related time;
• leisure-as-work.

Thus, to examine work and leisure has always been an important task for sociologists.

1 Work, leisure and unemployment

Sociologists have had difficulty in defining what is really meant by work. While we can common-sensically 'know' what work is, separating work from leisure and other activities is not always straightforward. There have been various attempts to identify slots of time which can be related to work, non-work or leisure, though, even here, there will be some interweaving of the elements of one in another. So, the relationship between work and leisure may best be expressed as a continuum, with the ideal types of work and leisure at either end and time-slots such as work-related time, non-work obligations and leisure-as-work placed along it. Even paid employment is not always easy to identify. It is usually associated with activity in a factory or an office but it also occurs at home under out-working arrangements, usually by low-paid, female workers. More recently, some home-working of a different type has developed, as new technology has enabled computer personnel and other types of worker to do their jobs from terminals at home.

Changes in work and leisure

The relationship between work and leisure has also been a focus of interest among sociologists. Some have argued that work is so important to

To develop your skill of application you will often be required to identify evidence that you can use to support points made. Read *Social Studies Review*, vol. 3, no. 5, pp. 175–9 (see [22], p. 337), and carry out these exercises:

1 What evidence does Critcher use to support the categories he employs in identifying the factors affecting leisure?

2 List the major points of each study you use.

EVALUATION

A central figure in the sociology of leisure is S. Parker. You need to be able to assess his work, not just describe it. Begin by listing its strengths and weaknesses in two columns:

Parker on leisure	
Strengths	**Weaknesses**
1 Focuses on inter-relationship between work and leisure	1 Study is relatively old

The first points are made for you.

individuals that it influences the types of leisure that they pursue, not only in the amount of time that they have to enjoy leisure, but also in the sorts of leisure activities that they choose to pursue. Others suggest that, with the growth of leisure during the twentieth century, it has become the primary focus of individuals' lives, so that they now choose an occupation for the leisure opportunities it can provide them with. Still others suggest that there is only a very limited relationship between work and leisure as they represent very different aspects of people's lives. However, what *is* important is the way that different types of people have different leisure experiences, differentiated by their gender, age, race and class.

For example, it is fairly clear that women have less leisure time than men and when they do relax, they tend to do so in different ways from men. Ethnic groups tend to have different cultural interests and different amounts of time available for leisure, largely through their position in the class structure. Leisure activities also vary systematically according to age, not only in the obvious physical dimension, but also because of the greater financial resources often available to older people. (See Coursework Suggestion 4.1 on p. 126.)

INTERPRETATION

You should be practised in interpreting numerical material. Look at the table on p. 141 of *Social Studies Review*, vol. 5, no. 4. (See [23]. p. 337.)

Describe the main differences in the patterns of male and female leisure shown in the table.

In order to evaluate the effectiveness of any sociological method you should begin by listing its advantages and disadvantages. Do this for unobtrusive measures:

Unobtrusive measures	
Advantages	**Disadvantages**

Do not ignore ethical issues.

Unemployment

It is not only the character of leisure which has altered. There have also been substantial changes in the work experience of the majority of the population. These changes, in particular the return of mass unemployment, have been the focus of much sociological debate. One interesting line of argument has been over the counting of the unemployed by government, and whether it is possible to produce accurate unemployment statistics with the effects of government interference, on the one hand, and the problem of fraudulent claimants, on the other.

The role of the young unemployed has been a central focus of the debate about unemployment. Some sociologists see training schemes for the young as genuine attempts to give young people the skills needed for

Statistics can be manipulated to show different things. To assess the usefulness of any statistic you need to be aware of the problems of collection and categorisation. So, list in two columns the reasons why unemployment may be under-counted and over-counted.

Measuring unemployment	
Ways in which it may be under-counted	**Ways in which it may be over-counted**

By looking at sociological material and summarising it you will develop your skill of interpretation.

1 Read *Social Studies Review*, vol. 1, no. 1, pp. 36–50 and *Social Studies Review*, vol. 4, no. 1, pp. 24–9. (See [24] and [25], p. 337.)What are the main explanations for youth unemployment?

As there are several, you need to assess their relative worth.

2 Which do you find the most convincing and why?

modern industry. Others argue that they are devices to keep the young off the unemployment register and, thus, to keep down the total unemployed figure (particularly as it is quoted in the newspapers).

It has been argued that the rise in unemployment has increased the importance of other types of economy, including the household economy and the informal economy, where those who no longer have formal, paid employment are not necessarily 'idle' but engage in unofficial, possibly illegal or barter-type work with payments in cash and avoidance of tax. This suggests then that the experience of unemployment in the 1980s and 1990s may not be the same experience as that of the 1920s and 1930s. Other sociologists have argued that the most important change in the economy has occurred in formal employment, including such features as the emergence of a growing self-employed sector, the decline in manufacturing, the growth of the service sector and, in particular, the emergence of the leisure industry to service the leisure needs of those in employment.

There has also been an interest in how individuals experience unemployment and the effects of long-term unemployment on families and individuals. It has been recognised that a whole series of consequences may emerge from unemployment, not all of them negative, as early redundancy can be an opportunity to embark upon a different type of

From your reading you should be able to identify the arguments of the market liberals and of the Marxists about unemployment.

What empirical evidence can you provide to support each side's argument?

The effects of an increase in unemployment can be seen on the state and on the individual.

Detail these effects in two columns:

Effects of unemployment	
On the state	**On the individual**
1 Increase in social unrest, e.g. urban riots	1 Loss of income

work or may be a release from unsatisfactory work. However, the main effects of unemployment seem to have been disruption of family life and even destruction of individual lives. The loss of employment highlights the importance of work for an individual's status and welfare, although it should not be assumed that the experience of work is always a pleasant one.

Leisure and choice

One of the effects of unemployment is a reduction in the range of choice for unemployed individuals in pursuing leisure activities. As society has become *postmodern*, leisure has moved from having had a mass basis towards being more individualised in the composition of pursuits. This has increased the opportunity for individuals to choose how to spend their leisure time. One of the contradictions involved in this change is that leisure itself has become dependent on large-scale organisations rather than individual autonomy and this has allowed the range of leisure pursuits available to individuals to expand. But, at the same time, leisure provision has become more standardised as the leisure industries offer similar leisure products.

Read *Social Studies Review*, vol. 6, no. 3, pp. 98–101. (See [26], p. 337.)

How does the article suggest that consumption is linked to leisure?

It has been argued that the state influences leisure patterns in several ways. From your reading identify the main ways in which this occurs.

INTERPRETATION

This can be seen in one of the more popular leisure activities – shopping. While the range of goods available in the shops has increased enormously and many products have come within the financial reach of employed people, the growth of national chain stores has meant that the same products are available throughout the country at standardised prices. This leads to the contradictory situation that individual choice increases, while national choices become restricted.

2 Work satisfaction and alienation

The interest of sociologists in the area of the experience of work has traditionally been focused on the relationship between structural conditions in the workplace and the satisfaction or dissatisfaction which people feel about their work. The central debate has focused on whether work is experienced as an alienating or satisfying phenomenon and how occupying a different position in the division of labour may produce different levels of satisfaction or alienation.

Variations in the experience of work

The major debate has been between those who see the possibility of organising work in such a way as to produce satisfied workers and those who argue that work, under capitalist relations of production, is an inevitably alienating experience. While it is likely that most people both enjoy and dislike their work at different times, there is strong evidence for a systematic variation in the levels of satisfaction experienced by dif-

From your studies, you should be familiar with the concepts of alienation and anomie.

KNOWLEDGE UNDERSTANDING

1 Give a definition of each.

EVALUATION

2 Which do you think is the more accurate description of individual situations in modern, capitalist societies?

APPLICATION

3 Give supporting evidence for your choice.

Provide a definition for each of the following:

- powerlessness;
- meaninglessness;
- isolation;
- self-estrangement.

ferent types of worker. This has usually been expressed as the further-up-the-hierarchy-the-more-satisfied-the-worker rule. The evidence suggests that those in positions of responsibility and trust are likely to be more engaged by their work than those for whom work is merely a way of earning money, with no intrinsic satisfaction at all.

The debate is important because it is linked to the productivity of industry, as satisfied workers are likely to work harder and produce more than those who are dissatisfied. Thus, there has thus been an enormous amount of research directed towards finding the best type of work environment in which to produce happy workers. This has led to the development of various job-enrichment programmes which seek to introduce variation into low-level, routine work, or to introduce a measure of responsibility for workers for their own work productivity. However, other sociologists argue that no number of employer schemes to improve working conditions and the engagement of workers in their work can alter the fact that, for most workers, work is a boring, mundane experience in which they can take no pride or satisfaction.

Another important variation in the experience of work is the way that different social groups may have quite separate work-lives. For example, work is clearly gendered in several ways. Many workplaces have labour activities which are traditionally the preserve of males *or* females so that often the shopfloor looks like a single-sex area. Women are much more likely to be found in part-time employment so that the level of income they receive and the time they spend at work are different from those of men. Similarly, young people are more likely to be in subordinate positions in work and experience little autonomy in their dealings with other workers.

Many members of ethnic minorities also find themselves in subordinate positions in work and are, therefore, likely to have different experiences from other groups of workers. In addition, they may encounter racist attitudes and practices in their work-lives which may limit their prospects for advancement. In particular, illegal immigrants in the industrialised societies may experience conditions of real exploitation and hardship as they have little recourse to legal remedy for abuses of working conditions.

You should be able to apply your sociological understanding of methodological issues to specific problems. For example, what difficulties might sociologists face in exploring the lives of illegal immigrant workers?

Alienation

The existence or otherwise of alienation – a condition where workers are separated from the fruits of their labours and experience work as a meaningless routine – has been a subject of strong debate between different types of sociologist. Alienation has been associated with private ownership of the means of production where the employer expropriates (or keeps) the outcome of other people's labour in the form of profits. Under such conditions, it is argued, there can be no pleasure in work as the employer will always seek to maximise profits by forcing workers to work harder. Thus, as capitalism develops, employers seek greater and greater control over the actions of their workers by taking away their skills and reducing work to routine, which is much more easily controllable.

Other sociologists argue that the existence or otherwise of dissatisfaction at work has little to do with the private ownership of the means of production and more to do with working conditions and the returns that workers receive for their work. By improving both, work satisfaction can be increased and any feelings of alienation eliminated. This does not mean that work will necessarily be enjoyable, as routine will still be present, but that routine can be experienced in a satisfying way as *traction*.

A third view of alienation argues that many workers experience neither satisfaction in, nor hostility to, their work because work is no longer their central interest in life. They have developed instrumental attitudes towards work in which their main focuses of concern are their families and leisure life outside of work, while work provides the income to support these other aspects of their lives. Workers such as these are prepared to put up with the tedium of work as long as they receive what they see as a sufficient reward for doing so.

Read *Social Studies Review*, vol. 1, no. 2, pp. 24–7. (See [27], p. 337.)

What features of part-time work described in the article might lead to feelings associated with alienation?

It is important that you are able to support points of view with appropriate studies. So, address the following points:

1 Read Haralambos and Holborn, pp. 401–3. Which of the sociologists mentioned see work as more important? Which see leisure as more important?

2 You should not provide long, detailed descriptions of studies if asked to support your decisions but relevant supporting points. So, summarise the main points made by each of the sociologists.

EXERCISE

Women in academic grades

By manipulating data you will develop your interpretation skill. Present this information in a different graphical form, one which illustrates the proportions involved.

INTERPRETATION

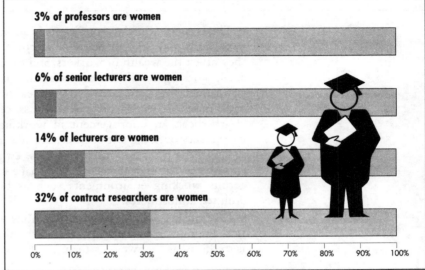

3% of professors are women

6% of senior lecturers are women

14% of lecturers are women

32% of contract researchers are women

0% 10% 20% 30% 40% 50% 60% 70% 80% 90% 100%

(Source: 'Goodwill Under Stress', Association of University Teachers, Autumn 1990)

Describe the pattern of female employment as shown in the diagram. What are the implications of these figures for women in middle-class occupations?

From your reading, list the main points of the explanations which sociologists have put forward to explain this gender distribution. Remember to focus only on middle-class occupations. If you come across an explanation for gender differences in working-class occupations, adapt it for middle-class occupations if you can.

Group differences in work

Another aspect of the debate about the experience of work is that of systematic differences between groups of workers in terms of their working conditions, fringe benefits and remuneration. There are clear class differences between manual workers in factories, lower middle-class office workers and higher-class managerial and employing groups. But there are also systematic variations between men and women and between ethnic groups. By and large, women and ethnic minority groups suffer worse conditions than men and whites both in terms of the income they receive and the conditions they endure. But it is also true that young workers and often older manual workers do not share the same benefits at work as those in young adulthood.

Ideas need to be supported where possible with appropriate empirical evidence. Read *Social Studies Review*, vol. 5, no. 4, pp. 157–61. (See [28], p. 337.)

What evidence can you extract from the article to support the idea that different social groups have different conditions of work?

The issue of working conditions is an important one, not just because conditions may lead to work satisfaction or dissatisfaction but because they affect the wealth of workers, and their health, sometimes fatally. As such, working conditions are often the subject of social policy through government legislation such as the Health and Safety at Work Act 1974. This raises issues of the effectiveness of such legislation. There has clearly been an improvement in working conditions in factories and workplaces over the last century, but nevertheless, work continues to be a dangerous place for many workers, either through the possibility of accident or through longer-term damage to their health because of dangerous working environments such as building sites, coal mines and polluted atmospheres.

One of the more significant variations which affects levels of satisfaction among workers is the type of technology that they work with and it is to this issue that we now turn.

Organising material systematically will assist your skills of interpretation and application.

Under the following three headings, list the features of work which may lead to satisfaction or dissatisfaction with a job.

1 Remuneration
2 Physical environment
3 Fringe benefits

Features of work			
	1	2	3
Satisfaction			
Dissatisfaction			

STRUCTURED QUESTION

Item A

Jobs for mothers

Cynthia registered her child for nursery school when she was six months pregnant, securing the last place for three years later. Norma had an ideal part-time job until she had to cancel it because she could not find a baby-sitter.

Cynthia and Norma live in contrasting areas of Newcastle upon Tyne but share the problems of women who are seeking to resume employment after having had families. Growing research shows that employers are ignorant or complacent about a potential business crisis.

The number of school-leavers will fall by almost a quarter by the mid-1990s, while numbers of working women will expand. Government figures suggest 90 per cent of essential middle-age employee growth will be provided by women returners in the next decade . . .

Possible solutions include tax allowances for childcare to encourage returners and increasing employers' enthusiasm for job-sharing and créche provision . . .

The researchers found almost as many women wanted to return to work for interest and to meet people as for supplementary income. More training and improved child-care facilities were the strongest factors helping returners.

The report called for an integrated approach by employers, including care options, flexible working systems and career breaks. It suggested equal benefits for part- and full-time workers and comprehensive child-care linked to training programmes.

(Source: adapted from Martyn Halsall, the *Guardian*, Monday 24 September 1990)

Item B

Golden oldies prove their worth in today's young folk's world

Greying British workers finding themselves on the receiving end of unwanted early retirement offers may have found a champion in the New York City-based charity, Commonwealth Fund.

The fund's study 'Age Works', which analysed the employment policies of three companies – one in Britain and two in the US – discovered that older workers are productive, cost-effective employees . . .

According to the Office of Population Censuses and Surveys, the early years of the 1990s will be dominated by a sharp decline in the number of teenagers and 20 year olds. The share of the population accounted for by 15- to 19-year olds will fall from 6.8 per cent in 1990 to 6.1 per cent 10 years later. The proportion of 20 year olds will fall sharply from 16.1 per cent to 12.3 per cent.

The struggle to recruit talented

APPLICATION

You need to be able to apply contemporary events to sociological issues. For example, how might the recession of the early 1990s affect the information in this item?

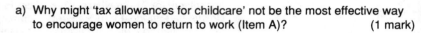

workers in the 1990s will take place on two fronts: firstly, companies will compete for the fewer young people available and, secondly, they will try to tap alternative labour markets, either older people or married women who are not at work.

Looking into the next decade, the market will be very bullish for older workers, especially skilled ones.

(Source: Nick Pandya, the *Guardian*, Friday 16 August 1991)

To gain the interpretation mark here, you need to carry out a small calculation.

a) Why might 'tax allowances for childcare' not be the most effective way to encourage women to return to work (Item A)? (1 mark)

b) What is the predicted percentage drop in the 15- to 19-year-old age group as a proportion of the population between 1990 and 2000 (Item B)? (1 mark)

'To what extent' means making an evaluation. You need to interpret the changes in the item, and then apply this interpretation and knowledge from elsewhere to the issue of falling unemployment.

c) Item A suggests that training will be an important factor in the 1990s. Assess government attempts to provide the workforce with appropriate skills. (7 marks)

d) Using material from the items and elsewhere, assess the extent to which the sociological evidence supports the idea that women and older workers are part of a 'secondary labour market'. (8 marks)

e) For each of THREE of the suggestions put forward in item A to encourage women returners, suggest ONE reason why it might have that effect. (3 marks)

f) To what extent might the demographic changes described in the items lead to a fall in unemployment? (5 marks)

3 Technology and automation

In looking at levels of work satisfaction or alienation, sociologists have focused much of their attention on the immediate environment and, in particular, on the machines which are present in industrial factories. Machinery has an obvious influence on the attitudes of workers, because the way it is organised affects such issues as the level of noise workers

To develop your skill of interpretation, read Haralambos and Holborn, pp. 322–32, noting the main sociologists mentioned, and the main points of their arguments.

endure, their ability to communicate with fellow workers and the physical actions they take, among other things. Technology has, therefore, been an attractive explanation for sociologists in looking at the levels of satisfaction that workers experience.

Technology and alienation

Some sociologists have looked to technology to explain such things as the levels of meaninglessness, powerlessness, self-estrangement and isolation felt by workers in different technologies. In support of this idea they have argued that alienation was also a feature of factories in the Communist world and, therefore, was the result of similar technologies being used in both capitalist *and* socialist societies. They believe that the worst form of technology for alienation, assembly-line technology, is on the decline and, as new forms of automated technology come to predominate, alienation will disappear. They believe that modern societies have moved into a 'post-Ford' era where the technologies which operate allow employers to organise work in such a way as to engage their workers rather than alienate them.

Other sociologists have argued that technology cannot be looked at in isolation from the wider society and that it is not the machines which cause the alienation but their deployment in a situation under capitalism where the workers do not share fairly in the results of the technology. There is, thus, a contrast between those sociologists who see alienation as a result of capitalism, regardless of the technology used, and those who see it existing in all industrial societies, regardless of who owns the actual technology. The difference between the groups is that the former does not believe we can get rid of alienation until the private ownership of the means of production is eliminated, while the latter believes that changes in technology may lead to the elimination of alienation.

With the failure of state economies in Eastern Europe and their adoption of private ownership and the free market as the most efficient way of producing goods, it seems that the absence of private ownership did not

---

Read *Social Studies Review*, vol. 5, no. 1, pp. 11–15. (See [29], p. 337.)

INTERPRETATION

1 Summarise the main features of work in the post-Fordist era.

APPLICATION

2 Attach appropriate studies to these features.

EVALUATION

3 To what extent do you think modern work is post-Fordist? List the arguments for and against.

What are the main characteristics of each of the following types of technology:

- assembly-line;
- automated;
- continuous process;
- machine minding;
- craft.

lead to individuals being less alienated from their work and, therefore, more productive. Moreover, the nature of ownership in the capitalist economies has also changed over the last century. There are fewer firms owned and controlled by individuals and share ownership is now more widespread throughout Britain, as individuals have bought shares in the recently privatised industries. While not all sociologists accept that the dispersal of share ownership has changed the patterns of control of industry, there is a general acceptance that institutions now own and control large amounts of modern industry and that this change has consequences for the way firms treat their work-forces. Yet, it remains to be seen whether new automated technologies will lead to a more satisfied workforce. (See Coursework Suggestion 4.2 on p. 126.)

Automation

The effects of automation on the attitudes and conditions enjoyed by workers are subject to great dispute among sociologists. This is because, in looking to the future, sociologists attempt to extrapolate present trends into the future and, not unnaturally, they see different things from one another. However, there are always new bits of evidence emerging to support or refute speculations. One of the most controversial debates has been over the effects of new technologies on the levels of employment in an economy. While it is obvious that automated machinery gets rid of some types of labour, it also creates new job opportunities in servicing and developing such machinery.

In your reading on automation, you will have come across the work of Blauner, Mallet and Naville.

To help you assess their work, note the most convincing and least convincing part of each of their arguments. Come to a conclusion as to which you think most closely describes the reality of the effects of automation.

Read *Social Studies Review*, vol. 2, no. 5, pp. 30–3. (See [30], p. 337.)

What does the article suggest will be the main effects of information technology?

INTERPRETATION

The dispute concerns the balance between the job losses and job gains and the long-term effects of this balance on society. Some have argued that the new technologies, far from consolidating the power of management to demand flexibility from workers, create opportunities for new forms of work organisation. These have focused on cooperatives of highly skilled workers which have emerged mainly in Italy. However, it is also suggested that female workers are more likely than male workers to lose their jobs to automated machinery and are least likely to acquire the skills needed to work with advanced technologies.

More difficult to measure is the effect that working with new technologies has on the attitudes of those workers who are employed in these industries. On one side, it is claimed that automation increases the responsibility of employed workers, creates a cleaner environment and enhances workers' skills so that their work satisfaction increases. On the other, studies have suggested that automation intensifies the meaninglessness of work, requires much (disliked) shift work and takes away the skills of workers, thus increasing the dissatisfaction of the workforce.

However, there is another sociological position which suggests that it is not automation which is the crucial issue but the way that individuals react to it both as managers and as workers. It is the intention of management, in introducing automation, and the reactions of workers to its introduction which are important. In other words, automated machinery is introduced as part of a social process. It creates constraints and opportunities for all participants. It may increase or decrease conflict in the workplace depending on the actions and reactions of all members of the organisation.

You should be developing your evaluation skills by being critical of anything you read. For example, read *Social Studies Review*, vol. 2, no. 5, pp 14–17. (See [31], p.337).

EVALUATION

Identify all the quotations from the article which you consider to be sexist, stating why you think they are.

KNOWLEDGE **U**NDERSTANDING

APPLICATION

1 What do you understand by the term *industrial sabotage*?

2 Suggest reasons why workers might undertake to engage in this?

4 Industrial conflict

Although we usually think of strikes when we discuss industrial conflict, the reality is that strikes are only one form of conflict. They do not form the main type of conflict, although they are the most obvious example of it. Industrial conflict can take many shapes; organised and disorganised, formal and informal, individual or collective, official or unofficial. The form that any industrial conflict takes depends on a whole range of factors but sociologists have attempted to come to a systematic understanding of the incidence of conflict, looking for explanations for the amount and type of conflict that takes place.

Conflict at work

In examining conflict in the workplace, sociologists have to take account of the legal framework within which conflict occurs. As an object of social policy, industrial relations has been a major focus of successive governments' concern, with laws regularly being passed to control and limit the amount of strike action undertaken by workers. Arguably, however, as strikes decline, alternative forms and expressions of conflict take their place so that labour turnover may increase, or industrial sabotage appear.

Because there is concern about the amount of industrial conflict that occurs, differing approaches to the problem are put forward by political

EVALUATION

From your reading you should know the functionalist, pluralist and Marxist perspectives on industrial conflict.

1 To begin to assess these perspectives, note the strengths and weaknesses of each, asking questions like these:

   i) Is it realistic?

   ii) What does it leave out?

   iii) What evidence is there?

2 In a separate conclusion, state which perspective you think is the most convincing and why.

parties and commentators. It is not surprising, then, that sociologists also take different lines on conflict and seek solutions in varying ways. Some tend to focus on the workers as a problem and examine ways in which workers may be better integrated into their firms. Others suggest that managerial practices are the main issue and that these need to be re-vamped in the post-Ford era. Still others argue that the relationship between managers and workers is the key to the whole problem and there has to be an efficient channel of communication and consultation to resolve disputes. On the other hand, there is the argument that conflict in the workplace is inevitable and natural as workers and managers have very different interests, interests which are always likely to come into conflict.

Strikes

Sociologists have had particular problems in defining and measuring strikes. They have used different ways of identifying the moment when a work stoppage becomes a strike, from the moment the workers are taken off the clock, to the moment the trade union becomes officially involved. There is a similar problem when looking at national strike statistics as different countries tend to use different rules when requiring employers to report stoppages to the government. This is important because one of the reasons that sociologists compare different countries' strike rates is to try to determine strike-proneness or the susceptibility of a country's workers to strike. By examining countries with low strike-proneness, some sociologists are hoping to identify solutions to striking and thus contribute to social policy in a positive way.

In so doing, sociologists have searched for the *causes* of strikes and have come to many different conclusions as to what these are. Some have emphasised the social characteristics of countries – their integration or industrial relations systems, for example. Others have focused on the characteristics of particular industries such as the technology used or the domination of an area by a single industry. Another emphasis has been on the inevitable nature of relationships between workers and owners in a capitalist society. The focus of others is on the different interests of workers and managers, their social situations and the tactics they employ to gain their ends.

With knowledge from your reading, answer the following points:

INTERPRETATION

1 Identify the main explanations for variations in strike activity.

EVALUATION

2 Which do you think is the most effective in explaining strike-proneness and why?

After looking at newspaper accounts of strikes, write a paragraph on the media's attitudes towards strikes and strikers.

INTERPRETATION

EVALUATION

1   Of the explanations for women's levels of strike activity identified in the paragraph below, which do you find the most convincing and why?

APPLICATION

2   Is there any evidence from your reading that you could apply to support your conclusion?

Most modern workers will never experience going on strike. However, involvement in strike action, such as it exists, varies according to social characteristics. The higher up the work hierarchy, the less likely individuals are to go out on strike. Statistics suggest that women are much less likely to be involved in strike action than men. In the search for explanations for this phenomenon, sociologists have suggested a range of possible reasons. Traditional explanations have focused on the more 'conservative nature' of women and their lack of membership of trade unions.

Others have argued that it is women's structural position, in low-paid, non-unionised jobs, which accounts for their lack of involvement in strikes. Still others disagree that women are more reluctant to strike, but argue that it is the ideology of domesticity, confining women to the home, which gives the appearance that women are less strike-prone. For example, although there are fewer women trade unionists, there is no evidence that they are less likely to join their male colleagues in striking.

5 Industrialisation and industrialism

For most people living in the West, industrialisation has been the most important process shaping the societies in which they live. Although the process is a very long one and, indeed, is still on-going, sociologists have been concerned, right from the beginnings of sociology, to assess its impact on society at large. The classical sociologists were living through some of the most dramatic changes which industrialisation set in train and examining what was happening became a central theme of their work.

APPLICATION

You should be able to apply your knowledge of events in the real world to issues such as falling strike activity. For example, what alternative explanations to those in Item A of the following structured question can you suggest for a fall in strike activity?

STRUCTURED QUESTION

Item A

In 1989 about four million days of work were lost through strikes, down from an average of 13 million in the 1970s. About thirty times as many days were lost last year through absence – people staying at home due to sickness, injury or not turning up.

Since 1979 the unions have had much less freedom to take industrial action. One of Margaret Thatcher's main election pledges that year was to curb union power. The Government has curbed union power by passing new laws. Unions now have to hold a secret vote among their members before they strike. They must also vote to choose new leaders, and to decide if they will send money to support political parties. During a strike, they are allowed to place only six members outside the workplace to try and persuade other workers not to break the strike by going to work – an activity known as picketing. Secondary action – where one group of workers strikes to support another – has been virtually eliminated. And employers have been given new legal powers to prevent unions striking or to claim financial penalties from them if they do.

(Source: adapted from Edward Pilkington, "Towards a striking new image", the *Guardian*, 11 September 1990)

Item B

Leading lives of leisure

The greatest strength of the Rapoports' approach is simply that age is the most reliable predictor of leisure behaviour. They are not insensitive to the way gender changes even the experience of the life cycle. They are careful to point out that policy-makers have failed to recognise the special needs of those with children or those confronting old age. More questionable is their assumption that the stages of the life cycle are inevitable human experiences. From adolescence to old age, the life cycle may be less a series of psychological and biological stages than sets of ideas about age-appropriate behaviour that we carry round in our heads. Why shouldn't grandma rock and roll? Part of the answer, of course, is that we don't expect her to and thus she doesn't want to (except to everyone's amusement at the family Christmas party).

(Source: Chas Critcher, *Social Studies Review*, vol. 3, no. 5)

Item C

British men work the longest day

Men in Britain are working longer hours than in any other European country, while British women are forced to fit their paid work around their family responsibilities, according to two reports by the Equal Opportunities Commission. They say that 42 per cent of men in the UK work more than 46 hours a week. This puts them just above Greece and Ireland and considerably above Germany, where only 14 per cent of men fall into this category.

It was found that employers often designed jobs around traditional assumptions that only men could work long hours and do overtime. Hence, in manufacturing, where most men are employed, pay was often enhanced by overtime or shift work. In the service sector, which employs many women, part time, often lowly paid work was the norm.

(Source: Keith Harper, the *Guardian*, Monday 10 June 1991)

a) What is the concept that sociologists use to describe the way that the leisure 'life cycle may be less a series of psychological and biological stages than sets of ideas about age-appropriate behaviour that we carry round in our heads' (Item B)?   (1 mark)

b) What is the percentage difference between the UK and Germany for the proportion of men working more than 46 hours per week (Item C)?
                                                                              (1 mark)

Note that you need to interpret the reason in item A and avoid comment on it.

c) Apart from the reason suggested in Item A, assess sociological explanations for variations in the level of strike activity.   (8 marks)

d) Referring to Item C and elsewhere, assess sociological contributions to an understanding of the relationship between household responsibilities and the types of paid work men and women do.   (8 marks)

e) Assess the relative importance of the social factors which may affect the leisure that people do. Refer to Item B and other sociological material in your answer.   (7 marks)

The causes and courses of industrialisation

Much early sociology employed the comparative method in a direct way to compare pre-industrial and industrial societies in the belief that the effects of industrialisation could then be identified. However, the classical sociologists often had different ideas about why industrialisation

Read Haralambos and Holborn, pp. 312–22.

What does the extract suggest are the main differences between industrial and capitalist societies?

came about and, therefore, what its likely results were to be. One tradition takes a determinist view of the process, arguing that industrialisation is the result of a long historical process involving the contradiction between the forces of production in society. This economic view has been criticised by a second tradition that emphasises the exercise of human will and choice in the process and looks in particular at how certain religious ideas were conducive to the practice of capitalism. A third view underlines the role of the entrepreneur and the spirit of enterprise within the autonomy of market forces. This last view is also deterministic in that it sees impersonal market forces as inevitably leading to the introduction of a capitalist system of industry.

Industrialisation is, therefore, not a uniform process. Historically, there have been various roads to an industrial economy. Industrialisation can take many forms, although we tend to take the capitalist form for granted. Sociologists have generally identified three main ways in which a society can develop into an industrial state. The first is the capitalist way, where private ownership is allowed to flourish with minimal government regulation. This tends to produce a large number of small- and medium-sized firms with a great deal of competition between them. The second is through central planning by the state with a minimal role for private enterprise and a maximum role for the state bureaucracy. This tends to produce large, state monopolies. A third route is the state capitalist road where private enterprise is subject to strategic planning by the state, tending to produce large, private monopolies.

INTERPRETATION   APPLICATION

Applying examples to sociological categorisations is an important skill to develop.

1   Give an example of a country for each road to an industrial state identified in the paragraph above.

Note that you will have to interpret these before you can apply an example.

EVALUATION

2   Which of the three roads do you think is the most effective in achieving industrialisation and why?

Note that you should give reasons for picking and one for rejecting the others.

EXERCISE

By reading newspapers you will pick up a great deal of useful information which can be applied sociologically. From a newspaper search, discover the functions of the TECs.

INTERPRETATION

From ET to Frankenstein

Employment Training was designed to offer 600,000 places a year (or a running total of 300,000 at any one time) for long-term unemployed adults with 18- to 25-year-olds the main target group and those up to the age of 50 as a secondary aim. The scheme was designed to provide quality training but it became evident early on that the programme was patchy.

Under the new contracts, there will be two new target groups. The long-term unemployed remain the main priority, calling on, on average, 85 per cent of funds and designated a mainstream group.

A non-mainstream group, comprising other recruits such as women returning to work, particular areas of skill shortages, victims of redundancy and enterprise trainees, has a call on 15 per cent of funds . . .

On the one hand, the new arrangements allow a greater degree of in-built flexibility for training providers, particularly Training and Enterprise Councils (TECs). But because of a period of panic last year, the reality is very different. As ET approached its first anniversary, it was clear that the programme was falling well short of targets. In June, Sir Norman Fowler, Employment Secretary, launched a concerted drive to push the numbers up to get the running total up above 200,000.

(Source: adapted from Simon Beavis, the *Guardian*, Friday 20 April 1990)

Write a report on what contributions sociologists could make to an assessment of the effectiveness of Employment Training (ET). In the report, you would need to discuss what the aims of ET were and what measures could be used to ascertain whether they had been achieved or not. You may need to consider both quantitative and qualitative measures of assessment.

When you have completed your report, look up sociological studies of previous training schemes such as the Youth Training Scheme, etc. Change your initial report so that it comes in line with any ideas or measures you find in these studies.

There is no doubt that any of these roads can begin the process of industrialisation given enough investment, private or public, and given the right market conditions. However, whether each road can sustain industrial development has been a cause of much dispute among sociologists. The problem is that capitalism, with its dependence on private enterprise, periodically experiences recessions in the classic *boom and bust* cycle. It is argued by some sociologists that the market cannot solve all the problems of a modern economy. For example, as new technologies develop there is a demand for more and more skilled workers. However, the labour market, despite large numbers of unemployed, cannot pro-

By placing the correct concepts in the appropriate cells of the diagram, you will develop your skill of application.

Fordist and post-Fordist features of production systems		
	Fordist	**Post-Fordist**
Types of technology		
Product types		
Types of labour used		
Type of work contracts		

APPLICATION

- Specialised and diverse;
- Payment by individual performance;
- Fairly autonomous;
- Mass and standardised;
- Fixed machinery;
- Multi-purpose machines;
- Little control;
- Collectively negotiated.

It might help you to begin by matching up opposing concepts and then seeing where they fit best.

duce these trained workers without some sort of intervention by the state. The existence of the Employment Training programme is often cited as evidence for this.

The socialist route becomes economically inefficient as the 'dead hand' of bureaucracy leads to over-staffing and the stifling of private initiative. Along the state capitalist road, the balance between the state and private enterprise has constantly to be adjusted to maximise production. Nevertheless, the collapse of the socialist economies of Eastern Europe in the late 1980s and early 1990s seems to have eliminated that model of industrialisation as a route for other countries to follow. Indeed, those sociologists who have argued that private enterprise is the only such way to a stable and democratic industrial society claim they have been vindicated by events.

However, capitalism, by its very nature, does not stand still, and sociologists have been interested in the way that early capitalism has given way to late- or even post-capitalist industrial society. The main focus of debate has surrounded the growth of different types of capitalist enterprise since the beginning of the twentieth century. For example, the growth of the joint stock company can be seen either as the dilution of individual, capitalist control through the dispersal of ownership, or as the concentration of more and more capital into private hands through the ability of a large minority shareholder to use the capital of larger numbers of small shareholders in the same company.

More recently, the growth of institutional shareholding and the globalisation of the activities of certain large companies have been issues of extreme interest to sociologists. The activities of multi-national companies are difficult to investigate precisely because they are so huge and powerful. Nevertheless, their operations are important for large numbers of people. For example, their investment decisions, often taken in a major commercial centre such as New York or Tokyo, can affect the employment prospects of thousands of people all over the world.

The consequences of industrialisation

The impact of industrialisation on individual lives is enormous and could not be adequately dealt with here. However, sociologists have highlighted various themes in their studies of the impact of industrialisation. For example, there has been some investigation of the change in the concept of time when a society moves from pre-industrial to industrial status. There is no doubt that the disruption that the process involves creates much misery and hardship for many individuals, especially for the powerless in society. While a small minority of the population may gain initial benefits, it is often at the expense of those dispossessed by the process itself. For example, those thrown off the land by enclosure in the eighteenth century were forced to migrate to the cities whether they liked it or not. Urbanisation itself is the major initial change that industrialisation involves. However, as the need for large concentrations of workers declines, and as new technologies reduce the labour force in the factories, postmodern societies may be seeing a 'flight from the city' to the suburbs and dormitory villages.

The long-term benefits of industrialisation, even so, are immense for

E VALUATION

1 Which of the two positions concerning the role of the West identified in the following paragraph do you think is closer to reality?

A PPLICATION

2 What sociological evidence could you use to support your view?

the majority of the population. The changes in the lifestyle and capabilities of individuals are enormous, ranging from the products that become available through mass production to the higher incomes which many people enjoy under capitalism, allowing individuals to travel or enjoy leisure pursuits previously beyond their means. Some sociologists argue that the benefits enjoyed by the mass of the population in the West are built on the misery and impoverishment of the majority in the Third World. Others argue that the West stands as an example for the rest of the world in terms of its standard of living and commitment to democracy.

The impact of industrialisation is uneven and affects different groups in different ways. The working class has gradually improved its social conditions either through peaceful agitation or violent action. But, working-class people have not benefited from industrialisation to the same extent as the rich and powerful in society who *have* been able, in the main, to defend their privileges and pass them on to their children. The poor still exist in Western societies with infant mortality rates in some Western inner cities rivalling those in the Third World.

It has been argued that women initially take the major burden of industrialisation with a deterioration in their legal and social position, although they eventually (largely through their own struggles) gain many of the benefits. Ethnic minorities, attracted to the capitalist societies by the promise of a higher standard of living, often find themselves in the most marginal of positions within those societies. Arguably, in the long run, it is the young who gain the most from the development of an industrial economy. They gain a large number of years where they have little responsibility and enough disposable income to create a distinct market niche whose needs industry seeks to fill. For example, the fashion and music industries are geared towards the youth market. In the postmodern world, the existence of the youth market, focused on leisure and the pursuit of happiness, will continue to be an important spur to industrial development.

INTERPRETATION

Often you will need to take evidence from a variety of sources. Read *Social Studies Review*, vol. 6, no. 5, pp. 186–8 (see [32], p. 337), and Haralambos and Holborn, pp. 387–92.

Chart the similarities between women and ethnic minorities in the labour market.

APPLICATION

You should be ready to apply your experience and knowledge of the social world to particular problems. For example, give THREE examples of conditions of work which are 'physically hazardous'.

Conclusion

Work remains a central aspect of individual lives, an important focus for their identity and a crucial source of income and satisfaction. Yet work also provides many negative experiences for individuals, not least of which is the fact that many places of work are physically hazardous or mentally stressful. Moreover, conditions of work are constantly changing as technology improves, governments introduce new legislation or old, heavy industries are supplanted by the new, sunrise factories. Because business enterprise is central to the operation of modern, capitalist societies and, therefore, creates many disputes in society, sociologists will continue to explore the area of work in all its facets from different points of view.

Important points to bear in mind

1 While work might blur into leisure, some people have less choice than others in whether they work or not, or what leisure activities they pursue.
2 Work is often satisfying and alienating at the same time. Most people have varying experiences at work.
3 Automation is linked to many enormous changes in society but it is human beings who create the new technologies and who decide when and how to introduce them.
4 Industrial conflict takes varied forms but most workers will never have been on strike.
5 Industrialisation causes great changes in societies but these are likely to affect different groups in various ways.

KEY CONCEPTS

It is important that you are familiar with and are able to use the concepts in this section in appropriate ways if you are to apply them effectively in the examination. Check your understanding of the concepts by carrying out this exercise.

For each definition, choose which of the two concepts is the closer one. Provide a definition for the other concept.

The process whereby responsibility for work tasks is given to the worker.

Work satisfaction *or* Job enrichment

Activities which are necessary for a person to carry out their employment but which are not part of the job itself.

Non-work obligations *or* Work-related time

The effect of premature retirement or redundancy on the unemployed.

Enforced leisure *or* Mass unemployment

An emphasis on state control of productive capacity.

Socialism *or* Capitalism

Machinery used to produce goods or services.

Automation *or* Technologies

The propensity to down tools.

Strike-proneness *or* Industrial conflict

The propensity for interactions to become worldwide.

Industrialisation *or* Globalisation

Productive activity which is not officially recorded.

Leisure industry *or* Informal economy

The feeling of being pulled along by the rhythm of a task.

Traction *or* Alienation

A social position of honour or prestige often linked to occupation.

Status *or* Central life interest

COURSEWORK SUGGESTIONS

4.1

Leisure activities are now a central part of individual lives and it might be interesting to explore the ways in which people use their leisure time. For example, it should be possible to carry out an unobtrusive observation of leisure space, such as a playground or a public house, looking for such phenomena as differential gender behaviour, patterns of behaviour, similarities and differences in behaviour. To give structure to observations you may need to carry out some preliminary observations in order to establish what it is you are going to concentrate on. It is pointless just to begin observations with no aim in mind.

Here are some aspects for you to consider:

1 If you are going to observe say, a public house, how are you going to observe without appearing to do so? This could be important as people may take offence if you stare. Are you over 18?
2 If you are going to look at a playground, what role will you adopt to give yourself cover? You cannot just turn up and hang around in case you worry the children. Someone in authority should know what you are doing, and the children should know that you are not a 'stranger'.
3 How will you systematise your observations? How will you record them when you are doing the observation?
4 How will you present your observations so that they convince other people that they are valid?
5 How are you going to relate your observations to sociological literature? For example, if you observe the number of times that a man or a woman goes to the bar in mixed company, you could relate your findings to the 'normal' roles of men and women in society.

4.2

If you have a part-time job you may be able to explore the feelings of your fellow workers through a series of informal conversations with them, on an individual level. You would need to work out a series of issues that you would discuss with them and ensure that you cover all the areas with every worker you talk to. There is a series of crucial decisions to be made, such as whether you tell your employer what you are doing, whether you tell the workers you talk to and how you are going to approach the topic with them.

Here are some points to take account of:

1 How are you going to simplify the sociological concepts that have been traditionally employed in this area, such as alienation, anomie or traction?
2 How will you resolve the ethical decisions you have to make? You will have to record the reasons why you choose the answers you do, and give sociological justifications for them.
3 Can you appear to carry out a 'normal' conversation with your subjects while actually probing them? How can you gain some practice at this?
4 How will you record your subjects' answers if they do not know what is happening?
5 Has a tape recorder any place in your project? This would affect the ethical problems you face.

CHAPTER 5

Stratification

In this chapter we will examine the arguments surrounding:

1 definitions of strata in society;
2 the importance of class;
3 social mobility;
4 developments in class structure;
5 global changes in stratification.

Before you begin any of the exercises you should have studied and should be familiar with at least one of the following texts:

Bilton, T., Bonnett, K., Jones, P., Stanworth, M., Sheard, K. and Webster, A. *Introductory Sociology*, 2nd edn (Macmillan 1987), chapters 2 and 3, pp. 121–8, 131–41, 149–57.
Giddens, A. *Sociology* (Polity 1989), chapters 7 and 8, pp. 597–600.
Haralambos, M. and Holborn, M. *Sociology: Themes and Perspectives*, 3rd edn (Collins Educational 1991), chapter 2, pp. 564–70.
O'Donnell, M. *A New Introduction to Sociology*, 3rd edn (Nelson 1992), chapters 5, 6, 8, 9 and 10.
Saunders, P. *Social Class and Stratification* (Routledge 1989).

In addition, you should have your notes on stratification in good order.

Introduction

When people talk about their place in society, they are referring to the commonly held notion that societies are made up of individuals organised or arranged in a certain way. So each individual recognises others who are for instance, *social superiors*; for example, many people would acknowledge that the Royal Family is in a higher position in society than nearly everyone else. Similarly, there may be others whom individuals think of as their 'social inferiors' and may 'look down' on them for one reason or another. Therefore, society can be seen as a hierarchy – a structure of individuals organised in a system of higher and lower positions,

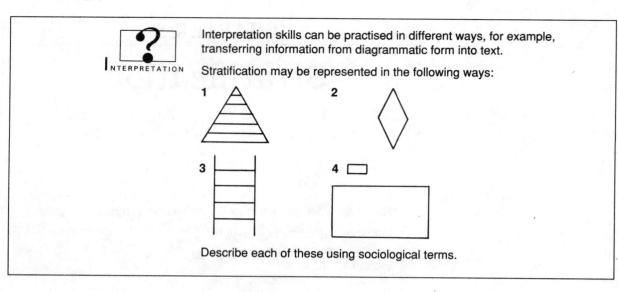

Interpretation skills can be practised in different ways, for example, transferring information from diagrammatic form into text.

Stratification may be represented in the following ways:

Describe each of these using sociological terms.

with those at the top of the hierarchy having more wealth, power and status than those at the bottom.

However, it is not just individuals who are arranged hierarchically in society; groups are too. When individuals share common features, such as similar lifestyles, occupations, ethnicity, gender or age, they tend to identity with one another and associate together. They form a stratum or distinctive group in society. This does not mean that everyone in a group knows everyone else, rather that individuals are able to identify with others of the same group whether they know them personally or not.

Being a member of a particular group or groups is likely to affect an individual's position in society. Generally, young people, such as teenagers, tend to be placed in an inferior social position when compared to older men and women. However, if a young person is also an aristocrat, this may counteract the age inferiority when he or she is dealing with an old person who is not an aristocrat.

Thus, society is made up of a complex pattern of groups in relationships of inferiority and superiority. Each individual is a member of several of these groups and the groups weave in and out of each other, varying in their importance depending on situation and context. For example, a female member of the aristocracy may be in a superior position to most middle-class and working-class males in society, but will still be in an inferior gender position with regard to men of her own class.

From your reading you should be familiar with caste, feudal, class or even hydraulic forms of stratification.

Summarise the main features of any TWO of these.

Gender and ethnicity are said to complicate class differences.

Write a paragraph on the 'cross-cutting' influences on the class structure.

This will help you to develop your skill of application.

A PPLICATION

1 Definitions of strata in society

Different societies are characterised by different types of strata. So, for example, Hindu society is defined by the castes into which individuals are born. Castes are traditional groupings based on a complex system of religious rules, occupational divisions and ascribed status. Apartheid is a system of stratification in South Africa, which is based on ethnicity and colour, though the system is undergoing fundamental social and political change as South Africa dismantles apartheid.

Social class

In modern industrial societies, like Britain or the United States, social class forms one of the main ways in which society is stratified. The definition of social class is not straightforward, and there are many disagreements about how to do it. There is also disagreement as to how many classes there are in society.

Some sociologists argue that there are only two major classes in industrial societies: those who own factories and wealth-producing property, and those who do not. Others suggest that the class system is much more complicated than this, with many different classes, distinguished by manual or non-manual labour, wealth, income, housing, etc. While the former viewpoint sees conflict between the classes as inevitable, the latter argues that social classes are an inevitable part of industrial societies, as they provide a legitimate structure of inequality, which motivates individuals to perform the more demanding tasks in society.

Read *Social Studies Review*, vol. 5, no. 5, pp. 193–6 (see [33], p. 337), and answer these questions:

I NTERPRETATION

1 How does Lenski attempt to synthesise Marxist and functionalist approaches to stratification?

E VALUATION

2 How successful do you think he is?

The Marxist perspective is important in the study of stratification. From your reading:

1 List the main features of the Marxist approach.

2 Begin to assess the approach by listing its main strengths and weaknesses:

Marxist perspective		
Features	**Strengths**	**Weaknesses**
1 Emphasises ownership	1 Draws attention to aspect which is often ignored or difficult to research	1 Over-emphasises ownership at expense of control
2	2	2

The first ones have been completed to help you.

Still others argue that above and beyond classes, there are important status groups which divide people from each other. These are distinguished by different consumption patterns and lifestyles, associated with certain jobs. These status groups are seen as the basis of people's social lives, because people spend their everyday lives in the company of people in similar status groups, both at work and in their non-work lives.

When carrying out research, sociologists have tended to rely on occupation as an indicator of people's social class, because occupation gives clues to people's income, lifestyle, housing, etc., and people are usually more willing to disclose their occupation than their income. However,

Evaluation often involves the comparison of two things to highlight their relative merits. For example:

Compare and contrast Weberian and functionalist views of stratification. Note that *compare* means identifying similarities and *contrast* means identifying differences.

From your reading on the measurement of social class, you will be aware of the controversy surrounding the use of the household as the unit of analysis.

EVALUATION

1 In two columns, list the main points for and against using the household as the unit of analysis.
2 Come to a conclusion as to whether or not it is acceptable to use the household in this way.

Using the household as a measure of social class	
For	**Against**
Conclusion	

occupation is an objective indicator, concerned with a person's external life, while people also have a view of class inside their heads, which is called *subjective social class*. Sociologists, therefore, try to assess an individual's social class in objective terms and in terms of what class the individual thinks he or she is in. (See Coursework Suggestion 5.1 on p. 155.)

Other bases of identity

However, people do not only identify with a social class. There are many characteristics which individuals possess that may form the basis of an identification or grouping in society. In many modern industrial societies, ethnicity is a form of stratification which is increasingly impor-

KNOWLEDGE **U**NDERSTANDING

1 Find out the categories of the Registrar-General's and Hall-Jones scales.

INTERPRETATION

2 Highlight the differences between them.

Sociology and biology often have contrasting views of issues. You should therefore be able to assess biological contributions to debates. So, in one paragraph, assess the argument that biological characteristics provide a basis for stratification.

Do not just describe the argument but put points for and against it.

tant. As Western societies have encouraged or been unable to prevent immigration from Third World societies, mainly to fill the labour shortages in modern capitalist societies, distinctive strata have emerged based on ethnic groupings. In Britain, blacks and Asians are the main ethnic groupings to emerge since the Second World War.

However, ethnicity is not just a question of differences in colour, as Poles, Irish, Italians, etc. are also separate groupings. Questions of ethnicity are often bound up with issues of colour and race. Some sociologists argue that race is not a natural biological phenomenon, but a social construction which serves ideological purposes in society. They therefore prefer to use the category *ethnic group* because this includes features other than some arbitrary biological classification.

Ethnic groups may differ in the extent to which they are integrated in the host society and may be distinguished by many other features, such as culture, language, cuisine, etc. Sociologists differ in the extent to which they believe the evidence shows that ethnic groups have been assimilated in British society. Some argue that there has been a gradual absorption of ethnic groups, as members have become distributed throughout the class structure. Others argue that the 'black British' form a distinctive underclass, who will be found in the worst jobs and the worst housing, with the least income, etc.

Read *Sociology Review*, vol. 1, no. 1, pp. 17–21. (See [34], p. 337.)

1 In three columns describe the three challenges to the centrality of class identity.

2 Provide examples to support your descriptions.

Read *Social Studies Review*, vol. 5, no. 3, pp. 86–90. (See [35], p. 337.) You should be able to apply sociological debates to contemporary issues. For example:

What implications does the Salman Rushdie affair have in terms of cultural identity?

Read Haralambos and Holborn, pp. 568–70.

What arguments could be made against Eichler's work?

Note that you need to interpret Eichler's work and then apply your sociological understanding to come up with some arguments against it.

There is also some disagreement among sociologists as to the extent to which young people form a distinctive generational subculture, sharing more things in common with one another than they do with their parents' generation. The emergence of a separate 'youth culture' has been associated with the rise of affluence after the Second World War, when young people had disposable income available to them, which created a rich market for the clothing, leisure and music industries. However, other sociologists suggest that class divisions are just as marked among the young as among their parents, so that the young are just as divided among themselves as any other group in society.

A similar debate has grown up concerning the position of women in society, with some taking the view that what unites all women – their situation of disadvantage when compared to men – is more important than the differences in income or circumstances which might divide them, while others stress differences between groups of women in society. Those who take the former view tend to look on gender as the most prominent division in society, while those who take the latter tend to emphasise class divisions.

So, modern industrial societies are difficult to characterise as simple class societies. Class divisions of one sort or another still exist, for example, in comparing the very rich with the very poor, but they are complicated by what sociologists call 'cross-cutting solidarities', such as gender, ethnicity, age and also language and culture, which at certain times and places can be as important as, or even more important than, basic class divisions. Nevertheless, class divisions still remain one of the more important ways in which people are differentiated from one another.

You should always be aware of the possibility of applying information in one area to a debate in another. For example:

1 Read *Social Studies Review*, vol. 4, no. 3, pp. 90–5. (See [36], p. 337.)
2 Extract the information on the elderly which can be used in other areas of sociology. State how you would use it.

STRUCTURED QUESTION

What evidence might Dr Rose have used?

APPLICATION

Item A

Don't wait for the revolution

[In calling for a classless society, Mr Major] is going to do what no socialist government, indeed no government in the whole world, has ever been able to do. He is going to give us equality of opportunity . . .

"It's quite clear," says Dr David Rose, a sociologist from the University of Essex, "he means that people can get to the top or fall to the bottom, that there's no bias" . . . But Dr Rose has been doing some research. "As a sociologist I can tell you that any politician who wants to create a classless Britain has got a big job on his hands," he says. "The evidence is absolutely clear that for as far back as we can go, which is the forties, there has been no change in the relative chances of people moving up and down the system, and there is no sign of it changing in the future."

It is not that the shape of the class system hasn't changed since the war. The surge of jobs in management and service industries has transformed it from being a triangle – with the Duke of Westminster at the top, and the hoi polloi sprawling at the bottom – into more of a rhombus, with the middle classes, the Majors and sociologists bulging in the centre.

(Source: adapted from Catherine Bennett, the *Guardian*, Friday 30 November 1990)

Item B

The bitter realities of being black in Britain

I had just turned the corner into my road and was alerted by a raucous noise from an approaching car full of youths. It slowed and I turned, to be greeted with a threatening chorus of "nigger come here". After an icy confrontation, the car sped on and I felt as if I had been the unwitting party in a low-budget promotional video for the National Front ...

It also reminded me of a time when at college I was encircled by five white youths wielding bricks and sticks. The reason for their venom is still unclear, but what became glaringly obvious was the reality of being black and living in Britain . . .

Discrimination takes many forms. A former girlfriend has a friend who was turned down for a job and told in confidence after the interview – presumably by someone who cared enough to pass on the information – that despite being the best person for the post she was refused employment because of her ethnicity.

The black woman who runs

Isis cosmetics told me of distributors who would discourage certain department stores and chain stores from stocking cosmetic products for black people because of a fear of increased shoplifting . . .

My friend's sister said that when she was 14 she was told during a spelling test at school to spell the word nigger. She was the only black girl in the class. "The apparent racism got worse," she recalled. "When I was about to start my A levels I told my career officer I wanted to be a solicitor. He told me I could not do it."

(Source: adapted from Richard Liston, the *Guardian*, Wednesday 13 June 1990)

a) What do sociologists mean by 'equality of opportunity' (Item A)?
(1 mark)

You need to interpret the method in the item and apply it to the question here.

INTERPRETATION   APPLICATION

'How far' implies that you must evaluate and come to a conclusion.

EVALUATION

b) Why might sociologists be reluctant to accept the information in Item B as conclusive proof of discrimination against black people in Britain?
(2 marks)

c) To what extent does the sociological evidence support the idea that 'people can get to the top or fall to the bottom' (Item A) in Britain today?
(8 marks)

d) How far do sociologists agree with the idea that the shape of the class system has changed in the way described in Item A?
(8 marks)

e) Assess any one sociological explanation for the existence of discrimination against black people in Britain.
(6 marks)

NEWCASTLE-UNDER-LYME COLLEGE LIBRARY

2 The importance of class

Many sociologists argue that, despite the emergence of new divisions in society, social class is still one of the most important ways in which individuals are organised into groups. This is partly because most individuals are willing to place themselves into a social class, with such phrases as 'I'm working class and proud of it', or 'I come from a middle-class home'. This suggests that most people have a *sense of place* in society, related to their class or occupational position.

EVALUATION

You need to use evidence to support your evaluations. Read Haralambos and Holborn, pp. 83–6.

How far does the evidence in the extract support the idea that there is a strong class identity among the working class?

From your reading, you will be familiar with the term 'class consciousness'. Define it.

Using evidence, to what extent do you think it exists?

Class cultures and lifestyles

Many sociologists go further than this and suggest that individuals who are in similar structural positions in society tend to mix socially with others in the same position, to share a culture with them and strongly identify their own interests with these others. Thus, in one society, there may be different 'class patterns of behaviour', one associated with the working class, one with the middle class and another with the upper class. The working class in different societies may have more in common with each other than with another class culture in their own society. When individuals show a strong identification with members of their own class so that they are prepared to act together to help each other, they are said to exhibit class consciousness.

Other sociologists argue that a class is far too large a structure for an individual to identify easily with and suggest that people with similar 'lifestyles' or ways of living are more likely to identify with each other, seek to mix socially with each other and act together in the social world. These sociologists believe that patterns of consumption are the key to these 'status groups', although obviously what people spend their money on will be determined partly by how much money they receive in the first place. So, class and status are linked together. However, other theorists argue that, in the postmodern world, consumption is increasingly used like a language by individuals and groups to mark out status differences between them. Other factors, like ethnic group, language or gender may also form the basis of status groups.

When you read, you may be tempted to skim over tables in the text. You should take the opportunity to practise the skill of interpretation. For example:

Using the tables on p. 99 of Haralambos and Holborn, describe the main patterns of attitudes towards distributional justice, according to social class.

EXERCISE

Inequality and stratification

The best known exponents of the functionalist theory of inequality are Kingsley Davis and Wilbert Moore who set out their views in a seminal article in the *American Sociological Review* in 1945. It stimulated much debate in the pages of sociological journals for many years after. We may set out the essential points briefly:

1 All societies need to attract the right people with the appropriate skills into functionally important positions and motivate those who occupy such positions to fulfil their duties effectively.

2 The appropriate skills are often in scarce supply.

3 Society must use differential rewards to encourage people to acquire the skills and attract them to the positions.

4 The greater the uniqueness of a position the more functionally important it is.

5 The more central the position, i.e. the more other positions depend on it, the more functionally important it is.

6 The more important a position the more highly rewarded it is.

7 The more scarce the skill the more highly rewarded it will be.

(Source: Malcolm Hamilton, *Social Studies Review*, May 1990, vol. 5, no. 5)

From your reading, add to this description of the functionalist position on stratification only those aspects which are not covered here. Write a paragraph on the strengths of seeing the stratification system in this way. Do not refer to any problems with the functionalist approach until you have done this. When you have finished the first part of this task, write a paragraph on the criticisms of it. Comparing the two paragraphs, come to a conclusion in another paragraph as to whether the functionalist view of the stratification system is a realistic one.

Nevertheless, large numbers of individuals in the same class do act together to achieve common goals. For example, sometimes classes act together in political parties to achieve social change or instigate a piece of legislation. For instance, aspects of the Welfare State can be seen as the result of working-class pressure for change. But it may also be true that organisations direct their attention to particular social classes in pursuing their aims. So, the government may *target* particular social groups to receive certain benefits. Political parties often gear their policies to particular social classes, usually expressed as occupational groups, such as manual workers or white-collar workers. Advertising agencies use social class groupings as a matter of course to identify potential markets for products.

What do sociologists mean by:

- functionally important;
- differential rewards;
- inequality;
- stratification?

Class differences

This brings us to another important aspect of social class. Classes are not just abstract sociological constructions; they represent real differences between groups. For example, classes have large differences in wealth and income, though there is some dispute as to the extent of these differences. The actual gulf between rich and poor will vary in time and between societies and will also narrow and widen as social policies affect the concentration of wealth in a society. It is also evident that there are differential amounts of power and status associated with particular class positions, which vary over time.

Members of classes also seek to pass on their wealth to their children through the system of inheritance which operates in a society. When a social class succeeds in passing on its privileges to the next generation, either materially through direct inheritance or by giving cultural advantages through family connections or private education, 'cultural reproduction' is said to have taken place. However, it is claimed by some sociologists that modern industrial societies are meritocracies, i.e. the upper class in a society does not reproduce itself exactly, that it is possible for those at the bottom of society to rise to the top through hard work and ability. Such societies are said to be 'open'.

1 Describe the difference between income and wealth.

2 What evidence is there that changes have occurred in either the distribution of income or of wealth?

Read *Social Studies Review*, vol. 4, no. 1, pp. 29–32. (See [37], p. 338.)

What are the implications of the information in the article for the idea that modern societies are meritocratic?

Note that *implications* means that you have to interpret the material and apply it to the idea.

3 Social mobility

One of the most basic debates which has occurred among sociologists is the extent of movement in the class structure which has taken place since the Second World War. The issue of social mobility is important because it goes right to the heart of what kind of society we live in; i.e. whether it is an open society, where it is possible to be born poor and rise to the top of society, or whether we live in a closed society, where most people are destined to live their lives in the class they were born into. For example, the Conservative Prime Minister in 1991, John Major, described his vision of Britain as being one of a 'classless society', where everyone could fulfil their talents, regardless of their class background, ethnic origin or gender.

The importance of mobility

These are important questions because they are bound up with ideas about 'fairness' and 'legitimacy' which we as individuals use to decide how much we accept or reject about the society in which we live. So, the amount of social mobility in a society will affect how stable and accepted a society is judged to be by its members. However, the relationship between social mobility and stability is not a straightforward one. In a society where tradition is valued, the lack of mobility may be seen as a source of strength and continuity. However, in a society where talented performance is given a high priority, high levels of social mobility are seen as desirable.

The amount of social mobility is also seen to affect class formation and class action in a society. Where there is a good deal of mobility, or movement in and out of classes, it is difficult for individuals to identify with one another and act together, as the people in similar structural positions are constantly changing. This does not mean that classes do not form or act, but that the chances of this happening are reduced when large numbers of people are socially or geographically mobile. Some sociologists have argued that it is the upper class or elite who are able to form the most stable class, though even here there is some movement, and that is precisely why they are able to act together to defend their own interests and pass on their privileges to their children through the process of 'class reproduction'.

When alternative positions are put forward, you have to make up your mind which you prefer and give reasons for your choice – it is more realistic, it fits the evidence, the argument is compelling, etc. For example:

Which do you find the more convincing description of modern Britain – that it is an open society or a closed society? Why have you come to this decision?

E VALUATION

Some topics are dominated by important studies which you need to understand.

Using two columns, list the main features of the work of Glass and that of the Oxford Mobility Group. Highlight any differences between them.

Social mobility studies	
Glass	**Oxford Mobility Group**
1 1940s	1 1970s

The first has been done as an example.

You should practise applying evidence to sociological ideas. For example:

Consider the effects of high mobility rates on social stratification systems.

You might ask questions like:

- How will they affect class solidarity?
- How will they affect class identity?
- How will they affect social stability?
- How will they affect class formation?

The problems of measurement

However, it is not always clear how we can measure social mobility in any meaningful way. The most common measures used are the occupational scales, such as the Registrar-General's, the Goldthorpe or the Hall-Jones scales. But there are many groups not represented in these scales and they tend to represent differences in income rather than differences in wealth or power. In particular, the scales tend to be 'gender-blind', focusing on male occupational status and assuming that women have the same status as their husbands or fathers. In a society where there are many single and married career women or female lone parents, this is clearly not adequate.

Moreover, it is difficult to identify the timescale involved in social mobility, i.e. whether sociologists can be satisfied with looking at short-term mobility (the career of one person) or whether there is a need for long-term study (over generations). There is also a debate concerning whether mobility is *apparent*, i.e. related to changes in the occupational structure so that there are simply more middle-class jobs available in

From your reading, you will be familiar with the term 'elite self-recruitment'. However, what evidence is there that elite self-recruitment exists?

Apply your understanding to the following problem:

What are the alternatives to using the male's occupation as defining a family's social class?

society, or *real* in that there is genuine movement of working-class children into middle-class jobs, as well as middle-class children moving into working-class jobs. Whichever is true, the study of social mobility is expensive because large numbers of individuals need to be surveyed to gain an overall view of the patterns of change that occur in society.

Nevertheless, mobility is an important issue for individuals as well. Upward mobility is the result of individuals seeking to 'better themselves' through qualifications or enterprise or will. But as individuals we may face obstacles to achieving our ambitions. It is not just a question of

In assessing social mobility studies, the methodology used is very important.

In two columns, list the strengths and weaknesses of the methodology used by most social mobility studies.

Social mobility studies methodology	
Strengths	**Weaknesses**
Effects on findings of studies	

Write a paragraph on how these features will affect the findings of social mobility studies.

how talented an individual is, but also involves the structure of opportunities which prevails in society and which may make an individual more or less likely to succeed in his or her ambitions.

4 Developments in class structure

Societies are never static but are constantly going through a process of change, so that sociologists have paid a great deal of attention to changes in class boundaries. While there has always been disagreement among sociologists about where social classes begin and end, the debate about the composition of classes has intensified as modern societies have experienced rapid social change.

The number of classes

While sociologists in the past have tended to see classes as fairly stable structures, they have disagreed over how many classes there were or what characteristics were most important in their formation. Some have stressed a fairly simple division of society with relationships between the classes being characterised by conflict. Others have argued for a more complex division of society with classes organised in relationships of superiority and inferiority, according to their function in society and with manual labourers at the bottom and professionals at the top. Still others argue that society is characterised by many competing groups who try to gain advantages for themselves through a variety of 'strategies of closure', such as increasing qualifications or the establishment of a 'closed shop'.

The classical theories of Marx, Durkheim and Weber have been adapted by their followers, as the nature of industrial societies has changed. All these theories seem to acknowledge the greater complexity of class structure in modern industrial societies, as social arrangements have become more sophisticated and industrially advanced. This involves an increasing specialisation of labour, the operation of more complicated technologies and a related change in the occupational structures of developed societies and the globalisation of the economies of the developed

Always back up your opinions with sociological arguments or studies. For example:

E VALUATION

1 Which of the descriptions of class in the paragraph above do you believe is characteristic of Britain?

A PPLICATION

2 What sociological evidence can you cite to support your view?

1 Marx, Durkheim and Weber: write a paragraph on each of these on the strengths of his approach to class.
2 Then write a paragraph on each on their weaknesses.

These paragraphs should not be just descriptions of the theories but analyses of the pros and cons.

3 On the basis of your analysis, state which approach best describes the British stratification system and why you think it is so. For example, you may think that Britain is a stable, harmonious society where everyone has a chance to get on. This would lead you to choose Durkheimian ideas.

world. However, the theories differ in their view of the number of classes that exist in modern industrial societies and in the nature of their relationship to one another, with some emphasising antagonism and others cooperation.

Other factors in stratification

Nevertheless, there has been a general acknowledgement that the modern class system cannot be seen solely in terms of occupational status or economic ownership, but as a complex interweaving of a whole range of social characteristics. In particular, gender has been put forward as a *cross-cutting solidarity*, so it can be argued that all women, regardless of their social class, share a similar position. Some sociologists have stressed the responsibility for child-bearing and rearing, which women have traditionally been associated with, as a basis for their disadvantage in society compared to men. The *domestic labour debate* has tried to show the importance of homemaking to the modern economy.

You may be asked to apply your understanding by offering alternatives to information. For example:

With reference to Sulaiman's article in the exercise on page 144, are there any other questions that you can think of which might be sexist in interviews?

Sociological concepts can be more or less useful in describing social phenomena. You need to assess how useful any concept is. For example:

To what extent is the concept of an *underclass* an accurate description of the position of women in society? You need to consider evidence for and against the usefulness of the concept.

Why can't a woman be treated more like a man?

...FINALLY, MRS SMITH— AND WE ARE ASKING ALL CANDIDATES IRRESPECTIVE OF GENDER— ARE YOU A WOMAN?

JOB SUITABILITY EXPERT

CHIC PIX

EQUAL OPPORTUNITY?

The Equal Opportunities Commission Code for interviewing stresses that candidates must be assessed solely on their qualities, knowledge, experience and personal qualities. 'Men and women should be assessed using identical standards based on their suitability for the job.'

Some employers try to work around the legislation by asking the same questions of men and women. 'I once challenged an interviewer who asked me about my child-care responsibilities,' says Jane Thurman. 'She replied very coolly that she was putting the same questions to the male interviewees.'

Paula Grayson, Personnel Executive at Luton College of Higher Education, points out that, as unwelcome as questions about child-care are, they are also outdated. With demographic changes, there is now a new area in which women can be discriminated against: women as carers of parents. 'These days more people are caring for elderly relatives than for children,' she points out. 'It is reasonable to ask candidates if they have any commitments which might make it harder for them to work regularly, but it should never be assumed that it is just women who have these responsibilities.'

What you should not be asked:

- Are you married or single?
- Are you planning to get engaged or married?
- Do you have children? How many? What are their ages?
- What is your husband's job?
- Do you live with parents/ alone/ with a boyfriend?
- What are your parents' jobs?

(Source: adapted from Sandy Sulaiman, the *Guardian*, Tuesday 9 October 1990)

You should always be aware of the 'real world' which sociology is trying to explain. Which legislation is the article referring to?

APPLICATION

What are the implications of the picture and the text for women's position in the occupational structure and therefore in the stratification system? Do the suggestions in the picture and text mean that women form a separate segment in the stratification system? What other sociological information would you have to gather to back up the idea that women are discriminated against in the labour market?

APPLICATION

For each of the positions described in the paragraph below, find one sociologist who supports it.

Similarly, the position of ethnic minorities has introduced complications into the modern class system. While individual ethnic minority members are found throughout the class structure, their concentration at the bottom of the hierarchy has led to the suggestion that they form a separate underclass in society, cutting across working-class solidarity. Other sociologists have suggested that women and ethnic minorities operate in a secondary labour market, characterised by part-time, casual, low-paid labour, which separates these groups from the primary labour market inhabited in the main by white males. Other sociologists argue that any disadvantages experienced by the ethnic minorities will disappear as they become assimilated into the class structure. It has been argued that all classes can be divided up into ethnic groupings, not just the working class. (See Coursework Suggestion 5.2 on p. 155.)

The occupational structure

Perhaps the most important change that has affected social classes has been developments in the occupational structure. With the decline in traditional heavy industries and the growth of service industries since the Second World War, the number of manual working-class jobs has declined and the number of middle-class white-collar jobs has increased. This has led to the suggestion that the class structure has become increasingly subdivided or fragmented into identifiable, but smaller, groupings. For example, instead of one traditional middle class, modern societies are now said to have a professional class, an intellectual class, a self-employed class and a routine white-collar class, among others.

APPLICATION

What are the implications of a changing occupational structure for a Marxist view of class?

Here you need to establish what a Marxist view is like and apply the changes to it.

In this exercise you must first interpret the information,

then apply it to the problem,

and finally come to a conclusion about it.

Read Haralambos and Holborn, pp. 56–9.

How far does the information in the extract support the idea that the upper class is fragmented?

Indeed, some argue that the traditional classes have always been divided along the lines of skill so that it has always been possible to identify an 'aristocracy of labour', a 'rough' working class and a lumpenproletariat. Others argue that, despite changes in the occupational structure, a clear hierarchy of classes still exists and the power of the ruling class has hardly been seriously challenged by developments.

However, some sociologists put forward the idea that occupation is now no longer the most important class division in society, and that other characteristics are now better indicators of attitudes and actions than the simple manual/non-manual division. For example, regional differences are quite marked among the working class, or housing patterns, particularly ownership patterns, might be better bases for social groupings than occupation itself. These changes in class societies are part of a much wider change that is sometimes claimed to be occurring worldwide.

5 Global changes in stratification

In the 1950s, a whole series of theories was developed which suggested that there was a *logic of industrialism*. What was meant by this was that as societies became industrial, they were forced to adopt particular ways of organising things, in order to produce efficiently and compete with other societies. These theories were developed in the context of the Cold

Read *Social Studies Review*, vol. 3, no. 2, p. 67–70. (See [38]. p. 338

What are the important dimensions of regional differences?

Events in the real world constantly unfold to support or undermine sociological ideas. You need to be able to apply these events to sociological theories. For example:

Do the events in Eastern Europe during the late 1980s and early 1990s support the idea of a logic of industrialism? Look for arguments against confirmation as well as for.

War between capitalism and communism, and should be seen as partly ideological and partly an attempt to trace the future development of society. Nevertheless, supporters of these theories based them on empirical evidence as well – they were not just the product of speculation.

Embourgeoisement and proletarianisation

One popular theory in the 1950s concerned the *embourgeoisement* of the working class. This was the idea that as manual workers became better off under capitalism they would become more and more like the middle class, so that Britain would end up as a predominately middle-class society. This idea was attacked from a variety of positions. For example, some argued that the working class was becoming more affluent, but still remained distinctly working class. However, it was 'incorporated' by its affluence, i.e. accepting capitalism as legitimate, as long as it continued to deliver the material goods.

Others argued that, far from the working class becoming like the middle class, the opposite process was at work. This was *proletarianisation* – that as many middle-class jobs became routinised and mechanised by technological innovation, the white-collar workers came to identify with, and act in a similar manner to, the manual working class. The theory of proletarianisation has come under attack itself, with some sociologists arguing that as white-collar work becomes proletarianised, it also becomes feminised, with the result that there is no increase in middle-class workers identifying with the predominantly male manual working class.

Another view suggests that, while middle-class jobs might be becoming proletarianised, middle-class workers do not experience proletarianisation, because individual middle-class workers are not de-skilled directly, but either retire early or move to other skilled jobs. Meanwhile, firms recruit other workers, usually women, to de-skilled jobs.

The argument concerning these processes continues to rage among sociologists. The debate has been intensified by the acceleration of automated processes in both manual and non-manual work. Some sociologists argue that manual workers in the so-called 'sunrise industries' which produce computer-related products in 'Silicon Valley' are virtually indistinguishable from middle-class people. Others suggest that the skill and power of non-manual workers, especially office workers, has been eroded by the development of information technologies.

INTERPRETATION   APPLICATION

For either proletarianisation or embourgeoisement, list the supporters and attackers of the concept, alongside the key points they make.

Proletarianisation	
Supporters	**Main points**
1	1 2 3 4
2	
Attackers	**Main points**
1	1 2 3 4
2	

INTERPRETATION   APPLICATION

Read *Social Studies Review*, vol. 2, no. 1, pp. 36–40. (See [39], p. 338.)

How could you apply the argument about corporatism to the idea that the power of workers has been eroded?

From your reading, you will be familiar with the idea of fragmentation. How convincing do you find this idea?

Give supporting evidence for your conclusion as to its power to explain the modern class structure in Britain.

Ownership and control

At the upper end of the social class hierarchy, a parallel debate has gone on about the nature of ownership in modern capitalist societies. Some sociologists have argued that the personal ownership of the means of finance, communication and production – the banks, the media, factories, etc. – is very much a minority feature of capitalism. Instead, ownership has spread to large numbers of individuals through shareholding. This process has been extended through the privatisation of large numbers of state nationalised assets such as British Gas, etc.

Others argue that the extension of share ownership is more illusion than reality and that there has actually been a concentration of ownership through the development of interlocking institutional ownership of firms. The individuals who own have become invisible through the apparent institutional pattern of ownership. Nevertheless, in the end it is individuals, not collectivities, who collect the profits from ownership. An interesting feature of this debate is the difficulty of investigating the ownership of capitalist firms, precisely because of the power of the people who own them.

Read *Social Studies Review*, vol. 1, no. 3, pp. 24–9 (see [40], p. 338) or any work on the managerial revolution.

1 Do you think that the managerial revolution has occurred?

2 What evidence can you use to support the idea or criticise it?

3 Which pieces of evidence are most convincing and why?

Your conclusion should always be based on a balanced consideration of the arguments for and against an idea.

STRUCTURED QUESTION

Do you agree with this theory? What evidence can you provide to support or undermine it?

EVALUATION APPLICATION

Item A

Giving capitalism an equal chance

Sociologists are having to rethink their attitudes towards capitalism because of the dramatic events in Eastern Europe. Until now, most have seen it as a system of inequality which inhibits the material and psychological potential of the majority of the population.

In the 1960s, when sociology became firmly established as a popular academic discipline, there seemed to be the possibility for constructing alternative forms of society. Eastern Europe offered some examples . . . But in the 1990s, sociologists are compelled to do more than simply offer a critique of capitalism, which seems to have won the day . . .

Sociologists are also having to rethink assumptions about the nature of opportunity in a capitalist society. Patterns of social mobility may be highly restricted, as measured in terms of the percentage of children from working-class homes who become professional and managerial employees, but in the overwhelming majority of families, children are enjoying better opportunities than their parents did.

(Source: adapted from Richard Scase, the *Guardian*, Tuesday 18 June 1991)

Item B

Crusade which failed to win converts

For all the ideological fervour with which the Tory government has pursued its privatisation crusade since 1979, the policy itself has always proved strikingly unpopular with the general public. With few exceptions, opinion polls have registered strong majorities against privatisations since the beginning of the 1980s.

But the attitudes of those who work for privatised companies have attracted next to no attention. Has their experience convinced them of claims that private businesses are necessarily more dynamic, efficient and consumer-sensitive than those con-demned to lumber along in the public sector?

The answer from the first detailed academic research into employee attitudes in privatised businesses is an emphatic *no*. In general only about a third had positive views about privatisation and most of those were managers or supervisors. The survey was based on a comprehensive questionnaire given to a sample of 422 employees at district offices, depots, sewage treatment works and a billing office. There was no pro-Labour bias in the respondents' voting intentions.

(Source: adapted from Seumas Milne, the *Guardian*, Saturday 27 April 1991)

One mark is for a definition of capitalist society and one for a definition of industrial society, as long as the difference is illustrated by your definitions.

a) What is the difference between a 'capitalist society' (Item A) and an 'industrial society'? (2 marks)

b) Why is it important that there was 'no pro-Labour bias in the respondents' voting intentions' (Item B)? (1 mark)

c) Assess the argument that the privatisation process mentioned in Item B has led to a greater separation of ownership and control in Britain. (7 marks)

d) Item A suggests that capitalism has 'won the day'. To what extent do the events in Eastern Europe support this view? (6 marks)

e) Assess sociological contributions to an understanding of the 'patterns of social mobility' (Item A) in Britain today. (9 marks)

You need to provide a series of explanations and evaluate each of them.

Convergence debate

Another debate from the 1950s which has gained a new lease of life in the 1990s is the *convergence theory* and the related idea of the *end of ideology*. This suggested that the logic of industrialism demanded that there was only one efficient way to produce goods, and that was through the free market economy, as exemplified by American capitalism, and the battle of ideology between capitalism and communism could only end with the victory of capitalism. In the 1950s, of course, there was at least one alternative example: that of the Soviet Union, which seemed to offer a non-capitalist road to modernity.

Opponents of convergence argued that it was far too simple to reduce a complex process such as industrialisation to a single path to modernity. However, the collapse of the Communist economies in the 1980s suggested that the convergence theory may have been right all along. Certainly, the Soviet model no longer held any power as an alternative road to development, through its own inadequacy and failure. However, the American and British capitalist examples are not without their prob-

To what extent does the evidence support the idea that the collapse of communism is a victory for capitalism?

You need to consider not just the collapse of communism but whether the world is becoming post-capitalist.

Read *Social Studies Review*, vol. 4, no. 4, pp. 153–5. (See [41], p. 338.)

Do national differences mean that there can never be convergence?

APPLICATION

lems, and attention has switched to the more successful economies of Japan and Germany for inspiration.

Others suggest that we now live in a post-industrial or post-capitalist society. That is, modern societies have moved towards a new 'convergence' which eliminates the worst excesses of old-fashioned capitalism, but which establishes the most efficient industrial societies as democratic, economically liberal and involving large number of individuals in the ownership of the means of production. Moreover, such societies are meritocratic and classless, with each individual being able to fulfil his or her talents, regardless of religion, class, gender or ethnicity. Whether this is occurring is still a subject of intense sociological analysis, with the New Right arguing that individuals have been empowered in post-modern societies and the New Left arguing that there are still enormous barriers preventing individuals from fulfilling their talents, because they come from a particular background.

Conclusion

Social class, then, occupies a central position in sociological debate, as it has an important influence on our life chances. The nature of class in capitalist societies affects our individual chances of health, wealth, housing and income, among other things. As a dynamic concept, changing as societies change, it is constantly under review by sociologists and is a subject of intense research and discussion. It is likely to remain so as long as there are large differences in wealth, status and power in societies.

EVALUATION

In evaluating ideas, the values of the holder of an idea may be important.

Read Haralambos and Holborn, pp.114–16.

How far do you agree that differences about stratification are differences in ideology?

Consider the arguments for the power of ideology and the arguments against.

Important points to bear in mind

1 Class cannot stand alone, only in relation to other important differences and similarities between groups.
2 Stratification systems change both in terms of system, and for individuals throughout their lifetimes.
3 Some individuals have no desire to be upwardly socially mobile because they are content in their community.
4 Class structure in Britain is affected by global changes in the world economy.
5 The influence of class may be declining, but it is still an important factor in the life chances of individuals.

KEY CONCEPTS

It is important that you are familiar with and are able to use the concepts in this section in appropriate ways if you are to apply them effectively in the examination. Check your understanding of the concepts by carrying out this exercise. Match each concept with the definition which most closely corresponds to it.

The awareness that a person has of the interests he or she has in common with others in a similar occupational position.	Youth culture
A situation where there is a great deal of social mobility.	Ownership
People in a similar occupational position form this.	Social class
What a person thinks he or she is in terms of social class.	Convergence
Associated with the behaviour and attitudes of young people, as opposed to older people.	Hierarchy
A situation where capitalist relations of production have been transcended.	Class culture
Having possessions which confer power.	Social closure
A system of superiority and inferiority.	Social mobility
Groups in the same structural position form similar value-systems, behaviour patterns and norms.	Subjective social class
Where the occupational structure is divided into the advantaged and the disadvantaged.	Dual labour market

The capacity to protect one's advantages through certification or solidarity tactics.	Class consciousness
The movement of people up and down the social hierarchy.	Fragmentation
The splintering of social classes.	Post-capitalism
The process whereby advanced societies come to resemble each other.	Open societies
A group which constitutes part of a reserve army of labour.	Under-class

COURSEWORK SUGGESTIONS

5.1

You could attempt a replication and up-dating of the Hall-Jones occupational classification (see *GCSE Sociology: A Conceptual Approach* by T. Lawson (Checkmate 1992), section 35), but employ more recent occupational categories. You would need to be careful to choose an appropriate panel composition in which to order your chosen occupations, and be careful to chart any differences or similarities systematically.

Here are some issues for you to consider:

1 Are you aware of the criticisms of the methodology of the Hall-Jones study? How can you seek to avoid the difficulties that other sociologists have found with the study?
2 How are you going to ensure the representativeness of the panel? What if some of the panel refuse to co-operate? What social factors are you going to consider to ensure a representative panel?
3 Which occupational categories will you include, and how many will you ask your panel to rank? With what criteria will you ask the panel to rank the occupations – for example, status, power, income? How will you find out what the results of the Hall-Jones exercise were?
4 How will you ensure that you fulfil the requirements of the skill domains? What sociological context will you provide?
5 How will you present the similarities and differences – statistically or by describing them? At what level will any differences between the Hall-Jones' scale and your results have any significance?

5.2

Social mobility studies usually involve many hundreds of individuals in large-scale surveys. It is obviously not feasible for an A level coursework project to attempt such a research project. However, you could develop a variation of this type of study by looking at the relationship between ethnicity, class, ambition and mobility. By comparing the parental occupations and subjective social class positions of a random sample of ethnic-minority and white teenagers, along with their career intentions, you might begin to chart the connections between ethnicity, class, ambition and mobility.

Factors to consider:

You will also need to address the skills dimension in your project, making sure that you include knowledge and understanding, interpretation and application, and evaluation.

1 You will need to set out a very precise hypothesis to test, otherwise your project may become formless and unwieldy. How will the questions you ask seek to test the hypothesis?
2 How are you going to identify the social class of the parents from the occupations that your samples give?
3 How will you ensure a balanced number of ethnic and white respondents? What techniques can you employ to gain such a balance?
4 Where will you get the sociological literature to provide yourself with an appropriate context for your study? Who can you ask for help on this issue?
5 Given that you will be attempting a fairly sophisticated analysis of the relationship between ethnicity and class, how will you separate the elements out to make sure that you present a feasible analysis, and not a fanciful one?

CHAPTER 6

Deviance

In this chapter, we will examine the arguments surrounding:

1 social construction of crime and deviance;
2 social factors, crime and deviance;
3 crime and power;
4 crime, deviance and ideological State apparatus;
5 suicide.

Before you begin any of the exercises, you should have studied and should be familiar with at least one of the following texts:

Bilton, T., Bonnett, K., Jones, P., Stanworth, M., Sheard, K. and Webster, A. *Introductory Sociology*, 2nd edn (Macmillan 1987), chapter 11, pp. 121–7, 179–86.
Giddens, A. *Sociology* (Polity 1989), chapter 5, pp. 181–98.
Haralambos, M. and Holborn, M. *Sociology: Themes and Perspectives*, 3rd edn (Collins Educational 1991), chapter 10.
Heidensohn, F. *Crime and Society* (Macmillan 1989).
O'Donnell, M. *A New Introduction to Sociology*, 3rd edn (Nelson 1992), chapters 13 and 15.

In addition, you should have your notes on deviance in good order.

Introduction

At some time or other in life, everyone will commit a crime or exhibit a deviant action, whether it is stealing from the pick-and-mix in Woolworth's or disagreeing with what everybody thinks on an issue of politics or morality. We all tell fibs socially, either to avoid embarrassment or be polite or get our own way. This does not mean that everyone is *bad*, but that what we see as deviant often depends on individual social position, background, context, morals or experiences. However, what is defined as deviant also depends on social factors, such as the attitudes of those who control the media, or politics or religion. They are in the upper positions of the *hierarchy of credibility* which give them more power to put forward certain definitions of deviance and have them accepted.

Identify one experience or action in your past which, if it had been noticed, might have ended up as a newspaper story. Decide whether it would have been *news* because it conformed to what people see as *good* news or because it would have been seen as *bad* news. For example, many people have engaged in petty theft at some time in their lives, with the risk of being caught and reported.

1 Social construction of crime and deviance

Definitions

Deviance is said by sociologists to be *socially constructed*, that is, formed by social factors and not immediately obvious, or unnatural in some biological sense. It all depends on the time and circumstances of the society in which the definition of deviance is formed. This suggests that any activity can be seen as *normal* in a particular society. For example, human sacrifice, repugnant in modern societies, has been seen not only as a normal activity in some societies, but as an honour for the individual sacrificed.

However, there is disagreement between sociologists about the extent of social influences on what is seen as deviant. Some argue that all activities can be seen as normal in certain circumstances and therefore it depends on the individual society's arrangements as to what is defined as normal. Others argue that certain patterns of behaviour are typical or normal, regardless of the individual society's arrangements, because they are the most efficient way of achieving human goals. For example, some sociologists argue that the nuclear family is the normal way of organising family life, and other forms are usually seen as deviant in some ways.

Although crime is easier to define formally, in that it is any action against the law, this does not mean that there is no social aspect to the process of law-making. Laws are human products and as such are not

In your reading you will have come across interactionist approaches to deviance:

1 Offer a definition of what sociologists mean by the phrase *deviance is relative*.

2 Support your definition by giving some examples of actions which are sometimes seen as deviant and sometimes not.

1 Explain the difference between the following:

   a) pure deviance;
   b) conformity;
   c) secret deviance;
   d) falsely accused.

2 Provide an example for each of them.

natural in the sense of *God-given* or *obvious*. Laws can be just or unjust depending on your point of view. Breaking the law does not guarantee that a person will be seen as a deviant. However, breakers of the law may come to be seen as deviant. Some laws may be seen as unworkable or oppressive by some sections of society. Some crimes are seen as socially acceptable, such as smuggling the odd bottle of spirits through Customs. Some laws are scarcely enforced, such as the Sunday trading laws.

Biological, psychological and social factors

Sociologists have usually rejected attempts to explain deviants by reference to their biological or psychological make-up alone. There are clearly psychological and even biological influences on our behaviour, but to explain all deviance in terms of these factors is far too simple. Sociologists argue that there are social factors which affect both the amount of deviance which is seen as existing in society, the types of deviance which appear and the form which deviance takes. However, there is no consensus among sociologists as to what these social factors are and how they affect the actions of individuals.

Read *Social Studies Review*, vol. 5, no. 2, pp. 66–8. (See [42], p. 338.)

Practise the skill of evaluation by assessing how far the evidence in this article supports the claim for the existence of a criminal subculture.

You will first need to interpret the information in the article and apply it to the idea, by making a list of which points support the idea and which do not. For example, Jack (the Lad) provides evidence for and against the idea.

Your assessment should be in a separate paragraph.

EXERCISE

Hidden crime

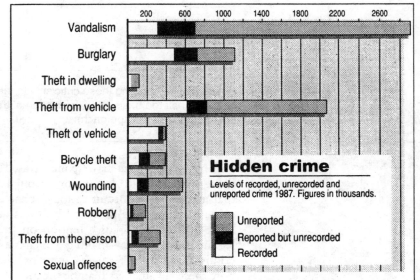

Choose three of the categories and present them in an alternative graphical form. In doing this, you will practise the skill of interpreting information carefully.

INTERPRETATION

(Source: British Crime Survey Estimates 1990. Reproduced with the permission of the Controller of Her Majesty's Stationery Office.)

The chart shows different categories of crime and the level of reporting for each of them.

Using the skill of interpretation, write a paragraph on the distributions shown in the bar chart, identifying which category has the greatest percentage of unreported crime and which has the greatest percentage of reported but unrecorded crime. Similarly, identify which has the least percentage of recorded crime.

Using your textbooks or your notes, write a list of reasons why certain crimes might go unreported, and identify any sociological studies which would provide evidence supporting your reasons.

E VALUATION

Sociologists are often critical of biology and psychology. In two columns, identify the main sociological criticisms of these two approaches to explaining deviance.

Sociological criticisms of alternative approaches to crime and deviance	
Biology	**Psychology**

Notice that by applying these criticisms to the two approaches, you are providing half the basis of an evaluation of them. The other half would be the strengths of the approaches.

Some sociologists have concentrated on the social backgrounds of those who commit deviant or criminal actions. Others have suggested that it is more important to look at the ways in which some individuals come to be seen as deviant by others and the effects this has on their lives. Still others focus attention on the workings of the processes of legitimation and law-making which seek to define what is deviant or criminal and *set the agenda* for a public discussion of these issues, and how these law-makers may be the most frequent law-breakers.

To say that crime and deviance are socially constructed is not to say that they are not real. Crime in particular is a topic of everyday conversation and a social problem for society as a whole. Most people commit a *crime* at many stages of their lives, but they are also the victims of crime and experience its effects directly. Some people are *professional* criminals, others are petty criminals. Some are occasional criminals, others make crime their career. The effects of crime can range from inconvenience to disability and death. Some effects are unfelt, because

A PPLICATION

Read *Social Studies Review*, vol. 2, no. 2, pp. 2–6. (See [43], p. 338.)

Practise the skill of application by considering if the evidence on heroin use supports the idea that deviance and crime are concentrated in particular social groups.

Read *Social Studies Review*, vol. 5, no. 1, pp. 2–6. (See [44], p. 338.)

The article describes control theory. You can begin an assessment of control theory by listing its strengths and weaknesses. On the basis of these, evaluate control theory directly. You can do this by answering the question:

'How far does control theory adequately explain deviance?'

ESSAY QUESTION

You will need to assess the strengths and weaknesses of both the biological and sociological evidence to come to a fair assessment.

Assess the extent to which deviance is socially constructed rather than biologically determined.

the victim does not even know that a crime has been committed against him or her, such as in price-fixing by companies. The State spends an enormous amount of time and money on trying to combat crime, not always with a great deal of success, as the number of crimes reported continues to increase. Crime is often the target of government campaigns in the media and the object of social policies to combat it, such as Neighbourhood Watch Schemes.

2 Social factors, crime and deviance

The statistics on crime suggest that the majority of opportunistic crime is committed by youngsters, especially teenagers. Therefore much sociological attention has been focused on the issue of delinquency and the reasons why it seems that young people are most likely to commit acts of vandalism and theft. However, there is also a class dimension to this research, in that it is usually inner-city working-class youths who are caught committing crimes, processed and included in the criminal statistics.

The area of football hooliganism has been of great interest to sociologists investigating youthful deviant activity, as it encompasses all the

I NTERPRETATION A PPLICATION

You will often need to apply sociological studies in support of or against specific ideas. To do this, you first need to interpret the studies correctly. So, from your reading, list the studies which support the idea of crime as a young person's activity and those which do not.

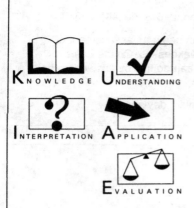

Read *Social Studies Review*, vol. 1, no. 2, pp. 3–5 or *Social Studies Review*, vol. 4, no. 1, pp. 6–10. (See [45] and [46], p.338.)

1   Either from your own knowledge or from the articles, list the social policies which have been put forward to combat football hooliganism.

Evaluation is partly about judging the success or failure of sociological explanations or social policies. So:

2   List the ways in which sociologists might assess the effectiveness of the policies put forward to combat football hooliganism.

social characteristics which seem to be involved in deviant and criminal activity. Even here, there are differences of emphasis, with some focusing on working-class culture as the cause of football hooliganism, and others taking a wider view which incorporates the activities of the police and football clubs themselves.

Social background

In looking at youthful deviance, different sociologists have turned to different levels of explanation and focused on different social processes. One main strand has been to examine the backgrounds of young offenders and seek to find what they have in common. A major contribution has been to look at the structural position of young working-class males and suggest that it is the gap between the aspirations they are encouraged to have and the realistic possibility of achieving them which turns them to criminal activity as an alternative means of achieving their goals.

A related tradition looks at the environment in which the groups identified by the statistics live, and suggests reasons why it might produce a high rate of crime among the young. These might include physical features like large estates with few amenities for the young, or cultural factors, such as anti-police attitudes passed down from generation to generation in deviant subcultures. These theories have mainly been criticised because they tend to assume that the criminal statistics describe the real rate of crime in society rather than just the criminals who are caught.

An important variation of this tradition has been to focus on the whole issue of youth subcultures and their relationship to deviant or criminal

Durkheim believed that crime has a positive function to play in society. What are the main points of his argument?

If asked to evaluate the idea that a criminal subculture exists, you will need to apply the studies that you are familiar with, which either support or criticise the idea:

1 List these studies in two columns, detailing the main points.

Criminal subcultures	
Supporters	**Attackers**
1	1
Conclusion	

2 Below your columns, come to a conclusion about whether such subcultures exist.

activities. Some sociologists have argued that there is a distinctive youth subculture in society, in which the mainstream values of society hold only a limited sway. Much deviant and criminal activity has been laid at the door of young people with too much money and time on their hands. Other sociologists reject the idea that there is a single youth culture in society, and argue that young people are as divided by class as were their parent generations.

Others have pointed to the existence of distinctive ethnic youth subcultures which suggests that there is no unified youth subculture. Moreover, the invisibility of young females in most studies of delinquent

Read *Social Studies Review*, vol. 6, no. 3, pp. 92–4. (See [47], p. 338.)

Develop your skill of application by referring closely to the article in answering this question:

What does the information in the article mean for the concept of youth subcultures?

You will have come across labelling theory in your reading. To assess the importance of this theory, answer the following question:

1 To what extent do you agree that deviance is a product of a labelling process? You will need to consider the importance of alternative theories to produce a balanced evaluation.
2 Support your points with appropriate sociological studies.

subcultures means that half the number of young people are assumed not to participate in youth subcultures. Still others have focused on the importance of symbols for many young people, with the use of *styles* of dress, music and rituals to carve out a distinctive grouping within the young generation. These symbols are seen as a form of resistance on the part of subordinate youth groups to dominant ideologies in society.

Agencies of social control

A second strand suggests that it is the way in which inner-city areas are policed and controlled which leads to misleading figures in the criminal statistics. A whole series of factors is suggested here, from the stereo-types that the agencies of social control have, through policing policies to the processes of labelling and self-fulfilling prophecies which occur with young working-class males. These arguments have been criticised for tending to absolve criminals from any blame for their actions. (See Coursework Suggestion 6.1 on p. 182.)

Thirdly, some sociologists are more concerned with social processes on a wider scale and how they affect working-class youngsters. They suggest that by focusing on working-class crime, the ruling class diverts

You should be familiar with the neo-Marxist account of crime from your reading.

1 List the main points of this approach.

2 How valid is this account? Answer in a paragraph.

3 List the studies you can use to support your answer to 2.

ESSAY QUESTION

'Relative merits' suggests that there should be a direct comparison of the two approaches mentioned, if you are going to give a balanced evaluation.

Some argue that deviance leads to social control; others that social control leads to deviance.

Discuss these two positions and evaluate their relative merits.

attention from white-collar and corporate crime. They thus argue that crime is *caused* by the capitalist nature of society, which encourages *acquisitive materialism*, but only selectively punishes those who break the law in pursuit of it. These theories have been attacked because socialist societies in Eastern Europe still have large levels of often unrecorded crime, despite having no private ownership of the means of production, unlike capitalist societies.

Social groups and deviance

A more recent variation has been a focus on ethnicity and crime, although this remains a controversial issue. The criminal statistics show that Afro-Caribbeans are disproportionately represented in the prison population. In the search for explanations for this, sociologists have become involved in a debate about racism and its effects upon the social processes which lead to the greater appearance of blacks in the criminal

From your reading and from *Sociology Review*, vol. 1, no. 2, pp. 20–3, (see [48], p. 338) carry out this exercise:

1 To what extent is the idea of the black criminal a stereotype?

2 List the studies that you would use to support your answer.

3 Why do you find these studies convincing? Answer in no more than a paragraph.

statistics. The focus of debate has centred around several issues: whether blacks are more likely to commit crime than other ethnic groups in society; whether the social class position of the Afro-Caribbeans accounts for the greater likelihood that they engage in crime; or whether the agencies of social control are either unconsciously or consciously racist in their practices and ideologies, and discriminate against black people in their investigation of crime. In particular, attention has focused on the operation of the *sus* and other laws, which give the police discretionary powers in their operations.

Sociological attention has also focused on women and crime, and the particular images and ideologies of femininity which operate when women come into contact with the law. On the one hand, many sociologists have focused on women as victims, in particular the victims of rape, and much light has been thrown by sociological investigation on what was previously a hidden area of social life. Another area of interest which has arisen is the sorts of criminal activity which women are assumed to be involved in. Focus here has been on shoplifting and prostitution as primarily *female* criminal activities. The processes employed by social control agencies in dealing with female offenders have also come under scrutiny, with some sociologists pointing to a contradiction in the activities of the courts and prisons, which corresponds to the conflicting images of *women-as-good* and *women-as-evil* operating in this area.

While the criminal statistics point to the young as the main offenders, some sociologists argue that deviance and crime are not the unique preserve of any one age, class, gender or ethnic group. For example, homosexual activity, both legal and illegal, occurs in all classes, ethnic groups, genders and age groups. However, it is argued that it is the powerful, who are also generally the older population, who engage in criminal activity as much as younger people but who do not get caught, and it is to the connection between crime and power that we now turn.

3 Crime and power

Sociologists have begun to focus on the connections between deviance, crime and power, because of an increasing awareness that processes which seemed to be obvious in other countries, such as the Soviet Union

1 List the ways in which feminism has influenced the study of crime.

2 In order to assess the impact of feminism on the study of crime and deviance, first write down the advances made by feminism. Secondly list the areas where feminism still needs to make an impact. Lastly, come to a conclusion.

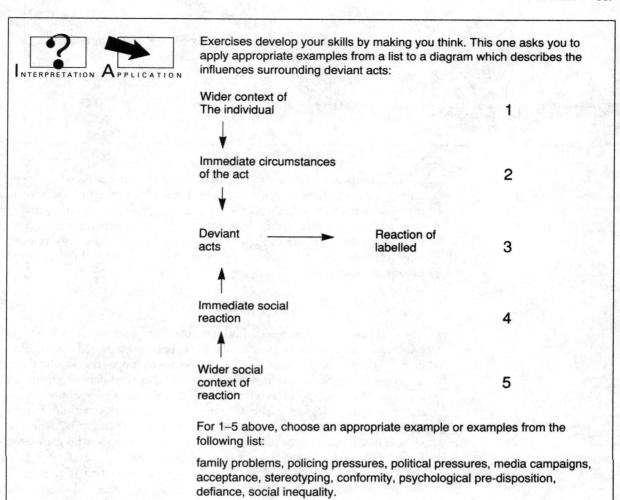

Exercises develop your skills by making you think. This one asks you to apply appropriate examples from a list to a diagram which describes the influences surrounding deviant acts:

Wider context of
The individual   1

Immediate circumstances
of the act   2

Deviant   ⟶   Reaction of
acts   labelled   3

Immediate social
reaction   4

Wider social
context of
reaction   5

For 1–5 above, choose an appropriate example or examples from the following list:

family problems, policing pressures, political pressures, media campaigns, acceptance, stereotyping, conformity, psychological pre-disposition, defiance, social inequality.

and South Africa, might also be important, though less visible, in Britain and the United States. In particular, it was the official statistics on crime which became the focus of investigation and raised questions about the effect of the powerful on the creation and manipulation of the criminal statistics.

Official statistics

Official statistics of crime have been criticised for their non-validity. The focus of attention has been on the high level of unreported crime which has been revealed through victim- and self-report studies. While some sociologists accepted that the official statistics represent a real rate of crime, in the sense that they count a representative sample of law-breakers, others have suggested that they are the product of the power of the police and the Courts to define who shall be caught, processed and convicted, and as such are a biased view of the activities of law-breakers.

Check your knowledge of issues concerning crime statistics by defining what sociologists mean by:

- the Dark Figure;
- the clear-up rate;
- self-report studies;
- victim surveys.

The day-to-day activities of the social control agencies, therefore, produce a view of crime which hides many real types of crime. The areas that have been focused on include stereotyping, routine activities, prejudice, and the negotiation of justice process, to try to explain why certain groups regularly appear in the criminal statistics but, more importantly, why other groups of law-breakers do not appear because they are never caught or processed.

The law

The everyday power to select those law-breakers who will be labelled as criminals is one aspect of power which has been investigated by sociologists. Another important area of concern has been the law-making activities of the State and how these are biased against certain groups in society. The concept of criminalisation is crucial to this approach to crime and deviance, with the argument that law is not neutral but an instrument used to control certain sections of the population, who are seen as threatening to the current order of things by those who gain most from it. This is to see the law as a tool of oppression.

Others are highly critical of this approach, arguing that it suggests a huge conspiracy by those at the top of society to control and deceive the rest of the population. It also seems to suggest that the law does not protect everyone. While some laws are said to protect only the interests of those with property, others would be accepted by the majority of people as *good for society as a whole*.

There is also the view that the law is an ideology which seeks to legitimise current social arrangements, by creating the impression that certain groups in society are the criminals, especially those at the bottom. Any group which threatens the legitimacy of the system as it stands will tend to be criminalised and will therefore be seen as outcasts. For example, homosexuals come to be seen as threatening to the biological reproduc-

Official statistics have often been criticised by sociologists but, to produce a balanced evaluative view of them, you should be able to show how sociologists make use of them. So, list three uses of official crime statistics by sociologists.

Marxists argue that the law is 'the servant of the ruling class'. From your reading, what evidence can you apply to support this idea? List the studies with their main points.

tion of the work-force and therefore legislation was passed to make their activities unlawful. However, critics of this view argue that this does not explain the decriminalisation (and subsequent re-criminalisation) of certain types of homosexual behaviour. Nor does this position always recognise the reality of criminal experience which is that many groups at the bottom of society are also disproportionately the victims of crime, especially *street* crime.

White-collar crime and corporate crime

Another aspect of the study of crime and power has been an increasing focus on white-collar and business (or corporate) crime. Though crimes of the middle class and crimes of the powerful are argued to be just as common as working-class crimes, they do not appear to such a great extent in the criminal statistics. This is partly because they are much less visible than working-class crimes and partly because those who commit them are much less likely to be caught or, if caught, reported to the authorities and processed as criminals. The types of crime included here by some sociologists vary from the small-scale fraud carried out by middle management, involving thefts from work of various items, to large-scale thefts, injuries and deaths occurring in large corporations in the course of their activities.

But they are very difficult to investigate because they are committed by powerful people in secret and often routinely, as part of their everyday practices, rather than being highly visible and prominent in media reports as street crimes are. Critics of this view suggest that there is little

The relationship between the law, the media and homosexual behaviour is complex.

1 Find one newspaper account of homosexuality and identify the attitudes to homosexuality which are implied.

2 From your wider reading, what sociological evidence can be applied to a discussion of the relationship between the law and homosexual behaviour?

3 What are the differences between media accounts and sociological accounts of homosexuality? Answer in a paragraph.

INTERPRETATION   APPLICATION

There is often confusion between white-collar crime and corporate crime.

Apply the knowledge that you have gained about these phenomena by listing the characteristics of each in two columns. Do not just give examples, but give characteristics of the two types.

Differences between white-collar and corporate crime	
White-collar	**Corporate**

sociological evidence to support these allegations and the whole issue has been blown out of proportion by politically biased researchers.

Crime and punishment

One of the most direct powers of the State is the ability to take away the freedom of those convicted in courts of law. Sociologists have been interested in the penal policies of the State and their operation in the prison system. Some sociologists have focused on the experience of those who have been in prison and their techniques for surviving in a *total institution*. Others have concentrated on the development of the prison as a system of punishment and what this tells us about the attitudes of the society in which we live – the *archaeology* of punishment. Other sociologists have focused on the prison as a Repressive State Apparatus, examining its use, for example, to control the Republican and Loyalist paramilitaries in Northern Ireland.

INTERPRETATION

Read *Social Studies Review*, vol. 4, no. 3, pp. 106–10. (See [49], p. 338.)

From the article you can interpret the reasons why business crime has been ignored by sociologists. List these.

Sociologists who have been interested in the relationship between law enforcement and crime include Chambliss, Pearce, Kolko and Gordon. Select one of these writers and read as much as you can about his work.

1 List the strengths and weaknesses of your chosen writer's work.
2 In a separate paragraph, come to a conclusion as to whether it is a fair analysis of law enforcement. In doing this you will be evaluating his work.

The government's performance in the area of the control of crime is often seen as a measure of the success of that government by the electorate. Therefore, the government's policies towards crime are important in affecting their electability. There are generally two positions adopted towards penal policy. The first stresses a punitive attitude, seeing the individual criminal as responsible for his or her own actions and involving the use of prison as a deterrent to others. The second emphasises removing the causes of crime, such as unemployment, and seeks to avoid custodial sentences in favour of community service.

4 Crime, deviance and ideological State apparatus

The Ideological State apparatus of religious institutions and the mass media is related to issues of crime and deviance in many ways. In the case of religion, the linking concept between religion and deviance is morality.

Morality and deviance

The effects of morality on the law and on deviance are subject to dispute among sociologists. Firstly, there are those who argue that there is a direct connection between the two, as it is socialisation into religious morality which provides a bulwark against law-breaking and deviant

From your reading

1 Describe the main points of the two positions outlined in the paragraph above.

2 List the studies which support each position.

Read *Social Studies Review*, vol. 3, no. 5, pp. 196–9. (See [50], p. 338.)

INTERPRETATION

From the article, identify different approaches to crime prevention, highlighting their main proposals. By using only the article, you will be employing the skill of interpretation. Using your own words rather than the article's will increase your skill.

behaviour. Secondly, others suggest that there is little connection between the two, as individuals are *practical moralists*, using morality as a support for their behaviour when appropriate and ignoring the *rules* when it suits their purposes better.

The relationship between morality and deviance can therefore be seen as a complex one, with some sociologists arguing that morals are the basis for social order and provide the definition of deviance, while others suggest that the idea of a moral order is part of the social control activities of society, and leads to varying definitions of deviance. Thirdly, it is argued that the effects of morality can only be seen in the activities of individuals, but that these effects are themselves complex. Religious people may carry out deviant activities; non-religious people may lead very conformist lives. Some religious people may be seen as deviant by virtue of their religious beliefs, while leading religious figures may be powerful agents in the definition of what is seen as acceptable in society. Other sociologists argue that deviant or conformist actions have little to do with religion or morality at all, but much more to do with other social agencies like the police and the mass media.

The mass media

The effect of the mass media, especially television and the newspapers, on the amount and type of crime and deviance in society has been a subject of keen debate among sociologists. This debate has concerned mainly whether the media amplify or make worse a highlighted deviant activity. While, on the one hand, it is argued that the media create folk devils out of particular reported deviants and cause *moral panics* among ordinary people, on the other, the media are said merely to be reporting events as they happen.

The dispute has largely concerned whether the reporting of events by newspapers and television can create a particular moral climate *and*

APPLICATION

From your reading you should have a good idea of what is meant by deviancy amplification and familiarity with examples such as drug-taking. On one side of paper, show how deviancy amplification can be applied to other deviant or criminal acts such as mugging, child abuse, inner-city disturbances or suchlike.

EXERCISE

Lager louts

It's 11 pm on a cold, drizzly Saturday night in Ilkeston, Derbyshire. Young men and women are staggering between the pubs that surround the market square. Policemen are stationed in every available doorway and corner, stamping their feet in a vain attempt to keep warm. There are sparks of expectancy in the air as the elaborate courting ritual takes place in front of police eyes. The boys eyeing up the girls.

Suddenly a police car screeches away. The police and the drinkers charge off in the direction of the Old Wine Vaults where a group of skinheads is on the rampage. With a few split lips and head wounds the police later return to the market square where two drunk youths are arrested. It's 11.20 pm and all the cells are full. at 11.40pm an ambulance is called for yet another casualty of the drinking crisis – a paralytic youth knocked down by a macho male.

"You can plan your duties on Friday and Saturday nights with tedious regularity," said Chief Inspector Norman Hartshorne of Ilkeston police. "Between 11 pm and midnight you have the fighting and disorder in the market square as everyone empties out of the pubs. Between midnight and 12.30 am they smash shop windows on their way home. And from 12.30 you get the domestics."

Ilkeston, a small market town with a population of 33,000, has a drinking problem. A 1989 Home Office report on drink-related problems in Britain's small towns and villages, *Drinking and Disorder: A Study of Non-metropolitan Violence*, pinpointed unemployment, a rise in the male population and under-age drinking as factors related to the upsurge in rural violence. But police in Ilkeston say unemployment is not the problem – the drinkers are well dressed and have enough money to pour up to 10 pints of beer down their necks.

(Source: adapted from Sarah Lonsdale, 'Crime', *Observer Magazine*, 17 February 1991)

What do you understand by the term 'macho'? Define this in no more than two sentences.

On one side of paper, answer the following questions:

INTERPRETATION   APPLICATION

EVALUATION

a) What other information would a sociologist need to know before *lager louts* could be seen as *a folk devil* subject to the amplification of deviancy spiral. Support your argument with appropriate sociological references.

b) What problems are there with the concepts 'folk devil', 'moral panic' and 'amplification of deviancy'?

change the actions of both the forces of law and order and the identified deviants themselves, and thereby create a *social problem*. While many sociologists argue that there is a measurable effect from the reporting of news about deviants and criminals, others argue that increases in those activities are caused by other factors such as the collapse of the family, weakness by the social control agencies, too much money in the hands of the young deviants, etc. (See Coursework Suggestion 6.1 on p. 182.)

INTERPRETATION

EVALUATION

From your reading and by reading *Social Studies Review*, vol. 3, no. 2, pp. 42–6 (see [51], p. 338), you should know what is meant by a moral panic. However, to evaluate its usefulness in explaining the incidence of crime, answer the following:

1 Write down its strengths and weaknesses, in two columns:

Moral panic	
Strengths	**Weaknesses**
1 Includes how people might react to reports of events	1 Does not show that all people react in a particular way
How useful is the concept?	

The first two are done for you.

2 On the basis of these, decide how useful the concept is, writing no more than a paragraph.

KNOWLEDGE

UNDERSTANDING

From your reading, list the advantages and disadvantages of content analysis in two columns:

Content analysis	
Strengths	**Weaknesses**

EVALUATION

From your lists, write a paragraph on how useful content analysis is to sociologists. In doing this, you will be evaluating content analysis.

Find out the main arguments of Geoff Pearson's work, either from your own reading or from *Social Studies Review*, vol. 3, no. 4, pp. 160–4. (See [52], p.338.) You can develop your skill of application by examining the implications of his work for the idea that juvenile crime is a recent phenomenon. Do this on no more than half a side of paper.

Another debate concerns the extent of copycatting of activities by those who watch television reports or read newspaper articles about certain deviant activities. Again, some hold that copycatting does occur, while others find little evidence of it. Others suggest that it is the labelling of activities in certain ways by the media which creates the appearance of an increase in deviant activity, such as happened when the newspapers introduced the term *mugging* into Britain from the United States. A similar debate on the effects of the media has taken place over the reporting of suicides, and whether the reports can create a *suicide wave* of individuals who follow a reported method when deciding to take their own lives.

5 Suicide

Individuals and suicide

The issue of suicide has been a central sociological one from the beginning of the discipline. The reason why a deviant action such as suicide should attract so much sociological attention is that it is the most individual of actions. Yet, sociologists argue that there are social factors at work in that individual action which are open to sociological investigation. For example, suicide is also a social problem, with much State money and many specialist medical and psychological personnel devoted to the treatment of attempted suicides.

This is saying more than that individuals may be *driven* to suicide by social pressures, such as failure to fulfil the expectations of their peers. It is also saying that, although it is the individual who *pulls the trigger* when committing suicide, different societies show remarkably stable suicide rates over time. Thus the rate of suicides (expressed as the number

If asked to assess Durkheim's contribution to an understanding of suicide, you must provide a balanced account. So,

1 Use your reading of the textbooks or *Social Studies Review*, vol. 6, no. 2, pp. 70–4 (see [53], p. 338), to prepare for the following task:

2 Write two paragraphs, one detailing the usefulness of Durkheim's work and the other highlighting the weaknesses. The paragraphs should be of roughly equal length.

ESSAY QUESTION

When you are asked to evaluate a view, you must consider arguments for and against it.

Evaluate the view that the official rate of suicide reflects coroners' decisions rather than the *real* rate of suicide in society.

per million population) in any one year stays roughly the same in most societies. But different societies also exhibit different rates, from high to low, which should be explained by social factors, not by individual decisions.

Explanations

In searching for explanations for these differences, sociologists have come to very different conclusions. Some argue that the suicide rates are real; that is, they count the actual number of suicides in a society, and compare the characteristics of suicides with those of non-suicides to identify differences between the two. They have come up with many diverse explanations including the degree of solidarity in the society, the social disorganisation of an area and even the weather. A more recent focus has been on the unemployed and their higher rate of suicide than employed people.

KNOWLEDGE   **U**NDERSTANDING

1 From your reading, list the points supporting the use of official statistics of suicide and those opposing their use in two columns:

Official statistics	
Points in favour	**Points against**
Should sociologists use official statistics?	

EVALUATION

2 From your lists, write a short paragraph stating whether sociologists should or should not use suicide statistics.

Other sociologists have argued that the suicide rate is not an objective fact, but a socially negotiated number, the result of a process of negotiation among many social actors, but especially coroners. The focus here is on the social processes that lead up to the inclusion of a death in the suicide statistics and the social factors which may or may not influence the official decision concerning a death.

To understand suicide, you will need to apply your knowledge to the whole process involved. To improve your application skill, place the following in chronological order and answer the subsequent question:

- police investigation;
- intention of suicide;
- verdict of suicide;
- medical investigation;
- preparation for suicide;
- discovery of body;
- evidence of family and friends;
- coroner's court;
- suicidal act.

At which points is labelling likely to take place?

Still others have argued that the whole notion of suicide is a tricky one, as most suicidal acts are *gambles with death*, aimed at both life and death and often leaving the outcome of a suicidal act in the hands of luck or of other people. Therefore, the determination of a death as suicide or as something else is difficult. This is precisely because the individual who can actually tell whether he or she intended to take his or her own life is dead, and it is a skilled performance to be able to put yourself in that person's place. It is the coroners or their equivalent who have the greatest expertise in deciding the cause of death, and therefore it may be that the suicide statistics do roughly count the number of those who actually meant to take their own lives.

Although suicide has been an area of sociological research for many years, other disciplines have also been interested. This is especially true of psychology, and psychologists have directed some attention to the issues of age, gender and suicides. However, a major problem with this

---

You may be asked to write in your own words what is meant by sociological concepts or ideas. This focuses on the skill of interpreting sociological material.

Write a paragraph on what sociologists mean when they argue that suicide is socially constructed.

EXERCISE

"Suicide is a very personal and dramatic final solution, which is very difficult for anyone else to influence."

(Source: 'Booth 1990' in *Weekend Guardian*, Saturday–Sunday 14–15 July 1990)

Suicide in Europe
(deaths per 100,000 population)

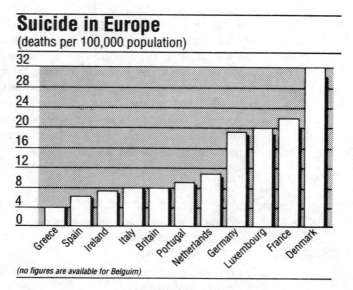

(no figures are available for Belguim)

(Source: the *Guardian*, Friday 7 September 1990)

From the cartoon, write a couple of paragraphs on how sociologists would disagree with the point of view expressed above. Using the table and the information below it as evidence, write a couple of paragraphs on the implications of the extract for the study of suicide, highlighting the reliability and validity of the statistics. Come to a conclusion about the worth of suicide statistics and whether they tell us anything about the real distribution of suicide.

You will need to evaluate sources of sociological evidence as well as the findings themselves. To practise this skill:

Write a paragraph on the value of cartoons as sociological evidence. Make sure that you give some arguments *for* using cartoons and also the difficulties there might be with them.

sort of psychological research is that it can only be carried out on attempted suicides or on failed suicides. Successful suicides can still communicate through notes or letters left, but there is a public dimension to these artifacts which might make them less than truthful. Sociological research on these issues has tended to concentrate on the statistical relationships between these social characteristics and the frequency of suicide. Those sociologists who try to investigate the intentions of individuals in suicidal situations have used the technique of empathy, with all the difficulties that this might entail.

Conclusion

Sociologists have taken an interest in issues of crime and deviance because, after war, these seem to pose the greatest threat to social order in modern societies. The fear of violent crime is a real fear in society and creates demands that something should be done about it. Deviance, by reinforcing people's sense of belonging to a *normal* group, helps to integrate individuals into society. But every single person in society is in some way criminal or deviant. It is the processes by which certain types of criminality and deviance become seen as threatening which have proved such a fertile ground for sociological research.

If you are at all familiar with psychology, you may wish to practise your skill of application by noting down what psychologists can contribute to an understanding of suicide. If you can also apply two examples of what psychologists have done in this area, you will develop your skill further.

Important points to bear in mind

1 Ideas about crime and deviance are bound up with stereotypes of the criminal or deviant. Sociologists are as subject to these stereotypes as anyone else.
2 Suicide is interesting to sociologists precisely because it seems to be the most individual and least social of acts.
3 The law and crime are like two sides of a coin – they cannot exist apart from each other.
4 Although organisations can commit crime, it is individuals within organisations who are the agents accomplishing it.
5 Deviance may be in the eye of the beholder, but some actions, like child abuse, attract more universal condemnation than others.

KEY CONCEPTS

It is important that you are familiar with and are able to use the concepts in this section in appropriate ways if you are to apply them effectively in the examination. Check your understanding of the concepts by carrying out this exercise.

Which is which?

Each pair of concepts is followed by two definitions. Attach the correct definition to each concept.

Crime   Delinquency

A. Unlawful activities
B. Misconduct

Labelling   Self-fulfilling prophecy

A. Attaching stigmatised status to an individual or activity
B. Conforming to a stigma or label

Corporate crime   White-collar crime

A. Illegal activities carried out by the middle classes
B. Illegal activities committed by large institutions

Invisibility   Criminalisation

A. Making a type of behaviour illegal
B. Where social groups are ignored or discounted by sociologists

Repressive State apparatus   Ideological State apparatus

A. Those institutions in society concerned with the exercise of social control through force
B. Those institutions in society concerned with the exercise of social control through ideas

Resistance   Conformity

A. Acceptance of dominant ideas
B. Negotiation of dominant ideas

Gambles with death   Suicidal impulses

A. Social forces influencing the level of suicide in a society
B. Where the outcome of a suicidal action is uncertain

Copycatting   Deviancy amplification

A. The heightened awareness and incidence of deviant actions by social groups through media exposure
B. The spread of deviant behaviour through following examples in the media

COURSEWORK SUGGESTIONS

6.1

It is possible to use photographs to explore the importance of stereotypes in identifying those thought to be criminal. By exposing people to a series of randomly arranged photographs of criminals and non-criminals and asking them to identify the criminals and why they chose whom they did, you can begin to build up a picture of the physical characteristics which define the *criminal type*.

Here are some problems for you to consider:

You will often be asked to apply knowledge from one area of the syllabus to another. To practise this, answer this question: what is the difference between photographs as a primary source of data and as a secondary source?

1 How will you get your photographs and ensure that they are of a good enough quality to use?
2 How will you select the people to ask and ensure their representativeness?
3 Will you draw the sample's attention to any particular features of the photos or will you allow them free expression?
4 How will you set up your hypothesis – in general or specific terms?
5 What will happen if there are no consistent results? Does this mean that your coursework has failed?

6.2

The representation of crime in the newspapers is an interesting area of study. You can carry out a content analysis of newspapers and the way in which they deal with crime. You may search for key words or concepts that are used, or look for different ways in which crime is represented in the various newspapers; for example, comparing tabloid treatment with broadsheet newspapers. You might examine whether ethnicity is a prominent feature of reports, or whether female criminals are treated differently from men.

Key decisions to be taken:

1 How many newspapers will you carry out your content analysis on?
2 How long will you carry out the content analysis for?
3 Will you buy all the papers yourself and incur the expense, or find some legal way of avoiding it?
4 What if you forget to get the papers one day? What alternative strategy will you have?
5 Will you include photos as well as text?

CHAPTER 7

Development

In this chapter we will examine the arguments surrounding:

1 developed, undeveloped and under-developed societies;
2 explanations of development and development policies;
3 social policies and development;
4 aid and urbanisation.

Before you begin any of the exercises you should have studied and should be familiar with at least one of the following texts:

Barnett, T. *Sociology and Development* (Hutchinson 1988).
Bilton, T., Bonnett, K., Jones, P., Stanworth, P., Sheard, K. and Webster, A. *Introductory Sociology*, 2nd edn (Macmillan 1987), pp. 141–5.
Foster-Carter, A. 'Sociology of development', in Haralambos, M. (ed.) *Sociology – New Directions* (Causeway 1985), pp. 91–205.
Giddens, A. *Sociology* (Polity 1989), chapters 16 and 20.
O'Donnell, M. *A New Introduction to Sociology*, 3rd edn (Nelson 1992), chapters 20 and 21.

In addition, you should have your notes on development in good order.

Introduction

The issue of development, usually defined as the transition from a rural to an industrial society, was a central subject of investigation for the early sociologists who were concerned with the ways in which Europe and the United States were developing through industrialisation in the nineteenth and early twentieth centuries. Development is important because of the many benefits it eventually brings to most of the individuals in those societies which are considered *developed*. These benefits are not without their costs, sometimes to individuals, sometimes to groups of people in developing societies and sometimes to the environment.

APPLICATION

From your reading about Marx, Durkheim and Weber, fill in the following table, listing the costs and benefits which each theorist identified about industrialisation:

Costs and benefits of industrialisation			
	Marx	**Durkheim**	**Weber**
Costs	1 Sweep away feudalism		
Benefits	1 Impoverishment		

To start you off, the first items for Marx's column have been given.

Contemporary sociologists, as well as theorists from many other disciplines, such as economics, politics, geography, etc., continue to be interested in the process of development, and in particular how it affects the relationships between the rich and poor countries of the world. Development issues are a major focus for social policy initiatives, not only in those countries which are attempting to industrialise, but also in those rich countries which need the raw materials of the poorer countries for their own industries. It is the emphasis on the inter-relationships between all the societies of the world and a renewed interest in environ-

EVALUATION

Assessment is not just about the evaluation of studies and ideas in sociology. It is also about wider theoretical and political issues concerning the discipline of sociology. For example, an interesting question arises from the sociology of development.

Should sociologists be interested in environmental issues? If they should, why? If not, why not?

Discuss this issue, writing no more than one side of paper. To come to a reasoned conclusion, you should look at both sides of the argument, listing points for and against an interest in environmental matters.

mental issues which have kept the topic of development at the forefront of sociological research.

1 Developed, undeveloped and under-developed societies

Types of society

Sociologists have tried to differentiate between societies at different stages of development. Some argue that the main difference is between the developed world and the undeveloped world. Others argue that there are also developing societies and therefore distinguish between the First (developed) World, the Second (developing) World and the Third (undeveloped) World. A different way to see the World is to divide it into the Western capitalist societies (First World), the socialist economies of Eastern Europe (Second World), which together make up the *North,* and the undeveloped countries of the *South* (Third World). Still others suggest that some Third World societies have actually been made poorer by the First World and these they call under-developed societies.

But even this does not cover all societies. In particular, some sociologists have argued for a further division between the advanced capitalist or postmodern societies of the West and the collapsing economies of the late Communist societies of Eastern Europe. The Communist system associated with the former USSR seemed to offer an alternative way of development to the capitalist system of the West. For example, the space achievements and war potential of the then Soviet Union suggested a powerful economic base. This has been shown to be less formidable as the economies and political systems of Communism have turned out to be inefficient in building advanced technological societies, while retaining some advanced sectors within them.

It is important that you keep up to date with world events, as this makes sociological study relevant. Also, the news is a rich source of evidence for you. For example, you could be asked:

EVALUATION

1 How far do you think the division of the world into three is an accurate reflection of the world in the 1990s?

APPLICATION

2 What events would you use to support your conclusion?

EXERCISE

As the Third World disappears, a new language is needed to describe poverty

The Third World is dead – at least, as a political and economic concept. It was an identity born of the Cold War and a shared sense among developing countries of their disadvantage in the global economy. Events of the 1980s and 1990s have brought its demise.

The virtual disappearance of the Second World in Eastern Europe has destroyed the old three-world matrix. And the emergence of a single superpower [the United States] has made "non-alignment" meaningless.

Economics is playing as significant a role in this as the ending of East–West divisions. During the 1980s, developing countries experienced marked divergencies in economic performance. This is giving rise to a two-track development which, if continued, will open up an increasing gap between the more successful group and those performing poorly.

Over the 1990s, the "high per-formers" should reduce, or at least maintain, the relative income gap between themselves and the industrialised countries of North America, Europe and Japan. But the "low performers" will continue to drop behind.

There are some economic commentators, such as Lord Bauer, who argue that the Third World was anyway only the creation of Western aid policies. If there was no aid, there would be only a spectrum of countries at different stages of economic development. This is not so. It ignores the common legacy of colonialism, with all the inherited economic distortions. It also ignores the existence of various international financial and trade mechanisms that have the effect of redistributing income. But whatever pressures created the Third World, there are today more powerful forces pulling it apart.

(Source: adapted from Melvyn Westlake, the *Guardian*, Thursday 9 May 1991)

What are the implications of the information in the extract for various theories of development? Note down the implications for each of the following: modernisation, dependency, ecological, New Right and Brandtian theories. List the strengths and weaknesses of each of the theories. Choose any one and provide an evaluation of its effectiveness in explaining the state of development of the Southern countries of the world.

Sometimes the wording of questions helps you to structure an evaluation correctly. For example:

Discuss the benefits and disadvantages of colonialism. Which are more important and why?

In answering these questions, try to follow the order of the question in structuring your response. This will make you look at both sides of the argument and come to a conclusion.

Some effects of development

Whether individuals are born into a developed, developing, under-developed or undeveloped society will have enormous consequences for their life chances and life styles. The characteristics of each type of society will affect not only the health and wealth of an individual, but whether people have enough to eat, how long they are likely to live, and their chances of improving their standard of living during their lifetime.

This does not mean to say that all members of Third World societies are necessarily poor and those in First World societies rich. Indeed, all societies exhibit large differences in wealth between those at the top and those at the bottom. But relatively, global wealth and power is concentrated among the elite of the First World and the population in the West enjoy a greater average income than those in the Third World.

For this exercise, you will have to read Giddens, pp. 520–30. The interpretation part of the exercise is to produce a list of the effects of development. You then need to apply your sociological understanding by arranging them under appropriate headings or categories. For example, *short-term* and *long-term* might be a useful way to view the effects.

What do sociologists mean by:

- Third World;
- Cold War;
- global economy;
- developing countries;
- relative income gap?

Check your understanding by writing a paragraph on each *before* you go to the texts to see if you are right.

The study of development often involves sociologists in a consideration of ethical issues.

Write a paragraph on whether sociologists should be concerned with the moral dimension of social life. Make sure that you consider arguments for and against involvement.

It is also important to recognise that there is a moral dimension to the issue of development. Disasters in the Third World tend to attract media coverage in the First World and tend to stir the conscience of the relatively affluent members of developed societies. Recurrent famines in countries such as Ethiopia or Somalia are often *news* in the West. This leads to charitable attempts to alleviate the situations presented in the media, sometimes associated with rock concerts, Comic Relief, and so on. However, it is also often assumed that development in the Third World would solve these problems and lead to a *better* world; that is, development is seen in positive moral terms and rarely presented negatively. (See Coursework Suggestion 7.1 on p. 203.)

However, there are negative aspects to the development process, not just in the Third World, but also in the First. The process of development involves much hardship and change for certain groups in society. It is not achieved without harm. For example, the development of the First World often involved the forceful displacement of peasants in the First World and often the near genocide of Third World peoples who stood in the way of the raw materials needed by the developing West. For example, the original inhabitants of the Americas have suffered greatly since their *discovery* and *development* by the Europeans. There are thus considerations of power to be examined when looking at development processes and it should be recognised that there are always both winners and losers involved.

There are also ecological costs attached to the development process. The exploitation of natural resources to produce goods has often destroyed natural habitats and resulted in spoiled landscapes, as the consequences of strip mining in the United States or deforestation in Brazil illustrate. Industrial production has often been hazardous, not just for the workers in the industry but also for people who live in the neighbourhood. While there have been prominent tragedies, such as the Bhopal or Chernobyl incidents, there are also much more subtle environ-

Using newspapers and magazines, such as *New Internationalist*, which is likely to be in your institution's library, build up a dossier of stories about the Third World. Depending on the source of these stories, look for ways in which Third World countries such as India, Pakistan, Kenya or Uganda may be stereotyped. This will help you to develop the skill of interpreting information and applying the concept of stereotyping to the information.

Carry out a newspaper or literature search to find a story which illustrates the negative aspects of the development process. You will need to use the skill of interpretation to spot the negative dimension. For example, the story of the development of Cocoa production in Ghana at the turn of the century is a good example here.

How might a sociologist use your story? It would be sensible to apply your information to a particular perspective on development to answer this question.

mental costs attached to development. For example, damage to the ozone layer has been caused by the protracted use of CFCs (Chlorofluorocarbons) in refrigerators and aerosols. The destruction of the rain forests and the disappearance of many animal and plant species also cause concern. This is not only because of some idealistic view of nature, but also because these natural resources form a reservoir of chemical and medical potential. Nevertheless, development is still seen as desirable by many people in the Third World, because it is associated with wealth, control over one's own life and happiness, etc.

2 Explanations of development and development policies

As in many disciplines, sociologists have suggested different reasons why development has occurred and have therefore been associated with different *paths to development*. Sociological explanations of development are linked to suggested policies for making countries in the Third World more developed. These differences are important, then, because the future of many people may be affected if an explanation is accepted and policies introduced on the basis of that explanation. Of course, in the real world, decisions about development policies are the result of many complex factors and not just sociological theories. Nevertheless, they do contribute to the debate about development and therefore carry some

1 What other academic disciplines can contribute to development policies?

2 Place them in rank order of importance, stating why you have placed them in their positions. For example, would economics be high on your list or low?

responsibility for the human and environmental consequences of those policies.

Roads to development

Some sociologists have stressed the importance of following the models of the developed societies as a means of achieving industrialisation. However, there is no one road to development, and different Third World societies have chosen different models. These models are *ideologies* of development, which are attractive to groups of differing political persuasions. The three usually chosen are the capitalist, the Communist and the State capitalist roads. With the collapse of the Communist economies, Third World societies which have chosen the centrally controlled *command economy* model, like Vietnam, may now be re-assessing their choices, although the model of one-party control still retains political attractions for the elites of the Third World. In the West, the role of technology has been the main emphasis of those who recommend following the example of the capitalist model. However, this has been criticised in many ways, not least of which is that the capitalist economies of the West developed in the past without competition from a more advanced section of the world, unlike the Third World today.

Another explanation of development has focused on the inter-relationships between the First and Third Worlds. Here, the argument suggests that the First World exploits the Third World through trading relationships, using its power to extract the maximum profit from the dependent nations. The issue of Third World debt to the West is an important part of this explanation, because debt repayments are seen as an important device for transferring funds from the Third World to the First. Thus, the policy suggestions from this perspective are to isolate the economies of the Third World from the First, so that they are given the time and opportunity to develop. This has been attacked as idealistic and unworkable, as the poorer countries need the technological expertise of the rich countries if progress is to be made.

E VALUATION

You will often be asked to evaluate a particular theory or approach to an issue. One of the crucial issues is how effective the theory is when put into practice.

Which of the three models of development identified in the paragraph above was the most effective in achieving industrialisation?

If you were asked the above question, you would need to state what your chosen model's strengths were, but also what was wrong with the other two. Only then could you arrive at a rational evaluation.

ESSAY QUESTION

The crucial word here is 'failed', but you must be careful to look at the pros and cons of the view and come to a conclusion about whether the statement is correct or not. Make sure that any studies used are applied to the question and not just described.

Both modernisation and dependency theories have failed to produce policies which benefit the Third World, and new theories are emerging.

Assess the evidence for and against this view.

E VALUATION

Other explanations

Other explanations have been less prominent but are often influential in certain areas of the Third World. One approach stresses the dualistic nature of development, arguing that in destroying the peasant economies and introducing an urban proletariat into the Third World, capitalist development has a positive role to play in bringing about industrial development. However, it can also be destructive of traditional cultures as the West engages in *Coca-Colonisation*, which is the transfer of Western consumption patterns to the Third World. First World goods attract a high status in this process, which has the effect of increasing First World profits and making it more difficult for Third World industries to compete.

This approach puts forward the political and cultural struggle of the masses of the Third World as the way to ensure an even development in which the poor do not lose out, and it looks to the Sandinistas of Nicaragua as a model. It has been criticised as a recipe for social conflict which will inhibit rather than encourage development.

Another approach is to emphasise the role of market forces in development, allowing for the freest possible trading conditions, so that development trickles down from the developed to the non-developed world. This tradition points to the *new international division of labour* as evidence for the success of *trickle down*, using Taiwan as a model. Here, the large populations of many countries in the Third World are not seen as one of the causes of poverty. Poverty will be overcome, it is argued, by development, which can only happen when Third World countries open their borders to capital investment from the West at maximum profits for all parties involved. Critics suggest that this would lead, not to development, but to an intensification of exploitation.

More recently, an approach which concentrates on the ecological issues has gained some support. The approach suggests that it is in small-

From your reading, you will have come across *world system theory*. Use the table below to answer the following:

1 Describe what it is.

2 List its strengths and weaknesses.

3 Use appropriate examples to back up points.

4 Assess its usefulness in explaining differences in stages of development.

World system theory	
Description	
Strengths	
Weaknesses	
Evaluation	

In answering these four questions, you will have practised four different skills.

scale environment-friendly intermediate developments that the future of the Third World lies. The over-exploitation of natural resources as Third World countries struggle to develop could lead to local or even global catastrophe and it is therefore prudent to think small, build small and develop slowly. This may be sound advice, but it is unlikely to be attractive to Third World governments looking for more immediate solutions to poverty.

Moreover, there is an approach which stresses the role of women in the Third World and examines the burden that development strategies tend to place on women, both in terms of health care, education and social issues, and in agricultural and industrial production. The criticism that has been levelled at this approach is that it is predominantly poor women and men who bear the brunt of many development policies, not just women.

Which sociological perspective will be most likely to be interested in the role of women in the Third World?

Here, you are asked to apply your knowledge of perspectives to a specific issue.

Whichever approach is adopted by the Third World, the consequences will not be entirely as predicted. Social science is just not able to predict consequences with precision because human beings possess free will and consciousness, and the range of factors which influences events can be enormous, and often unpredictable. Unintended consequences are an inevitable part of policy implementation and therefore policy needs to be reflective (looking back to see the effects of policies) and reflexive (responding to events effectively). This does not mean to say that sociology should have no role in development policies at all. On the contrary, it is the attempts to predict and control events through the rational analysis of society which have made for progress in the past, and therefore sociology, in its many aspects, will continue to contribute to debate in the area.

3 Social policies and development

Globalisation

One feature of the post-war period has been the increasing globalisation of economies and societies. Through this process, economies become increasingly interdependent, so that they operate within an integrated world-wide system. In part, this is the result of the emergence of a global monetary system and the development of leading-edge technologies, such as robotics and microchips, which are geared to global markets. This has led to a greater economic interdependence of national economies, which has consequences for the possibility of development in the Third World. There has also been a localisation of national economies, as units of the national economies become tied to global mar-

To do this exercise, you need to have access to *Sociology Review*, vol. 1, no. 2, pp. 10–14. (See [54], p. 338.)

In no more than one side of writing, highlight the main points of Foster-Carter's four *rock-pools*.

Taking succinct notes like this helps you to develop interpretation skills by making you identify key points only.

Globalisation is a fairly new concept in sociology. However, by applying your knowledge of the world and your sociological judgement:

APPLICATION

List three limits to the process of globalisation.

You might find some hints in the textbooks.

kets, often through the activities of multi-national companies, such as the huge car companies of Japan and the United States. The development of the Nissan factory in the Northeast of England is an example of this process.

There has also been a globalisation of culture and politics. In terms of culture, many events put on by the mass media are world-wide events, transmitted simultaneously through satellite technology. In politics, the United Nations' action in Kuwait in 1991 demonstrated the possibility of joint military action. This globalisation tends to reduce the independence of societies, making development dependent on supranational organisations, such as the dominant multi-national corporations, the World Bank or the International Monetary Fund. With the collapse of the Soviet Union, it is argued that the United States is now the dominant global power.

One of the most important issues concerning the Third World is the crisis in food which frequently affects the poor countries of the world, especially sub-Saharan Africa. Sociologists have tended to argue for longer-term solutions to the ecological and meteorological disasters which affect large parts of the world. However, there are many different approaches within sociology and other development disciplines. Some argue for large-scale development projects which will alter the flow of rivers or preserve water stocks more effectively. Others suggest that smaller-scale projects, geared to the provision of clean water sources and land preservation, are the long-term solution to the problems. Still others suggest that population control provides the only sure way of avoiding periodic famine. Another approach emphasises the need to resolve the political and social struggles which often occur in drought-ridden countries and which often hinder relief efforts.

Read *Social Studies Review*, vol. 2, no. 3, pp. 2–6. (See [55], p. 338.) The article suggests reasons for famine in Africa.

EVALUATION

Practise your skill of evaluation by stating which you find most convincing and why.

In assessing the strengths of your favoured explanation, do not neglect to state what is wrong with the other explanations.

EXERCISE

Development in the balance

What other measures of progress or deprivation could you apply to this chart? Use the same column format in your answer. Be careful to avoid measures already given. This means that you will have to exercise your skill of interpretation.

PROGRESS

DEVELOPING COUNTRIES

LIFE EXPECTANCY
- Life expectancy increased by one third between 1960 and 1990. Now 63 years.

HEALTH
- Proportion of people with access to health services has risen to 63 cent.

NUTRITION
- Average calorie supplies as percentage of requirements rose from 90 to 107 per cent.

EDUCATION
- Adult literacy in developing countries rose from 46 to 60 per cent 1970–85.

INCOME
- Income per head grew annually in 1980s by 4–9 per cent in east Asia.
- More than one in four people live in countries with growth rates above 5 per cent.

CHILDREN
- Under five mortality rates halved over last 30 years.
- Immunisation coverage increased dramatically in 1980s.

RURAL/URBAN
- Proportion of people in rural areas with access to adequate sanitation has doubled in 10 years.
- 88 per cent of urban dwellers have access to health care and 81 per cent have access to safe water.

INDUSTRIAL COUNTRIES

LIFE EXPECTANCY
- Expectancy 75 years.
- Virtually all births attended by health workers.
- Two thirds of population covered by public health insurance.
- 8.3 per cent GNP spent on health care.

EDUCATION
- 6 per cent GNP spent on education.

DEPRIVATION

- 10 million older and 14 million young children die each year.

- 1.5 billion lack basic health care or safe water. Over 2 billion without safe sanitation.

- One fifth of the world's population still goes hungry every day.

- One billion adults illiterate and 300 million children not in school.

- More than 1 billion live in absolute poverty.
- Income per head has declined in the last decade in Latin America and sub-Saharan Africa.

- 14 million children die before they are five years old and 180 million suffer chronic, severe malnutrition.

- Only 44 per cent of the developing world has access to basic health care.
- 2.4 people per habitable room (three times that of the North).
- One urban dweller in five lives in nation's largest city.

- Adults smoke average 1,800 of cigarettes and consume four litres pure alcohol a year.
- More than 50 per cent likely to die of circulatory and respiratory diseases linked with sedentry lifestyles and nutrition.

- Almost one in four lack secondary education.

INCOME
- GNP per capita increased 1976–88 almost 300 per cent.
- These countries produce 85 per cent of global wealth.

- The wealthiest 20 per cent receive almost seven times as much income as poorest 20 per cent.

SOCIAL SECURITY
- Social welfare expenditures now 11 per cent GNP.

- About 100 million people live below the poverty line.

SOCIAL FABRIC
- Communications: one radio per person, one TV and telephone for every two people.

- Many industrial countries experiencing a fast change in their social fabric.

POPULATION
- Growth rate around 0.5 per cent.
- Almost everyone enjoys access to safe water and sanitation.

- Up to 50 per cent dependency ratio.
- 433 persons in 100,000 are seriously injured in road accidents every year.

(Source: from John Vidal, the *Guardian*, Friday 24 May 1991)

Prepare a report on the differences between the developed and the developing world from the information in the chart. For each of the categories in the chart, prepare a list of the social problems which the developing countries face in these areas. Suggest a policy to combat each of these problems.

North and South

There is also an ethnic dimension in the sociology of development. This occurs in two ways. Firstly, the North–South divide is to all intents and purposes an ethnic divide. The rich North is predominantly white and the poor South mainly non-white. The division between poor and rich countries is therefore complicated by the realities and ideologies of race and colonialism. The poor Third World is largely an ex-colonial world and it carries the burden of the colonial years, both in economic and psychological terms. The colonial authorities often used ethnic divisions to

When you are asked to evaluate something, you are being asked to exercise your personal judgement. But good sociologists always back their judgement with sociological evidence. For example:

E VALUATION

1 How important do you think racial stereotypes are in the Western view of the Third World?

A PPLICATION

2 What sociological evidence can you cite to support your view?

From your reading, you will have found that some sociologists believe that education is the key to development, while others disagree. Therefore:

Assess the importance of education in fostering development in Third World countries.

Here you need to consider education compared to other factors which may be equally, or more, important. Then you should come to a conclusion about the importance of education in a separate paragraph of your answer.

divide and rule, and the second dimension of ethnicity is the importance of those ethnic rivalries within the decolonised countries, as they often lead to communal violence and political instability.

The demographic balance in the North and South is also different. The rich North has a greater proportion of the elderly in its populations, with all the social problems that this entails, such as the provision of adequate health care for an elderly, dependent population. In the poor South, the population balance is weighted towards the young because of the higher birth rates and low life expectancies in these countries. This brings its own set of social problems; notably, the provision of education for large numbers of the young becomes difficult in societies where the Gross National Product (or national income) is low. But even where a society succeeds in educating its young people to a fairly high level, it cannot always provide jobs with the appropriate levels of skill and pay for the educated youngsters. This may, in turn, lead to social discontent or unrest. In societies where there is a lack of opportunity for upward mobility for the educated poor, emigration becomes an attractive alternative, with the consequent loss of talent in those societies which can least afford to lose it.

4 Aid and urbanisation

A central strategy of development policies has been to deploy resources from the rich nations of the world to the poor through aid. Aid takes a variety of forms, including charitable aid, development aid and tied aid. Aid may be donated from private, governmental and supra-governmental sources. The role of aid has been a subject of debate among sociologists, with some seeing it in a positive light and others suggesting that its effects on the poor countries are negative.

It is important for sociologists to engage in *real* issues and not just theoretical thinking. So, use the following exercise to apply your sociological sense to a political issue:

Write a paragraph which argues the case for the abolition of all charitable Third World agencies. Be careful not to defend the agencies in your paragraph.

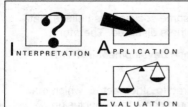

The texts on aid suggest that there are both positive and negative aspects to Third World countries receiving aid. From these points and from your reading:

1   Evaluate aid provision, stating whether it helps or hinders the Third World. Make sure that you address arguments both for and against the provision of aid.

2   Include any sociological evidence that you can to support your points.

Advantages and disadvantages

The positive view of aid tends to emphasise the development that has occurred as a result of the transfer of funds from the rich to the poor countries. There are many examples, both specific and general, which show that progress has been made through the receipt of aid. This progress can either be measured in the real improvements to people's lives in the Third World or by reference to growing Gross National Product (GNP) and manufacturing industry in those countries.

The critics of aid programmes come from several different positions. Some argue that any government intervention in the development process has unhappy effects because it distorts the natural workings of the market, which are the only way that development will be achieved. They suggest that aid is inefficient because it is directed towards non-development projects, such as supporting the poor. Moreover, there is much corruption in the administration of aid, with a great deal of funds being siphoned off by Third World elites, or going to pay the salaries of the well-to-do in the Third World. The *disappearance* of emergency relief in places such as Somalia has been used to support this viewpoint.

A second approach argues that aid is actually of benefit to the First World rather than the Third World. It is suggested that aid is directed

ESSAY QUESTION

Though this essay is similar to a previous exercise, notice that the wording is different. Your evaluation needs to take account of this. In particular, your conclusion must refer directly to the specific question asked.

Assess the argument that aid to the Third World has more negative than positive consequences.

towards projects that develop the infrastructure to support exports to the rich North, or imports into the Third World countries from the developed world for the building of specific roads or harbours. It is also put forward that much aid is tied to the purchase of First World products and expertise. The terms of aid donations are often tied to the pursuit of certain economic policies which tend to benefit Western industries, such as the privatisation of State industries.

A particular line of criticism has been associated with the activities of the multi-national corporations (MNCs). Some argue that MNC activities are a prerequisite for development because they provide the necessary capital and technological know-how for the emergence of an industrial base in the Third World. The economies of Singapore or South Korea are used as examples here. Others suggest that the role of the multi-national corporations in the Third World is primarily exploitative, either extracting raw materials cheaply or taking advantage of the low-wage economies of the Third World to shed expensive labour in the First World, thus increasing profits. The activities of the tobacco industry have come under particular criticism, as they have targeted Third World countries to offset declining sales in the First World.

Urbanisation and development

A similar debate has concerned the role that urbanisation in the Third World plays in the global economy. It should not be assumed that cities are a new phenomenon, only associated with industrial development.

When reading sociological work, you should not just be learning a description of it but asking yourself evaluative questions about it, such as question 2 in the following exercise:

1 Through a newspaper search or from your reading, describe an example of the activities of an MNC in the Third World.

2 Is the effect of that activity beneficial or not? Give reasons for your answer.

I NTERPRETATION   K NOWLEDGE

U NDERSTANDING   E VALUATION

Many works on development give examples of particular cities in the Third World; for example, Delhi and Mexico City.

From any description of a Third World city you can find, apply its characteristics to the issue of the role of cities in Third World development.

A PPLICATION

Cities have grown up historically as centres of commerce or administration, but they are characteristic of industrial societies and inextricably associated with their state of development. However, the role of cities in the Third World is not clear-cut, nor are all cities there likely to adopt the same role. There is a great deal of variety in different cities of the world and, even within one city, various differences will be present. But sociologists have focused on the city as a central issue in the debate concerning development.

On the one hand, some sociologists say that cities are often the motor of development, being a magnet towards which cultural attitudes favourable to development are attracted. They form the epicentre of development, spreading out capitalist practices into the rural hinterland and ensuring that progress continues to be made. Others argue that, generally, cities represent outposts of the First World in the Third World and are the vehicles of exploitation, ensuring the smooth transfer of resources from the poor to the rich. A third approach suggests that some cities of the Third World are the links that bind all economies into a global economic network, dominated by capitalist modes of production.

However, the reality of cities in the Third World is best summed up in the concept of *over-urbanised*. For the mass of people in the *barrios* or *favelas* of the Third World, life can be extremely stressful. Much migration into cities is forced because of the failure of peasant agriculture, but much is attracted voluntarily through the better standard of living for which many hope. This demographic pressure produces a situation where there is growth without development, with a consequent pressure on housing and infrastructure which reduces the conditions of life in the cities for the majority of the poor. Where this was systematised, as in the

E VALUATION   A PPLICATION

In assessing different explanations of the same phenomenon, the role of evidence is crucial in convincing someone that one of the explanations is the most likely.

If you were asked to choose one of the three explanations of the role of the city in development, identified in the paragraph above, what evidence would you produce so that you could say you knew your answer was correct?

I NTERPRETATION   K NOWLEDGE

U NDERSTANDING   A PPLICATION

Apart from those mentioned in the paragraph above, what other problems exist in Third World cities? List each one and apply a short definition to each.

migrant labour policies of the apartheid regime in South Africa, rigid seg-regation of populations in cities may result, and the rural hinterland pro-vides a source of cheap labour which is pulled into *dormitory* accommo-dation when needed and sent back when no longer necessary.

NEWCASTLE-UNDER-LYME
COLLEGE LIBRARY

Conclusion

Thus, the sociology of development offers a continuing contribution to the important problems of global relationships and the development of the world economy. While sociology is unlikely to provide all the answers to those problems, by emphasising the social as opposed to the economic dimension, it draws attention to an important and necessary aspect of the debate. As contributors to the arguments, sociologists have increasingly co-operated with members of other disciplines with a conse-quent enrichment of them all.

Important points to bear in mind

1 Aid can be double-edged; while many countries could not survive without it, giving aid does not always lead to the desired development but can increase dependency.
2 All Third World countries are not the same but have their own histories and cultures.
3 Population pressure in the Third World is subject to different pressures compared to the First World. While birth rates remain high, the AIDS epidemic in Africa is reducing life expectancy sharply in some countries.
4 The world economy is increasingly interrelated but this may also result in the localisation of markets, undermining national sovereignty.
5 Policy decisions on development take account of the political and economic interests of the people and countries involved, both in the First and Third Worlds, and are not just influenced by morality.

KEY CONCEPTS

It is important that you are familiar with and are able to use the concepts in this section in appropriate ways if you are to apply them effectively in the examination. Check your understanding of the concepts by carrying out this exercise.

For each of the following descriptions, choose the most appropriate concept from the list:

1 A concept used to describe the switch of manufacturing from high-wage Western economies to low-wage economies in the Third World.

2 The process whereby the bulk of the population of a country moves into cities and towns.

3 One way in which funds may be transferred from one part of the world to another.

4 The process used to describe American economic domination of other countries.

5 The transformation of a society from a traditional to a contemporary state.

6 The process whereby Third World societies have been impoverished by colonialism.

7 The transformation of society from a predominantly agricultural to an industrial state.

8 The process, whereby a society shows improvement in such factors as gross national product (GNP), life expectancy, etc.

9 The emphasis on the environment as an important element in development.

10 The process whereby the world is increasingly seen as a single unit.

11 A concept emphasising the geographic division of rich and poor countries.

12 A description of business organisations which have a global role.

13 A system based on State control of the economy.

Modernisation	Under-development	Industrialisation
Communism	Ecological dimension	North–South
Coca-colonisation	Globalisation	Development
Urbanisation	New international division	Aid
Trans-national corporations	of labour	

COURSEWORK SUGGESTIONS

7.1

Development issues are difficult to investigate using primary methods, for the obvious reason that the Third World is so far away. However, there may be students in your institution who have had direct experience of, or cultural links with, a Third World society, having lived there or visited extensively. Having identified any such respondents, you could carry out an in-depth interview with them, with the aim of examining some of the stereotypes that exist about such societies.

Here are some pointers to help.

1 You may need to advertise in the college magazine or through the pastoral system for your respondents.
2 You may need to identify the stereotypes of the Third World by looking at newspaper reports about such countries. You will need to be precise about the stereotypes you are investigating so that you can ask the right questions in the interviews.
3 You may enlist some students to gain access to their parents or grandparents if they would be a more useful source of information. You may need help if there are any language differences.
4 You may find it useful to use a tape recorder during the interviews so that you can refer to information later on.
5 It will be important to keep a field-work diary so that you can record the events of your research as they happen.

7.2

You may be able to investigate the work of an organisation which operates in the Third World, either as an aid or as a relief agency. One point of access may be at the national level through organisations such as Oxfam or Christian Aid (you can write to them for information). However, many organisations have local branches where you might be able to get an interview with a representative. If it is possible, you could compare the activities and attitudes of two or three different agencies, perhaps identifying if they favour one particular approach to development over others.

Here are some points to consider.

1 How will you establish an aim for your project? With such *global* issues, it is easy to be over-ambitious and your project will suffer from the lack of *bounded* aims.
2 You may be dependent on the availability of local organisations. You will need to find out if they exist before you commit yourself to this project.
3 How far will you be able to claim that any local representative's views are typical of the whole organisation?
4 How are you going to distinguish between publicity material for the organisations and their *real* activities?
5 How long can you reasonably wait for national organisations to reply? Should you send them a reminder?

CHAPTER 8

Health, welfare and poverty

In this chapter we will examine the arguments surrounding:

1 health issues;
2 poverty;
3 welfare.

Before you begin any of the exercises you should have studied and should be familiar with at least one of the following texts:

Bilton, T., Bonnett, K., Jones, P., Stanworth, M., Sheard, K. and Webster, A. *Introductory Sociology*, 2nd edn (Macmillan 1987), pp. 65–77, 128–31.
Giddens, A. *Sociology* (Polity 1989), pp. 235–40, 587–97.
Haralambos, M. and Holborn, M. *Sociology: Themes and Perspectives*, 3rd edn (Collins Educational 1991), chapter 4.
O'Donnell, M. *A New Introduction to Sociology*, 3rd edn (Nelson 1992), chapters 7 and 16.
Stacey, M. *The Sociology of Health and Healing* (Unwin Hyman 1988).

In addition, you should have your notes on health, welfare and poverty in good order.

Introduction

The issues of health, welfare and poverty are important for individual life chances, as the circumstances of people's birth, their home background and their state of health will affect what they are able to do with their lives. The welfare system acts as a safety net for those individuals who need some sort of support at different stages in their lives, as well as providing, through the education system, for example, the social reproduction of society from one generation to the next. Moreover, these issues are a central focus of social policy, with the government prepared to invest billions of pounds in the health and welfare services and with voters often seeing these issues as important indicators of a government's performance.

Health, welfare and poverty are interesting, from a sociological point

What do sociologists mean by:

- life chances;
- safety net;
- collective provisions;
- fatalistic attitudes?

of view, because they are issues which are experienced individually but which also have a collective existence. When individuals feel ill, they may seek remedies through collective provisions. If they treat themselves, they are likely to use chemical products developed by pharmaceutical firms, which have their actions restrained by laws. If they seek medical help, it will be through collective provisions, such as doctors, trained by university medical schools, working in the National Health Service or private hospitals. Poverty is also experienced collectively in families, although the effects show themselves in individuals through poor health, fatalistic attitudes, mental illness, etc.

1 Health issues

Social and biological factors

One of the basic insights of the sociological approach to health and illness is that illness is not just a biological issue. Health and illness are said to be socially constructed, that is, affected by the society in which they occur, and therefore what is seen as a healthy state or an illness actually varies from society to society and across time. While there is a general agreement that both social and biological factors are at work in determining health and illness, there is no consensus about the relative importance of these factors.

Some argue that biological factors are paramount, with only some social effects on the margins of medical science. Others argue that it is in the area of mental illness that social effects can be identified most

From your reading, you will have come across the idea that health is a social construction.

What evidence can you provide to support this idea? Make sure that you apply both examples and sociological studies.

strongly, although even here biological factors, such as hormone imbalance, may be present. Still others suggest that there is a strong social element in the definition of health and illness. This is not to deny the existence of biological phenomena, such as bacteria and viruses, but our reactions to these are influenced by social factors, such as how others see them, how medical science approaches them, the state of medical knowledge at the time, etc.

EVALUATION

In comparing biological and social factors of health, make sure that you give adequate consideration to the claims of biology. For example:

How important do you think biological factors are in determining levels of health and illness? List the pros and cons of the biological argument in two columns:

Biological explanations of health	
Pros	**Cons**
1 Hereditary diseases prove that biology influences health	1 Cannot explain differences in health between social classes

The first two are done for you to start you off.

Some sociologists have focused on the way that individuals adopt the *sick role* for certain social reasons, even though they may not be biologically ill. This does not make their pain any less real, but illustrates the potential that some ailments, such as a bad back, have for variable interpretations. Others have charted the debate between those who see medical advances as the main reason for growing life expectancy in the West and those who suggest that public health reforms, such as sewerage, are far more important. Another aspect concentrates on the power of the medical profession, its gender bias and the interaction between medical personnel, such as nurses, and those in their care. (See Coursework Suggestion 8.1 on p. 224.)

APPLICATION

When reading sociological material, you should be seeking to apply it to various debates. For example:

Read *Social Studies Review*, vol. 6, no. 4, pp. 128–30. (See [56], p. 338.) What does the article contribute to the debate about the nature of the doctor–patient relationship?

INTERPRETATION

APPLICATION

From your reading:

1 List the reasons why the working class appears to suffer ill-health more than the middle class.

2 How can these reasons be systematically classified? You need to think up appropriate categories under which to organise them.

Patterns of health and illness

While ill-health is experienced individually, there are clear patterns of group ill-health which often reflect patterns of inequality in the wider society. Sociologists have been particularly concerned with class differences in health, such as the different chances of dying early, which are clearly shown in the statistics, and which connect to debates about wealth and poverty in society. Regional variations are also linked to the different material conditions in parts of the country.

However, there are also gender and ethnic variations, which have been identified through careful analysis of the statistics. Women have different health problems from men, partly because of their different biological make-up, but also because of their different life experiences. The debate among sociologists has mainly concerned how important these differences are and how best to deal with the them. Similarly, different ethnic groups have specific forms of illness attached to them, partly associated with genetic differences and partly a result of lifestyle differences. The careful charting of these differences and the suggestion of solutions have been an on-going focus of medical and sociological investigation.

Explanations

The most intense debate has centred on explanations for these differences. The issue is important because the type of explanation which is emphasised will influence the sort of solutions put forward. It is here that the social policy implications of the sociological study of health become apparent. Those responsible for introducing social policies concerning health are likely to be influenced by the research carried out in the area by doctors, economists, sociologists and others. The sociological study of health and illness has, therefore, been one of the areas that the government has increasingly funded during the 1980s as it searches for solutions to health problems.

INTERPRETATION **A**PPLICATION

From your own experience and from your reading:

Identify the main differences in men's and women's patterns of health and illness.

ESSAY QUESTION

Notice that you should pay equal attention to class and ethnicity. You should ignore gender differences unless they are relevant to class or ethnicity.

Evaluate sociological explanations for differential levels of health and illness between social classes and different ethnic groups.

The explanations put forward are many and varied. Some argue that the differences between social groups are more apparent than real, being a product of the way that health statistics are collected and reported rather than the result of any actual differences in health chances. However, it is difficult to show that differential ages of death according to social class and gender are not real. Another related approach suggests that, in a meritocratic society such as Britain, those with ill-health will be unlikely to achieve well in the education system, or gain good jobs, and will therefore gravitate towards the bottom of the class structure. Between men and women, however, differences in health chances are apparent regardless of class position.

Another type of explanation focuses on class or ethnic behaviour or culture, arguing that the different practices and knowledge about health of the social groups, especially concerning smoking, stressful activities, exercise, etc., lead to varying rates of illness and life expectancy.

INTERPRETATION

Read *Social Studies Review*, vol. 4, no. 3, pp. 116–20. (See [57], p. 338.)

Use the figures in the article to describe the patterns of health inequality in Britain.

APPLICATION

You should be able to apply your knowledge of the real world to provide good examples for sociological ideas. For example, answer these questions:

1 What other social activities may be harmful or beneficial to health?

2 Are any of these activities both harmful and beneficial and, if so, which ones?

EVALUATION

3 What determines whether these activities are harmful or beneficial?

Sociological concepts from one area can be applied to others. For example, labelling can be used to explain how medicine delivers different treatment to different people.

E VALUATION

1 How far do you agree that labelling plays an important part in the medical delivery system?

A PPLICATION

2 Give examples to support your view.

Note that you should consider other factors which might be important.

Developing this theme is a further type of explanation which tends to stress the structural dimension, looking at issues like unemployment, types of work and patterns of diet to explain these variations.

Policy implications

In general, some of these explanations tend to *blame the system*, while others tend to *blame the victim (individual)* and, depending on the level of explanation chosen, they will lead to different strategies for tackling ill-health among the population. Two important dimensions of these strategies are the focus of policy and the health care delivery system used. In the first case, a debate has emerged over the relative effectiveness of preventive medicine and medical intervention strategies. Traditionally, health policies have been geared to making medical interventions, after a problem has been diagnosed, more effective. More recently, there has been a move towards more 'lifestyle' and preventive measures as a focus of policy. Thus, the government's changes to the general practitioner service have, in part, been an attempt to shift the emphasis to prevention, using such strategies as 'Well Woman' clinics, etc.

In terms of the ways in which health care is delivered, there has been an ideological disagreement over whether private or public health services are the most efficient system. While the State-supported National Health Service still retains immense public support, the growth of private health insurance and private hospitals has also been remarkable. The issue is not just one of funding, although this is important. The disagreements are also over privileged access to health care, waiting lists for the State system, the seemingly limitless demand for a *free* service, especially as the population contains an increasingly large proportion of old people with old people's ailments, and the cost of increasingly complicated medical technology. Changes in the Health Service in 1991 aimed to introduce *market principles* into its operation in an attempt to increase efficiency through competition between *opted-out* hospitals and health units, which are allowed to attract private sources of funding and not just rely on public funds for revenue. Whether the reforms succeed or not and how success should be measured has become another source of intense sociological research.

Listing the pros and cons of an issue is the first step to evaluation.

1 In two columns, list the advantages and disadvantages of the Health Service reforms described in the paragraph above.

2 What evidence can you cite?

Health Service Reforms	
Advantages	**Disadvantages**

Poverty

While there have always been poor people in society, it is only in relatively recent times that the relief of poverty has been a major object of social policy. The poor have always been a 'problem' in that they tend to be discontented and therefore a potential source of unrest and social disorder. Until recent times, the emphasis has been on controlling the poor, through legal sanctions, rather than supporting them or seeking to *cure* poverty through policy initiatives. While poverty may seem to be obvious and has some physical manifestations in the worst cases – poor housing, malnutrition, ill-health, etc. – there is actually a sociological and political dispute concerning the definition of poverty.

1 What other features of poverty can you think of?

2 For one of these features, either from your own knowledge or from the text, find some recent statistics concerning its incidence.

EXERCISE

Death rates show wider health gap between North and South

The health divide is continuing to widen, according to official figures yesterday which show worsening death rates in much of the North, and improvement in most of the South.

The 1989 area mortality statistics for England and Wales, produced by the Office of Population Censuses and Surveys (OPCS), came a week before expected publication of the Government's Green Paper on plans to set targets for cutting death rates from common diseases.

The statistics reflect regional differences according to a standardised mortality ratio (SMR), adjusted for differing age structures, where the national average is 100.

As in previous years, the Northern region has the worst figures, with an SMR of 113 for both men and women, compared with 113 for men and 112 for women in 1988.

Worse figures for 1989 compared to 1988 are reported for Yorkshire and Humberside, with 107 (106) and 104 (104) for men and women respectively . . .

By contrast, figures for the South are broadly encouraging. East Anglia has the best rates, with 91 for both sexes. The Southeast has 92 for men and 93 for women in 1988.

The OPCS also gives SMRs by leading causes of death. In the Northern region, the rates for heart disease in 1989 were 119 for men and 126 for women, compared with 85 for both sexes in the Southeast. Equivalent rates for lung and throat cancer were 129 and 141 in the Northern region, compared with 79 and 82 in the Southwest.

(Source: adapted from David Brindle, the *Guardian*, Wednesday 15 May 1991)

How do you think these statistics were collected? Do you think they are reliable or valid?

Describe in your own words the pattern of illness shown in the extract. Without reference to any textbook, suggest two possible explanations for the differences. Then look up in a textbook any sociological explanations of these regional differences and compare them with yours. If there is a match, note down the writers and books as supporting evidence for your ideas.

Definitions of poverty

Although this may seem to be a dry academic argument, it is a crucial one. How poverty is defined will affect who will be counted as poor. Who is counted determines the total number seen to be in poverty and, therefore, how many will be the object of social policy. The definition of poverty thus has implications for public expenditure and the types of poverty programme adopted by any government. But the political dimension of poverty is more than this. Whether the gap between the rich and the poor is increasing or decreasing is one way in which voters

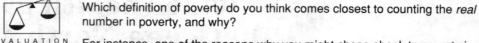

In evaluations you need to be able to come to a decision and give your reasons for it. For example:

Which definition of poverty do you think comes closest to counting the *real* number in poverty, and why?

For instance, one of the reasons why you might chose absolute poverty is because it is objective. However, you would need to consider if it is really objective.

may choose to measure the success of any government. Some voters will be looking for greater equality in society and others will accept that the solution to poverty depends on the economic activities of the rich creating enough wealth and job opportunities to trickle down to the poor. So, whether poverty is perceived to be increasing or decreasing may be an important political calculation for the electorate, especially for individuals who are falling into poverty.

The dispute is between those sociologists who argue that there is a *poverty line* – an amount of income below which people can be defined as in poverty – and others who suggest that what is seen as poverty depends on the society in which the calculation is made. For the latter, poverty exists where there is not enough income for an individual to carry out the activities which the majority of the society takes for granted. It is the loss of potential for involvement in everyday actions which is the hallmark of being poor. A third definition stresses the subjective aspect of poverty, in that those who feel they are poor may be counted as poor. This allows for such phenomena as *genteel poverty*.

Policy effects

Taking different definitions would lead to different numbers of families and individuals in poverty, and this has political implications. Both

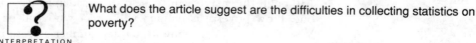

Many sociological debates include a discussion of methodological issues of which you need to be aware:

Read *Social Studies Review*, vol. 5, no. 3, pp. 115–16. (See [58], p. 338.)

What does the article suggest are the difficulties in collecting statistics on poverty?

ESSAY
QUESTION

'To what extent' means that you
have to come to a definite
evaluative conclusion.

To what extent do the official statistics on poverty describe the real rate of
poverty in Britain?

politicians and sociologists disagree among themselves as to the proper
target for social policies on poverty. Some argue that expenditure should
be focused or targeted on those relatively few families who have the
greatest need. This would avoid the *poverty trap*, where those just below
any poverty line find it difficult to climb out of poverty, because as soon
as they are given help, they immediately begin to pay more taxes and so
lose out. On the other hand, others suggest that benefits should be given
to all those below the poverty line, as this would ensure that the reluc-
tance to claim benefits by the poor would be overcome.

Explanations

After defining poverty, sociologists have tried to explain the existence
and persistence of poverty. In rich societies like the United States and
Britain, the focus is on a society which can afford to send people to the
moon and yet allows the existence of impoverished ghettos.

An important aspect of sociological research is its relationship to social
policy. You should apply theories to real world problems and try to assess
their effectiveness. For example:

1 Identify three approaches to *solving* poverty.

2 Identify the main criticisms made of each.

Which of the explanations of poverty below do you find most realistic and
why?

To start off, list the strengths and weaknesses of each explanation and
then compare them.

Various explanations have been developed by sociologists in answer to these problems. The first suggests that the poor are largely to blame for their own poverty, as they have certain personality traits which lead them into feckless ways. A second approach examines the culture and behaviour patterns of the poor, arguing that poverty is passed on from generation to generation through the cultural socialisation of children into the habits and practices of poverty. Others suggest that the position of being poor limits the possibilities of getting out of poverty, with poor people having few resources or skills to drag themselves out of the situation in which they find themselves. A further explanation focuses on the relationship between the rich and the poor, arguing that the wealth of one depends on the poverty of the other.

The explanation preferred will affect the solution put forward, from improvements in welfare provisions to schemes which seek to increase the number of jobs in areas of high poverty. Policy programmes to combat poverty have had varied levels of success, with some initiatives generally perceived as useful and others at the centre of much political controversy. However, policies regarding poverty are constantly under review as the groups which are 'in poverty' change as society develops. In particular, since the Second World War, the *New Poor* have emerged. Traditionally, the poor consisted of the unemployed and low waged, and tended to be made up of family units where the father or mother was in a certain type of manual job, or where the family unit did not have a member in work.

New Poor

In the 1980s, new groups of the poor have emerged, such as lone-parent families, where usually mothers have the sole responsibility for the support of children, either without any job or with a low-paid one. Other groups of the New Poor are the old, who are living longer; for many of them this means a fall into greater poverty. Similarly, many young people have to face homelessness and poverty as the operation of the rules for claiming financial support from the State are said to encourage an early departure from the family home, often to the 'bright lights' of the cities.

The conclusions you come to should be supported by appropriate evidence. For example:

Read *Social Studies Review*, vol. 5, no. 3, pp. 112–14. (See [59], p. 338.)

1 How far do you agree that there is a *culture of poverty*?

2 Refer closely to the article in your answer.

KNOWLEDGE UNDERSTANDING

EVALUATION

1 Describe one policy programme designed to combat poverty.
2 How successful do you think it has been? Begin by listing its successes and failures, in two columns. Income support has been shown as an example but you need not be limited to this policy.

Income support	
Success	**Failure**
1 Targets 'poor'	1 Does not always reach target

Come to a conclusion, separately from your lists.

The increase in part-time and temporary work has meant that there has been an increase in the number of families with a restricted income to spend. The emergence of these groups is the product of changes in social arrangements, changing moral climates and the different ways in which the provisions of the Welfare State operate.

3 Welfare

Taxes and the Welfare State

The Welfare State system in Britain is arguably one of the most advanced and comprehensive in the industrial world. Its provisions cover a large number of areas of social life, from education through the health services

APPLICATION

You will often be required to apply general sociological concepts to specific problems. For example:

In what ways are the social characteristics of age, gender and ethnicity important in the study of poverty?

To assess a research method, begin by identifying its strengths and weaknesses. For example:

List the advantages and disadvantages of the formal interview, in two columns.

In a separate paragraph, come to a conclusion about the usefulness of formal interviews. It might help to ask yourself questions such as: When might formal interviews be used and when might they not? What type of information do they produce? Which respondents might not like formal interviews? Are there cost and time implications?, etc.

Formal interviews	
Advantages	**Disadvantages**
Evaluation	

to the benefits system. As such, the Welfare State calls upon a large proportion of the resources of the State and has to be paid for by general and specific taxation. Thus, the more provisions of the Welfare State offered, the more taxation has to be raised to pay for it. This relationship has been the focus of much political debate between those who argue for a low-tax economy, so that individuals can provide for their own needs, and those who argue for the protection and extension of Welfare provisions as a

In your reading, you will have come across the work of LeGrand. Though you need to know this work, you also need to relate subsequent developments in the real world to the issues that LeGrand discussed.

1 Identify the main areas of welfare benefits discussed by LeGrand.

2 In what ways might his findings have changed in the 1990s?

Social theories are constantly evolving as new ways of looking at problems develop. You should apply your understanding of these developments to identify the implications for sociology. For example:

In what ways has the New Right challenged sociological assumptions about the Welfare State?

APPLICATION

basis for the functioning of the economy. So, the provision of crèches is, on the one hand, seen as a matter of individual choice creating the demand for child-care, which should be met by private sources, and, on the other, the provision of crèches by the State is seen as necessary if industry is to attract skilled labour when there is a shortage.

Private and public provision

The Welfare State was created over a large number of years, and there is a dispute concerning the reasons for its creation. Some see it as a concession by the ruling class in an attempt to incorporate the working class into capitalism, so that they accept the legitimacy of the private ownership of the means of production. As such, it is always possible to claw back welfare provisions if alternative sources of legitimacy, such as wider share or home ownership, become available. Others see welfare provisions as the result of the political and industrial struggles of the working class, which continue to be waged as workers try to improve and defend those provisions.

There is thus a fundamental cleavage between those who wish to assess the effectiveness of State provisions in order to improve them, and those who wish to evaluate State welfare in order to propose alternative private, rather than public, arrangements. This cleavage is ultimately an ideological one. Those who are in favour of State provision argue that this is the most effective way that a 'safety net' can be provided for those unfortunate enough not to be able to look after themselves in a society where the market can unfairly discriminate against some individuals.

You should also be prepared to assess sociological approaches to problems. For example:

Read *Social Studies Review*, vol. 2, no. 4, pp. 36–40. (See [60], p. 338.)

1 Which of the three perspectives do you find the most appealing?

EVALUATION

2 Support your conclusion with appropriate argument.

APPLICATION

ESSAY QUESTION

Make a list of the studies for this view and a list of those against. Show how you will apply each study to the debate in the question; i.e. how will you use each study and not just describe it?

'The Welfare State was created with the aims of eliminating poverty and redistributing wealth. It has patently failed to do so.'

Assess the sociological evidence for and against this view.

Those in favour of private welfare provisions, where individuals buy their needs through insurance schemes, argue that State welfare creates a *dependency culture*, where those who rely on State aid cannot help themselves to solve their own problems; they become dependent rather than 'standing on their own two feet'. This leads to two different conceptions of *citizenship*. The first argues that individuals need a minimum standard of living if they are to participate fully as citizens in society, engaging in community struggles for improved collective provision. The second suggests that the *active citizen* is one who contributes individually and privately to helping others less fortunate through charitable and 'good' works.

Re-distribution

Another ideological dimension concerning welfare is that the original aim of the Welfare State was to re-distribute resources away from those with plenty towards those in need. The aim then was to create a more equal society, in which privilege and inherited wealth should not so advantage some that the majority were condemned to a life of uncertainty and early death. Opponents of this idea suggest that not only does re-distribution not work, in that the rich can always afford to buy the financial advice which enables them legitimately to avoid taxation, but that universal benefits actually help middle-class people more than working-class families, who are less likely to claim from or be able to work the system. Still others argue that the main beneficiaries of the Welfare State are the thousands of middle-class professionals who are employed in administering and operating the provisions of the Welfare State.

What do sociologists mean by:

• wealth;
• trickle down;
• polarisation;
• living standards?

EXERCISE

Who is poor?

How many people are poor, and just how poor are they? Answers vary according to how poverty is defined. Below are some different attempts to quantify and analyse poverty in the UK.

Convert these bar charts into tables of numbers and thus practise the skill of interpretation.

INTERPRETATION

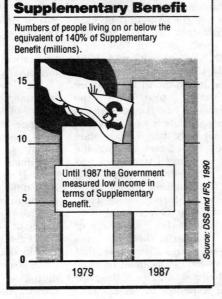

Defined in terms of Supplementary Benefit

Numbers of people living on or below the equivalent of 140% of Supplementary Benefit (millions).

Until 1987 the Government measured low income in terms of Supplementary Benefit.

Source: DSS and IFS, 1990

1979   1987

Defined in terms of average incomes

Numbers of people living on or below 50% of average income (millions).

Groups such as the Child Poverty Action Group prefer this measure of poverty.

Source: DSS, 1990

1979   1987

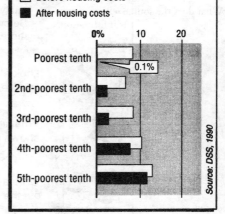

Still poor

The Government's preferred measurement is the change in real income of the poorest 50% of the population, which rose between 1979 and 1987.

☐ Before housing costs
■ After housing costs

0%   10   20

Poorest tenth   0.1%

2nd-poorest tenth

3rd-poorest tenth

4th-poorest tenth

5th-poorest tenth

Source: DSS, 1990

(Source: adapted from Edward Pilkington, the *Guardian*, Tuesday 2 July 1991)

The trickle of wealth that dried up

Hostilities are about to break out on yet another front of government policy. One area that has been relatively calm of late has been its record on the poor. At the end of last week the Government ran into trouble on this front too when it was forced to withdraw the official figures which had for so long supported its boast that the poor too had done well out of economic growth. Wealth, it was said, would trickle down.

It is important to be clear on the extent to which the Government has remodelled the traditional debate on poverty. From an early date it made plain its lack of interest in counting heads. It claimed that there was no agreed definition of poverty, and official figures of the numbers on low income were axed. Nor was the Government concerned about the polarisation of living standards between rich and poor. The claim was that there would be optimum increases in living standards of the poor during a period of record economic growth.

In place of official data on the numbers on low income, Mrs Thatcher substituted a new analysis entitled Households Below Average Earnings. Here, increases in the standard of living in each of the bottom decile groups were provided for in the 1979–1985 period.

The figures when first published seemed to support the Government's contention for the period when the economy was growing most rapidly from 1981 onwards. The rich had certainly grown richer but the increase in the living standards of the poorest 10 per cent of the population had grown at a greater rate than any other group. . .

The Government has now had to admit that its official publication of Households Below Average Income was misleading. Two major errors have been found . . .

A much more accurate way of judging how well the poorest have done during Mrs Thatcher's period in office is to look at what has happened to the living standards of the millions of people who exist on this level of benefit year in and year out . . .

Far from the poor benefiting during a period of economic growth, these figures show that their living standards rose most in real terms during the 1970s, when the overall economic performance of the economy was less impressive than since 1981.

(Source: adapted from Frank Field, the *Guardian*, Tuesday 24 April 1990)

What does the source tell you about the information?

INTERPRETATION

Look at the three charts. Identify whether each constitutes an absolute, relative or subjective definition of poverty.

APPLICATION

What implications does the information in the text have for the figures shown in the charts?

EVALUATION

Write a paragraph on each of the three ways of defining poverty, pointing out the advantages and disadvantages of each.

In a final paragraph, come to a conclusion as to which you find the most convincing and why.

When reading about developments in society always look for how you can apply information.

Read S*ocial Studies Review*, vol. 4, no. 3, pp. 110–11. (See [61], p. 338.)

How could the concept of the active citizen be applied to changes in the way in which welfare is viewed by people in society? You could begin by considering the difference between collective and privatised provision.

A PPLICATION

Policy implications

This ideological divide has real effects in the policies adopted by different Governments. The post-war consensus concerning welfare has broken down into strong disagreements over the proper way to deliver welfare provisions. For example, in the 1980s, there was a move to take back the care of the mentally ill to the community, with the closure of the large mental hospitals and the emphasis on family care or placement in sheltered accommodation. The pressure for change came from many different sources, but has also been attacked as ill-thought out, badly funded and carried out at the expense of women in the family who carry the burden of care. This reflects a debate about the care of the elderly in the family or by private or State homes.

There have also been huge changes in educational and health provisions which mirror the ideological debates over welfare. The pressure to take schools away from local education authority control through opting out, the grant-maintained status of post-16 education and the development of the City Technology Colleges (CTCs) are paralleled in the health service through the introduction of market principles in the provision of health care. Those in favour of these moves argue that they will make welfare provisions more efficient in that they will deliver what customers want more closely if 'money follows the patient (or schoolchild)'. Others argue that these changes will be irrelevant in determining what is delivered to clients, the main effect being to increase the salaries of those who run the opted-out units. Still others suggest that the changes will lead to worse provision, cutting consumer choice, as there cannot be a 'free market' in schools and hospitals in the same way as there may be with soap powders. Sociologists will be examining the effects of these changes and attempting to provide evidence in order to come to a rational conclusion about them.

When you have different arguments laid out, as in the paragraph above, you should try to identify evidence which can be applied to each of them. For example:

What sociological evidence can you gather to support any of the positions mentioned above?

A PPLICATION

Conclusion

Issues concerning poverty, health and welfare are often at the forefront of the political debate in Britain. Sociologists, therefore, have an important contribution to make by providing evidence and arguments for this debate as objectively as possible. The importance of these issues for people's lives can hardly be exaggerated, as people spend much of their time and energy looking after their health or seeking to avoid the worst aspects of poverty. Indeed, the link between poor health and poverty has been recognised by sociologists, and proposals have been put forward to try to combat its effects.

Important points to bear in mind

1 Individuals are concerned with their state of health on a day-to-day basis but there is also a health industry which caters for individual health needs.
2 Poverty is not usually self-inflicted but it may be a choice that some groups, such as monks or nuns, make freely.
3 The division between private and public provision is subject to political influences and choices.
4 To explain poverty or ill-health, sociologists need to look at personal circumstances and structural situations.
5 The social characteristics of the individual will affect his or her chances of being poor or being poorly but this does not mean that all the poor or the ill share the same characteristics.

KEY CONCEPTS

It is important that you are familiar with and are able to use the concepts in this section in appropriate ways if you are to apply them effectively in the examination. Check your understanding of the concepts by carrying out this exercise.

Provide a definition for each of the concepts, and include the words which follow:

Welfare State	– unemployment benefit, National Health Service
Sick role	– socially acceptable, norm
Ill-health	– biological, socially constructed
Artefact explanation	– statistics, reality
'Trickle down' theory	– rich, poor
Universal benefits	– child benefit, means-tested
New Poor	– old, lone parents
Active citizenship	– charity, State-dependency
Community care	– institutions, carers
Victim-blaming	– individual, fecklessness

Internal market	– NHS, budget-holding
Dependency culture	– benefits, over-reliance
Poverty line	– absolute poverty, poverty trap
Relative poverty	– material conditions, comparison

COURSEWORK SUGGESTIONS

8.1

It might be possible, through contacts or the work experience programme of your institution, to work-shadow a member of the medical profession, most probably a nurse. From this vantage point, you could observe the inter-relationships between nurses and patients, or perhaps between doctors and nurses. You could then fit this into the literature about male and female work roles and the power of the medical profession. You would need to identify the issues you are concerned with before you entered the work-shadowing and seek to ensure that you can gain access to appropriate information. A project which did not manage to gather much useful information would still be worthwhile, as long as you were self-critical and evaluative about your performance and the difficulties you faced.

Here are some factors for you to consider.

What ethical issues might confront you if you were to gain access to medical consultations or reports?

1 What aspect of the nurse's role are you interested in and can you be sure that you will gain access to the appropriate situations?
2 You are unlikely to gain access to medical consultations or to patient records. How will you record and interpret this in your report?
3 Will you have enough time to carry out your research if you are on work experience?
4 What reading will you have to do before you go into your work shadowing? How will you relate it to your research?
5 Will you plan your report around the skill domains of the marking scheme or will you find another format?

8.2

The formal interview is one of the techniques open to you in your project, and it can be effectively used if you want to interview someone in an official position. For example, if you wanted to explore the impact of changes in Social Security rules on those in receipt of benefit, you could seek an interview with an official from your local Department of Social Security as part of your research. He or she would be an *expert witness* for you to question.

Here are some aspects for you to consider.

1 You will need to be fairly knowledgeable about the workings of the Social Security system before you go into the interview.
2 With a formal interview, you will have to have an interview schedule where you have worked out your questions beforehand, as there can be no going back to seek clarification.
3 For the same reason, your questions need to be carefully thought out in relation to your hypothesis or aim so that you obtain relevant information.
4 It is not unusual to think of more useful questions when it is too late, but these might form part of the evaluation of your project so do not waste them.
5 You will need to determine at what level of officialdom you wish to have the interview, and make firm arrangements which you then keep. You need a contingency plan if no-one is willing to talk to you.

CHAPTER 9

The media

In this chapter we will examine the arguments surrounding:

1 the scope of the mass media;
2 the effects of the mass media;
3 ownership and control;
4 the issue of mediation;
5 the media and ideology.

Before you begin any of the exercises you should have studied and should be familiar with at least one of the following texts:

Barrat, D. *Media Sociology* (Routledge 1986).
Bilton, T., Bonnett, K., Jones, P., Stanworth, M., Sheard, K. and Webster, A. *Introductory Sociology*, 2nd edn (Macmillan 1987), pp. 427–44.
Giddens, A. *Sociology* (Polity 1989).
Glover, D. 'Sociology of mass media', in Haralambos, M. (ed.) *Sociology – New Directions* (Causeway 1985), pp. 439–46.
O'Donnell, M. *A New Introduction to Sociology*, 3rd edn (Nelson 1992), chapter 18.

In addition, you should have your notes on the mass media in good order.

Introduction

One of the most prominent developments of the modern world has been the emergence of the media industries. Much leisure time for individuals is now spent enjoying the products of the media industries, from the cinema to video. This development has been seen by sociologists and others as one of the most distinctive characteristics of the modern age, and there has been a great deal of research into its effects. One of the problems which such research faces is that it is often combined with common-sensical, journalistic and moral comment about the media. Concern about the effects of television, for example, can be found among politicians, 'moral entrepreneurs', like Mary Whitehouse, and media personalities as

You should be clear about the difference between sociological and other approaches to issues if you are going to assess accounts fairly.

Write a paragraph on what distinguishes sociological accounts from journalistic and common-sense ones.

well as sociologists. Their concern focuses on the potentially enormous power to influence the way in which individuals think and behave. There is also the fear that the media exercise a great deal of power over politicians, and unduly influence social policies through comment on issues of importance. This is compounded by the fact that the media are also industries which make a great deal of money for those who own and control them.

1   The scope of the mass media

Sociologists have always been concerned with communication because they have always been involved in publishing and lecturing. The ability to communicate messages to large numbers of people has been the goal of religious and political leaders for thousands of years. While word-of-mouth has been the traditional method of communication, the invention of writing and then printing allowed the possibility of reaching audiences far beyond those whom an individual can personally contact.

Technology and the media

Clearly, then, the ability to communicate with mass audiences depends on the technology available and it is the technological developments of the nineteenth and twentieth centuries which have proved to be of interest to sociologists. Early interest focused on such media as photography and cinema as well as magazines and newspapers. But it was with the overt exploitation of these media by the totalitarian regimes of the Nazis in Germany and the Communists in the Soviet Union that sociologists (and psychologists) began to consider the effects of the media in detail.

You should be prepared to assess social developments as well as developments in sociology. For example:

How far do you agree that television has replaced the press as the major medium of the modern world? Consider arguments both for and against this idea.

Similarly, you should apply your knowledge of developments to particular questions. For example:

Make a list of the ways in which modern media technologies have changed the way that people live their lives.

APPLICATION

Modern technologies have increased the scope of the media enormously, with the growth of information technology since the 1970s having particularly marked effects. In terms of individual lives, much leisure time is now taken up with 'privatised' leisure, using videos, computer games, television, etc. Moreover, individual work lives have been transformed by the fact that information technology has destroyed some jobs and created others, so that education must teach students new skills in preparation for their work roles. The advent of new media technologies has also allowed social groups to create and control their own leisure lives to some extent. For example, ethnic minorities may use video technology to gain access to minority language films, which would never be released in the cinema. Also, older students gain access to educational qualifications through the Open University programmes on television.

Globalisation and images

It has been argued that the growth of modern media technologies has also changed the nature of modern societies in more fundamental ways. The major effect of satellites, telecommunications, optical fibre links, and the like, has been the globalisation of the world economy and culture. This has had many effects. Firstly, modern communications have created a *global village*, in which events in one part of the world can be beamed to many others as they happen. But, secondly, they have allowed the development of a global economy, in which funds can be transferred around the world at the push of a button. This has had an enormous effect on the way in which societies cooperate at the international level. Countries are now so inter-dependent that their economies can no longer

Although the idea of globalisation is a fairly new one, you need to be aware of how it can be used and what evidence can be deployed. From your reading:

EVALUATION

1 To what extent do you agree that globalisation of the media leads to First World domination of communications?

APPLICATION

2 What evidence can you use in this debate? You might find Giddens, pp. 542–7 useful here.

EXERCISE

The *Sun* does it again

Two weeks ago, Yvonne Roberts of the *Observer* spent a day with Helen Gourdie, whose three sons are serving in the Gulf. Helen talked with pride about their Army careers, and her enormous regret that they had all been sent to the Gulf and might now face battle.

Four days after the article appeared in the *Observer*, the same story was published in the *Sun*, under the headline, "Pride of mum with three sons in the frontline". It now contained inaccuracies and injections of *Sun* speak, but still carried Yvonne Robert's byline.

On the day Yvonne Roberts visited Helen Gourdie, a woman from the *Sun* telephoned Helen to ask how she would be told if anything happened to her sons. Helen, who long before the Gulf war refused to have the paper in her house, said she had nothing to say on the subject and put the phone down. Undeterred, the Scottish edition of the *Sun* the next day carried an "interview" . . . much of it inaccurate and all of it bogus.

(Source: *New Statesman & Society*, vol. 3, no. 136, 1 February 1991. © *New Statesman & Society*)

Between the lines

How might sociologists use the *Satanic Verses* events in examining the media, or religion or ethnic minorities?

The aubergine story – where the seeds of the plant were revealed to spell out "Allah" – appeared on the front page of the *Independent* . . .

It angers me that the dangerous, narrow-minded view that many white people hold, of Muslims being wacky fanatics, is being consolidated by such articles.

Negative attitudes towards the Asian community, typified by the press treatment of the Muslim situation, have got to be countered by the Asian media. We need to defend ourselves by examining the real issues like the uprising against the *Satanic Verses*.

As the white press continues to philosophise on the merits of free speech, we need to explain that young Asians are being torn apart by British society: while on the one hand we are successfully integrating, on the other, disillusionment with the indifference to years of racist abuse has led us to . . . protect a religion that most of us do not practise.

(Source: Abdul Montaqim, the *Guardian*, Monday 23 April1990)

Write a paragraph on what the information in the extracts suggests about the working practices of the newspapers, and the effect they may have on the content of the paper.

Using your texts or your notes, suggest reasons why these practices exist.

Find sociological material which supports your ideas.

To what extent do you agree with the claim that information technology can be used to control individuals?

E VALUATION

You will need to consider the case for control and the case for liberation.

be treated as independent units, but must be considered as part of a complex whole.

It has been argued that another effect of the development of modern media technologies has been to establish the dominance of the cultural over the economic. This suggests that politics and economics are reduced to the images that appear on the television or computer console screen and the potential of individuals to control their lives is diminished by the sheer complexity of the modern world, hidden behind superficial images. Others argue that the information revolution has the potentiality for control but it also has the capability of giving power to individuals, by providing them with knowledge. Modern technologies allow the possibility of fragmented rather than mass markets, with every individual finding satisfaction for his or her needs.

So, whereas mass markets seek to erode differences between people to appeal to the 'lowest common denominator' (and thus maximise profits), modern media technologies allow interest groups, such as young blacks, the New Christian Right, gays or women, to have their needs for information and entertainment met. The fragmentation of the world of pop and rock into distinctive styles, such as rap or Indi-pop, is symptomatic of the effectiveness of modern media technologies.

2 The effects of the mass media

From the 1930s onwards, much sociological research has been directed towards the effects of the media on individuals. In the early stages, attention was focused on the newspapers but, with the development of a mass market in television, sociologists switched their studies to that medium.

Sociology often challenges notions which people take for granted. You need to make up your mind as to how valid such criticisms are. For example:

1 To what extent do you agree with the idea that the media are 'free'?

E VALUATION

2 Give examples to support your conclusions.

A PPLICATION

You might consider areas such as the law, the market, ownership and control.

One of the first distinctions made by sociologists was between effects on behaviour and effects on attitudes. In the former case, effects may be relatively easy to measure, in that there is a behavioural outcome which sociologists can observe. In the case of the latter, attitudinal shifts are much harder to measure and may appear only in behavioural shifts which can be caused by phenomena other than the media.

Media, sex and violence

In terms of behaviour, sociologists and others have concentrated on political behaviour, especially voting, and sex and violence. In the case of sex and violence, moral entrepreneurs have been quick to condemn scenes of sex and violence on the television and cinema as the cause of a perceived increase in real levels of sexual permissiveness and violence. Sociologists have been much more cautious about the alleged effects of the media, relying on the accumulation of evidence rather than the assertion of a causal connection.

On the one hand, some sociologists argue that there is likely to be some effect, given the statistical connection between the growth of television viewing and the rise in crimes of violence. The process is often described as 'copy-catting' and is used to explain, for example, the spread of inner-city riots to parts of urban Britain in the early 1980s. A particular viewpoint stresses the link between the availability of pornographic videos and the incidence of rape. Others suggest that there is no necessary causal link between the two, and any rise in violence can be attributed to other developments in society, such as the rise in unemployment or poverty. In particular, the theory of copy-catting is criticised because riots did not occur in every city where pictures of rioting had been broadcast, so it cannot be the only cause. Moreover, sexual activity is much more likely to be influenced by factors such as the spread of AIDS rather than visual images of sexual activity, limited as they are, on the major channels.

Still others challenge the very notion that there has been a rise in crime or sexual activity at all, and maintain that these are 'moral panics' or illusions created by the moral entrepreneurs in order to justify their

---

Sociology does not rely on personal opinion but on evidence. You will need to supply the evidence for any area you are interested in, and decide how to use it. For example:

INTERPRETATION

1 Choosing *either* violence *or* permissiveness *or* urban riots, research sociological studies in that area.

APPLICATION

2 How are you going to apply the studies you have found to the arguments put forward in the paragraph above?

As with all methods, you should list the advantages and disadvantages of participant observation in two columns. This is the beginning of evaluation. A more sophisticated approach might identify the strengths and weaknesses of different types of participant observation:

Participant observation (PO)		
	Advantages	**Disadvantages**
Covert PO		
Overt PO		

attempts to control the media. The creation of the Broadcasting Standards Council is seen as the consequence of this entrepreneurial activity. This position argues that attributing incidences of violence or sexual permissiveness to television watching is to reduce complicated phenomena to simplistic explanations, which serve political ends rather than produce real understanding of the media. For example, urban riots were a feature of modern British life long before television was able to broadcast scenes of violence directly into people's homes. (See Coursework Suggestion 9.1 on p. 244.)

Media and politics

In terms of political activity, the interest of sociologists has stemmed from the large sums of money which the political parties spend on advertising themselves. Sociological research has suggested that there may be some short-term effects during the course of an election campaign, but what is much more important are the long-term influences which the media have on attitudes, through creating a climate of opinion or through exposing wrong-doing or scandals involving politicians. The debate continues as to how far the power of the media extends and the relative influence of the newspapers, which are usually partisan, and television, which is required to stay neutral.

However, in seeking to examine the effects of the media, sociologists have had to recognise that there is no simple one-to-one relationship between the media and those who consume their messages. Rather, the media exist as industries set in a social context and producing messages which individuals may or may not choose to take note of. Any attitudinal effects are, therefore, the product of a complex process involving many factors, not least of which is the issue of who owns and controls the media.

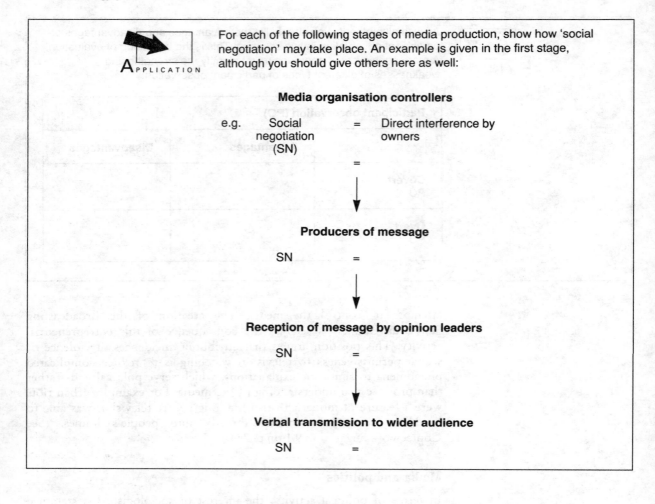

APPLICATION

For each of the following stages of media production, show how 'social negotiation' may take place. An example is given in the first stage, although you should give others here as well:

Media organisation controllers

e.g. Social negotiation (SN) = Direct interference by owners

=

↓

Producers of message

SN =

↓

Reception of message by opinion leaders

SN =

↓

Verbal transmission to wider audience

SN =

3 Ownership and control

The issue of who controls the media has always been of interest to sociologists, but it was only during the 1970s that the problem of ownership became a subject of sociological debate.

Ownership

The problem of ownership had always been a matter of political concern, because politicians were keen on keeping the press and the newly emerging media of radio and television on their particular side. Indeed, many societies have kept ownership of the media in the hands of the State in order to control the information that the population receives. In many capitalist societies, the press was initially controlled by private individuals who made no secret of their interference in the content of their newspapers. However, with the advent of joint stock companies and the growth of democratic feeling in capitalist countries, owners increasingly

ESSAY QUESTION

Note that you have to deal with both attitudes and behaviour. You will need to choose at least one appropriate example of each.

To what extent do you agree that the media directly affect the attitudes and behaviour of those who use them?

In coming to a decision about an issue, you should always consider at least two sides of an argument. For example,

Read *Social Studies Review*, vol. 2, no. 4, pp. 15–20. (See [62], p. 338.)

Does the pattern of ownership of the media restrict the choice of media experience that individuals have in modern societies?

EVALUATION

---

claimed that they allowed editorial freedom to their editors and journalists. The emergence of television highlighted the issue of interference by owners and, in Britain at least, a legal requirement of impartiality is laid on both public and private broadcasting.

Control

The danger that is seen in the control of all the media by one particular interest group or class is linked to the perceived effects of the media on individuals. By controlling media output, it was feared that alternative viewpoints would be squeezed out from the public domain and this would lead to anti-democratic political control. Hence Channel 4 is required to cater for minorities in its programme planning. But sociologists were interested in much wider issues than political control.

On the one hand were those who saw the media as elitist, putting forward a particular view of culture which alienated the mass of the population. On the other were those who saw the media as levelling down culture to the lowest common denominator and leading to a narcotisation of

---

It will often help you to produce diagrams of important social processes. For example:

Read Bilton *et al.*, pp. 431–8.

Produce a diagram to represent the social production of the news.

INTERPRETATION

the masses, who became unable to distinguish fiction from reality. A third view suggested that both these views were elitist, in that they treated individuals as robots, rather than living beings capable of making up their own minds about the content of the media. They argued that the main effect of the media was a privatisation of social life; a turning into the home by individuals searching for pleasure and leisure in the private rather than the public world.

Newspapers

Much of the debate about ownership and control in Britain has focused on the newspapers rather than television. Partly this is because of the more conspicuous owners of the press, such as Rupert Murdoch and the late Robert Maxwell, and partly because the newspapers are more visibly biased than television programmes. Sociologists have come to different conclusions about the influence of the newspaper proprietors on their newspapers. One strand suggests that the bias of the newspapers reflects the tastes of the market, that is, the newspapers merely produce what their readership want, and therefore the influence of the proprietors is negligible.

A second view suggests that the intervention of the owners is constant and pervasive. They use their power to determine the editorial line that their papers pursue and to push their particular interests, both political and economic. A third view argues that the direct influence of the 'press barons' is rarely exercised because it does not need to be. The system is so structured that editors and journalists produce 'copy' acceptable to the owners without ever being told to do so.

One of the difficulties in examining the issue of ownership and control is that the actual exercise of power is often hidden from view or operates at different levels. Powerful proprietors are unlikely to allow sociologists access to their exercising power. There is also a difference between operational or day-to-day control of newspaper production, held by editors, and the allocative control of appointing editors and resources to the newspapers, held by the owners. Nevertheless, there remains a problem of how the allocative control exercised by the proprietors translates itself into the everyday content of the newspapers or television programmes.

EVALUATION

1 Which of these three views above about the importance of ownership of the newspapers do you think most closely corresponds to social reality? Why have you chosen your view?

APPLICATION

2 What evidence supports your choice and is there any counter-evidence?

Read *Social Studies Review*, vol. 6, no. 1, pp. 12–15. (See [63], p. 338.)

1 Which of the three theories of the media do you agree most with?
2 Give reasons for your answer, which should include the strengths and weaknesses of each one.

4 The issue of mediation

The process of mediation refers to the ways in which certain ideas or ideologies are taken from specific ruling groups in society and are adopted by media personnel, so that they appear in the content of the media product and thus find their way into the beliefs of the mass of people in society. This process is a complex one and there is much disagreement among sociologists about it. Nevertheless, certain important issues are raised by a consideration of mediation.

Gate-keepers and agenda-setting

One area of debate has concerned the role of gate-keepers and the process of agenda-setting in the media. Because the collection and distribution of the news is a human process, there are choices made at every stage. Modern technology allows thousands of news items to find their way to newspaper offices, and it is the job of certain gate-keepers to filter out some of them, include some and headline others. These gate-keepers are usually editors or sub-editors, and it is argued that they tend to choose news items which fit the world-view of the proprietor who appointed them. Journalists are socialised into a set of professional values about what constitutes 'good' journalism and serves the interests of powerful groups in society.

Against this, the idea of gate-keepers has been attacked as reducing news-gathering to a conspiracy theory. Moreover, many editors themselves deny the influence of proprietors either directly or indirectly. It is also pointed out that the journalists' values are the product of long experience of what their readers want, and not a reflection of ruling-class ideology.

As for agenda-setting, it is argued, on the one hand, that the media, especially television, tell us what to think about. In setting the agenda of political discussion the media are interfering in the political process and defining a particular view of the world for people. For example, by choosing to highlight particular issues of social policy, such as child abuse or AIDS, the media bring particular ways of looking at problems into public debate. On the other hand, it is pointed out that there is a great variety of media sources in modern societies and it is unlikely that they would all set the same agenda or take the same position over any

ESSAY QUESTION

Assess the extent to which the techniques and processes of news-gathering affect what is presented as 'news' by the media.

INTERPRETATION   APPLICATION

Working out the order of things will help you to develop your skills of interpretation and application, because you need to work out what each stage means and apply your understanding to ordering them correctly. For example:

News-gathering

Place the following in chronological order:

1 Prime reporter decides whether to report to news agency.
2 Original event in the real world.
3 Publication of event as news.
4 Presented to prime reporter by original source.
5 Telegraph it to news agency.
6 Editor decides to use it.
7 News agency offers it to media organisations.
8 Selected by prime reporter.
9 Item bought by media organisation.

Why is this described as a social negotiation process?

social or political issue. Individuals can choose which media outlets they will use and which agenda they will expose themselves to.

Amplification and selection

In one particular aspect of agenda-setting, the media is claimed to have a large role and that is in the amplification of deviance. Those who support the idea of amplification suggest that, by creating moral panics about folk devils, the media, in seeking to maximise their circulation and profits, make situations reported on worse than they originally were. This theory relies on the notion that people take notice of what the media say about them and act accordingly. Critics of the theory suggest that it is deterministic, offering a far too automatic view of the influence of the media and assuming that individuals absorb and respond to media messages without reference to any other social influence.

Applying the appropriate studies to support points of view is an important skill.

List the studies, with their main points, which support the view that the media affect behaviour and list those which do not. Use the following format:

Media effects on behaviour	
Some effects	**No effect**

This has turned attention among sociologists towards the audience who receive the messages of the media. Sociologists have long recognised that people do not experience the media in isolation, but bring to the messages their past experiences, value-systems and social contexts. However, some argue that many individuals receive messages indirectly through opinion leaders.

Others suggest that people engage in selective exposure, interpretation and retention of media messages. Still others argue that the messages put out by the media, even if successfully and consistently encoded by the producers, need to be decoded by the audience. These messages can be decoded in several different ways, depending on the previous experiences and value-systems of those exposed. This negotiation process of the text by the audience may lead to a reinforcement of dominant values, but may equally lead to an alteration or even a rejection of them.

Read *Social Studies Review*, vol. 6, no. 5, pp. 174–7. (See [64], p. 338.)

Note that *implications* means that you have to apply information to a particular problem and suggest consequences.

What are the implications of the information in the article for theories concerning the effects of the mass media in people's lives?

You should be prepared to assess individual contributions to a debate. For example:

1 Read *Social Studies Review*, vol. 2, no. 1, p. 8. (See [65], p. 338.)
2 On the basis of the argument in the article, how reliable do you think the work of the Glasgow University Media Group is? Give reasons for your answer.

5 The media and ideology

The idea that the media reflect and reinforce dominant values has led sociologists to investigate the bias of the media in the way that it represents different groups and issues in society. There is little doubt that the newspapers are politically biased but the discussion of the role of ideology in the media goes much wider than this. The role of ideology in the production and dissemination of media messages is of increasing concern to sociologists examining the media, because it is likely that the way the media represents particular groups and issues is the most effective way in which the media influence individuals in societies.

Bias in the press

The newspapers are clearly politically biased in that they consistently push support for a particular political party. In Britain, the majority of the press support the Conservative Party. But the existence of Labour-supporting papers makes any simple accusation of bias difficult to sustain. However, sociologists have tried to show that, regardless of party persuasion, newspapers consistently put forward images of certain groups in society which have long-term effects on the way in which those groups are seen by most people. This is reinforced by other media, such as television, which also accept dominant ideologies concerning particular groups and reproduce them in their images.

Much sociological interest has focused on how women are represented in a stereotyped way by the media and the effects that this has on how society views the role of woman, and also on how women see themselves. Some sociologists suggest that the media are one of the main agents of gender role socialisation, setting up role models for young girls. Others see the media as important, but only one among many influences; while another point of view suggests that the importance of the media is minimal when compared to agencies such as the family or schools.

Read *Social Studies Review*, vol. 5, no. 1, pp. 17–22. (See [66], p. 338.)

According to the article, how does the popular press present class, race and gender?

EXERCISE

Women's roles in TV ads 'sexist'

The portrayal of women in television commercials shows "the very unacceptable face of sexism", according to a study into sexual stereotyping in advertising.

Stereotyping is robust, "lending strong support to the concern that women exist in what is essentially a man's world," says Dr Guy Cumberbatch, who carried out the study for the Broadcasting Standards Council. Women in commercials are younger and blonder than men and less likely to be shown in a professional setting, the study showed.

Men outnumber women by almost two to one in advertisements, and the vast majority of adverts – 89 per cent – use a male voice . . .

Men were more than twice as likely to be shown in paid employment: when men were shown in work settings, how they performed in those jobs was an integral part of the advertiser's message, but when women appeared in work settings, their relationships were emphasised.

In nearly half of the commercials examined, relationships were impossible to "code". But women were twice as likely to be shown married than men.

(Source: adapted from Georgina Henry, the *Guardian*, Wednesday 21 November 1990)

Identify two different ways in which the extract suggests that ads are sexist.

What would sociologists need to know before they accepted the view that such ads affected the attitudes of those who received them?

In the light of your answer, and using supporting evidence, evaluate the effectiveness of stereotyping in influencing people's attitudes.

E VALUATION

Although you will be familiar with the way in which women are represented in the media, a more systematic way of showing this is through content analysis.

What problems might there be with content analysis as a way of researching representations of women in the media?

Advertising

The process of stereotyping is a complex one and one major area of research has been on advertising. One point of view sees advertising as one of the primary characteristics of postmodern society, its archetypal activity. The exploration and satisfaction of fragmented markets in the postmodern world is the aim of the capitalist economy and it is through advertising that capitalist firms are able to target and reach their audi-

E VALUATION

To assess a phenomenon, you should look at both positive and negative aspects of it. For example:

1 In two columns, identify the positive and negative features of advertising. Come to a conclusion as to whether, on balance, advertising is a 'good' or a 'bad' thing for society. What should your conclusion be if you cannot decide between positive and negative?

Advertising	
'Good' points	**'Bad' points**
1 Gives information, e.g. new products	1 Can unduly influence, e.g. cigarettes
Conclusion	

The first points have been given to help you.

A PPLICATION

2 What evidence or examples can you use to support the points you make? Does this evidence help you to assess advertising more easily?

ences. However, in so doing, it is argued that advertising produces distorted or stereotyped images and this is especially so when women are used.

The images of women are many and varied, but a large number project a subordinate role either as housewife or siren. Even where feminist imagery is used, it is often subverted, so that any serious attempt to deal with women in an equal way to men is swamped by traditional representations. Of increasing interest has been the way that men are also stereotyped in advertising, creating an image which many men fail to live up to. (See Coursework Suggestion 9.2 on p. 244.)

Other representations

Other social groups are subject to this process of stereotyping also. In the case of ethnic minorities, although there is legislation which bars discrimination, the media images are often of a stereotyped nature. Moreover, the representation of ethnic groups in areas such as soap

In applying information to issues, you should be clear about the focus of your comments. For example:

Write two paragraphs – one on the invisibility of ethnic minorities in the media and the second on the stereotyping of ethnic minority groups in the media.

operas is either invisible or marginal. The effect of this is to reinforce the marginal position of the ethnic minorities in society at large. Some sociologists see this marginalisation as a result of the hidden or overt racism of Western societies, while others argue that the position is changing towards assimilation as more ethnic minority actors and programmes appear on television. Still others suggest that the negative images of ethnic minorities in the media are devices to ensure that the working class remain divided by racism, rather than unite around their common class position. It is also suggested that, as ethnic minority populations spread throughout the class structure, their representation in the media will also change.

Similarly, homosexuals are represented in stereotypical ways, although here gays themselves have taken those stereotypes and subverted them for their own ends; for example, in producing 'camp' comedy.

Young people are also subject to stereotyped treatment by the media. In the main, young people are often connected by the media with crime or with permissive sexual activity; for example, in the media's portrayal of muggers as young blacks.

However, some sociologists have argued against the effectiveness of stereotypes in the media. For example, they have argued that, where stereotypes clash with real experiences, it is the stereotypes which have lost out. As social actors, individuals can recognise and acknowledge stereotypes for what they are without necessarily absorbing them wholesale. Nor are stereotypes consistently put over in the media and given the variety of media outlets. There is no guarantee that every individual in society is exposed to the same stereotyped images.

Signification

More recently, attention has turned to the ways in which ideology is represented in the media through signification, which is the means by which

You should not take stereotyping for granted. Even if you think the media do stereotype, you should consider the arguments and evidence that they do not.

Using sociological evidence to support your argument, evaluate the importance of stereotypes in media messages.

How far do you agree with the idea that the media encode messages which have to be decoded by the audience?

Your personal experience as a member of the audience may be a starting point for your assessment here. But you must look for sociological evidence also.

cultural signs, such as pictures and words, are used to create meanings. For example, advertisers evoke *naturalness* by picturing their products in rural settings, thus drawing on deep-seated myths in individuals. Therefore, television does not just offer a 'window on the world' showing us reality as it really is, but is a text, which is encoded with ideological meaning and has to be decoded by those it reaches. However, this approach has been criticised because it assumes that these meanings exist at some deep level, and therefore it cannot be shown that they do actually exist and are employed by individuals in reading the text of the media.

Conclusion

Although most sociological work has concentrated on the newspapers and television, there are many more aspects to the media than these. It is the use of new media technologies by organisations, in both economic and ideological ways, which may form the focus of further research in the area. In particular, the growth of information technology, and the potential it creates for global fraud and increasing control of populations through its manipulation, may prove to be a legitimate area of sociological interest.

Important points to bear in mind

1 People are not 'empty sponges', mindlessly soaking in the products of the media.
2 The production of media messages is a human process, with all the problems, conflicts, compromises and contradictions which that implies.
3 The media are likely to have some effect on the way in which people behave and think, but it is difficult to separate these out from other factors.
4 Ownership of the media exhibits complex cross-cutting patterns, which often hide real centres of control.
5 Journalists and producers do not necessarily share the sociological view of their work but they often use sociological concepts in their work.

KEY CONCEPTS

It is important that you are familiar with and are able to use the concepts in this section in appropriate ways if you are to apply them effectively in the examination. Check your understanding of the concepts by carrying out this exercise.

Fill in the blanks with the most appropriate concept from this list. Determine which concept has not been used:

Media industry	Information technology	
Media technologies	Global economy	Agenda-setting
Gate-keeping	Ownership and control	Allocative control
Operative control	Narcotisation	Media bias
Mediation	Selection	Moral panic
Folk devils	Signification	

Because we now live in a _____ _____, where production is organised on a world-wide basis, _____ _____ have had to become more sophisticated to cope with its demands. Yet, the effects of the media tend to be on the individual level and sociologists have been particularly interested in the way that the media may influence the public at large. Accusations of _____ _____ take many forms, from direct corruption to more sophisticated models, where the media determine what should enter into public debate, i.e. the power of _____ _____. Thus, editors of newspapers are said to have the power of _____ _____, deciding what shall be presented as news or not. Other models of influence focus on popular responses to news stories, where the papers create stereotypes of social groups called _____ _____, which cause the public, in a _____ _____, to demand that something should be done about them. Other effects which have been suggested include _____, where the public are made complacent and quiescent by the activities of the media. Another strand of sociological interest has focused on the fact that the media are a _____ _____, made up of organisations which are also businesses and therefore have a dimension of _____. In particular, the influence of the owners and the power they have to determine the resources of their organisation, their _____ _____, has been a source of interest. While the day-to-day running of these organisations (_____ _____) may be left to editors and the like, the problem of _____, how the values of the owners come to dominate media output, has been examined. But one of the many problems with these approaches is that, though images are presented by the media through a process of _____, individuals do not have to accept them or interpret them in the way they were intended to. Instead, a process of _____ goes on, where individuals make choices about what they expose themselves to and use the media for their own purposes.

COURSEWORK SUGGESTIONS

9.1

An interesting, but probably fraught, exercise would be to carry out a participant observation study of your own family's television viewing. You could look at what programmes were watched and how this was decided. Any disagreements could be noted and the ways in which they were resolved. You would need to be careful not to mix your role as viewer with your role as observer. This may interfere with your ability to watch the programmes you want to watch.

Here are some points for you to consider:

1 This exercise might be difficult to carry out because it is so close to home. How are you going to be objective?
2 What timescale will you establish and how many observations will you carry out?
3 Will you tell your family what you are doing and what might be the implications for your study if you do?
4 How will you feel about revealing details of family rows? How might you keep them anonymous?
5 What sociological theories and concepts will you use to provide a context for your study?

9.2

A popular choice for coursework is likely to be the way that women are represented in adverts and the stereotyping that they receive. While this is a valid exercise, content analysis of advertising can be more adventurous than this, incorporating men as well as women and extending into a consideration of ethnic images as well as gender. The problem is to collect enough images and then to present a sociological analysis of them, rather than just a description. The way forward if you choose this area is to have a strong sociological context to place your work in, to ensure that analysis takes place.

Apart from these stereotypes, what other social groups might you investigate?

Here are some aspects for you to examine:

1 From which newspapers, television programmes or magazines are you going to glean your images?
2 Will you ignore the images which contradict your hypothesis or will you include them in your analysis?
3 Which sociologists will you include in your context? Will it only cover feminist work or will you look further afield?
4 How will you attempt to evaluate your project? Will you just say it is obvious that women, blacks, gays, etc. are stereotyped, or will you provide a discussion of whether they are or not.
5 Will your information be purely qualitative, or is there a way of introducing a quantitative dimension to it?

List the relevant studies with the main points beside them.

CHAPTER 10

Community

> In this chapter we will examine the arguments surrounding:
>
> 1 definitions of community;
> 2 the 'loss of community';
> 3 housing;
> 4 the inner city.
>
> Before you begin any of the exercises you should have studied and should be familiar with at least one of the following texts:
>
> Giddens, A. *Sociology* (Polity 1989), chapter 17.
> O'Donnell, M. *A New Introduction to Sociology*, 3rd edn (Nelson 1992), chapter 19.
> Slattery, M. 'Urban sociology', in Haralambos, M. (ed.) *Sociology – New Directions* (Causeway 1985), pp. 218–300.
>
> In addition, you should have your notes on community in good order.

Introduction

The early sociologists were concerned to explore the process of industrialisation and its causes and effects. One of the main phenomena they were concerned with was the associated process of urbanisation, and what this meant for the sense of community which they believed formed

---

Summarising information from texts is an important component of the skill of interpretation.

Read O'Donnell, pp. 431–3.

INTERPRETATION

1 Outline what sociologists have meant by community.

2 Support your description with quotations from appropriate sociologists.

APPLICATION

the basis of social solidarity and identity before industrialisation. Because industrialisation involved enormous changes in the way that individuals lived their lives, occurring at what seemed a fast and furious pace, all sources of authority and stability seemed to be under threat. This state of modernity, in which urban living becomes the dominant form of social life, was therefore often associated, by the early sociologists, with the loss of community and its attendant phenomena of anomie and alienation.

1 Definitions of community

The problem with the concept of community is that there is no general agreement as to what it means. It is an important concept, because it provides a key to one answer to the central contradiction in sociology, which is the relationship between the individual and the collective (or social). If community is seen as the result of many individuals' sense of belonging to a group which is wider than the individual's immediate family, the existence of a community creates an identity for the individual which binds him or her to social arrangements. (See Coursework Suggestion 10.1 on p. 264.)

Problems with the concept

However, the problem is the variety of groups which may emerge as the focus of individual identity and satisfaction. Different sociologists tend to focus on different groups, or different processes, when trying to define community. Some suggest geographical units as the natural basis for

E VALUATION

To begin to assess a method, you need to identify its strengths and weaknesses.

In two columns, list the advantages and disadvantages of questionnaires.

Questionnaires	
Advantages	**Disadvantages**
1 Are large-scale	1 Questions may be difficult to understand

The first ones have been done for you.

The work of Talcott Parsons is important in the study of community, so you should make up your mind about its significance, by answering this question.

How far do you think Parson's work is an accurate description of traditional and modern societies? Give reasons for your answer.

communities. This is usually associated with small rural areas, where the knowledge of, and contact with, other people are limited by geographical isolation.

Others suggest that certain types of social arrangement form communities, usually small-scale hierarchies, with clear roles and statuses for everyone within the community. Still others suggest that it is certain types of relationship which lead to communities, that is, close and intimate or *gemeinschaft* relationships.

There is another problem associated with the concept of community. While most definitions are concerned with the ways in which individuals might subjectively identify with groups, the evidence for the existence of a community is usually shown by objective collective actions. It is difficult to get inside other people's heads and find out whether they identify with a particular group or community. In asking individuals if they have a sense of belonging, sociologists cannot be sure that positive responses mean the same things to all respondents. Yet we do know from our own experiences that most people prefer to belong to wider groupings and do not wish to live a solitary life.

These wider groupings can take many forms and need not be communities in the geographical sense. However, as societies become more complex and communications improve, the chances of contacting others with whom we might identify become greater. Of course, there have always been wider groups with which individuals have identified. For example, religion has often been the locus of individual identity, and trans-national communities have formed. Thus, the Muslim world binds millions

As a member of society, you are a member of several communities.

1 From your own experience, list the communities you are part of and describe your relationship to them. This might include how much you feel you belong to a given community, the extent of the inter-relationships in it, the formal or informal organisation of it, etc.
2 Evaluate how your experiences of community compare with sociological descriptions of communities.

together through common rituals and beliefs. It can also divide people of the same religion but different versions, such as Sunni and Shiah Islam.

The social basis of community

Whereas social class has often formed the basis for communities in industrial societies, the importance of other social characteristics should not be overlooked. Ethnic groupings are said to form communities in modern Britain through a common identity, background, language or religion. Although the members may be scattered, they tend to form their own organisations, political groupings, lifestyles and values. This does not mean that ethnic minorities form a unified community because, though they may share a similar structural position in society, there are many differences between them.

It is also sometimes argued that young people form a distinctive community in society, with different ideas, values and lifestyles from older members. Moreover, these similar tastes lead young people to identify with each other in many ways so that they adopt similar clothing, musical preferences, etc. The identification of young people with each other is said to occur regardless of other differences between them, such as class or ethnic origin.

This idea has not gone unchallenged. Some sociologists argue that there are many class and ethnic differences among young people which prevent the emergence of a distinctive youth culture. Moreover, there are many different styles of youth culture, rather than one single community of the young, and young women tend to be ignored in the debate about whether young people form a separate community. The central role of the media in forming the idea of a distinctive youth subculture has led some sociologists to suggest that the media are also used to construct (or articulate) 'imaginary communities', with which the postmodern citizen can identify and find a sense of belonging.

As a young person, you may or may not have had some experience of a youth subculture. Using any experiences you have had:

1   How far do you agree that a distinctive youth subculture exists?

2   What sociological studies can you cite both for and against its existence?

APPLICATION

From your reading, you should be familiar enough with empirical studies to apply them to the 'loss of community' thesis.

List the studies, with their main points, of those sociologists who support the idea of a loss of community and those who disagree with it. Use the following format:

Loss of community	
In favour	**Against**

2 The 'loss of community'

Central to the debate about the effects of industrialisation is the idea that the change to urban forms of living leads to the loss of community, which was supposed to exist in rural areas. There is a contrast implicit here between the warm and close relationships of people in a stable hierarchy associated with village life and the fleeting, impersonal relationships associated with the masses living in towns and cities. Many early sociologists saw the swift social change of industrialisation as leading to disorder and 'footlooseness' and compared this with what they saw as the stable conditions of the rural past.

The ideological power of the myth

The notion that there is a fairly straightforward cause-and-effect between a society industrialising and individuals losing their communities and their sense of community has been the subject of much debate in sociology. The idea is a powerful and attractive ideology, because industrialisation undoubtedly involves change, and often swift change, which can appear disruptive and threatening, and indeed is often accompanied by misery as well as material advances. Individuals who live through periods of rapid change may turn to an idealised past to provide an anchor, a source of stability. Others may choose religion as a basis of identity, or may embrace the changes wholeheartedly.

Nevertheless, this turning to the past often creates powerful myths, so that dissatisfaction with present conditions may show itself as a longing for a past which is better than the uncomfortable present. The idea of a loss of community has been attacked for representing the past as some sort of 'Golden Age of the Village Community' and also for denying the opportunities for community living which exist in urban areas. Therefore, much of the sociological debate has focused on the real nature

You should be on the lookout for evidence from many sources.

1 How do the contemporary media portray village life?

2 What programmes or articles can you use to support your view?

of village life, in the past and the present, and whether urban life is as isolated and individualised as is often suggested.

For the loss of community

Those sociologists who support the loss of community idea tend to polarise the difference between the village and the town, suggesting that there are many differences between them which are wide and always to the detriment of the town. In summary, they argue that rural areas allow for the whole being of the individual to be fulfilled, so that life is lived *holistically*. On the other hand, urban areas tend to show various *pathological* symptoms; for example, high levels of crime, which are indicative of an individualistic value-system at odds with the collective sentiments associated with a community.

Other sociologists, while agreeing that there are many differences between urban and rural living and that urbanism is a distinctive way of life, do not accept that this necessarily involves a loss of community. They point to the existence of urban neighbourhoods as a basis of communities in towns, though these in turn may be subject to loss through urban planning and redevelopment.

A central concept associated with this idea is the concept of anomie, which is the state of normlessness, or that condition where individuals are not sure how to behave or think, because they do not live in a traditional unchanging community. However, the idea of knowing one's place can be both attractive to individuals, because it provides them with psychological, emotional and physical support, and unattractive, as it is restricting and frustrating to individual desires and ambitions. In other words, there are aspects of power connected with the idea of community which are sometimes ignored.

What do sociologists mean by:

• dormitory village;
• cyclical poverty trap;
• welfare services?

Write a paragraph on each.

EXERCISE

Hard times in the country

Rural poverty is an issue politicians have found it convenient to ignore, particularly when increasing numbers of well-heeled middle-aged and elderly people are buying holiday and retirement homes amid the peace and greenery of the countryside. This influx of the wealthy and the privileged has only made matters worse, by intensifying the two-tier nature of rural society and helping to hide the plight of the poor.

[A report by Brian McLaughlin] found that one-quarter of all rural households and just under twenty per cent of the population were living in or on the margins of poverty . . . The study tells a sad story above all of impoverished and forgotten old people. They are the ones who are left suffering in obscurity as the young people move away seeking education, training,

jobs and homes that are not on offer in rural areas . . .

The most deprived people in rural areas find themselves in a cyclical poverty trap. They have little money and no car. The public transport networks are thinly spread, especially since deregulation which has meant that private companies compete for the busiest routes at the busiest times to the neglect of the others. Unable to reach competitively priced supermarkets, they are forced to shop at the village store or at mobile stores where food and household goods are much more expensive. They are often cut off from welfare services, and end up spending money instead on professionals, like local solicitors.

(Source: adapted from Sarah Boseley, the *Guardian*, Wednesday 10 January 1990)

Write a paragraph or two on the implications of the information in this extract for the theory that there has been a 'loss of community' in modern industrialised societies.

Search your textbook or notes for other material which might help you to evaluate the 'loss of community' thesis. Organise your material in four columns, headed 'Lack of community in the city', 'Lack of community in the village', 'Community in the city', 'Community in the village', and arrange your evidence in the appropriate columns.

Assess whether the 'loss of community' thesis is a valid one or not, giving your reasons for your choice.

Note where else in your course this extract might be useful.

Against the loss of community

The attack upon the idea of a loss of community has come from many sides. In particular, the idea of a solidaristic village past has been undermined through the rediscovery of conflict and division in the countryside of old. Moreover, present-day rural areas do not exhibit the same close-

Carrying out an exercise like this will improve your application skill.

For each cell, attach the appropriate concept from the following list to the description within it.

Particularism, Achievement, Self-orientation, Collective orientation, Affectivity, Ascription, Affective neutrality, Role specificity, Universality, Role diffuseness.

Differences between traditional and modern societies	
Traditional societies	**Modern societies**
Status is by birth	Status is by effort
Life is emotional and public	Life is emotionally constrained and private
Rules are broad	Rules are specific
Personal contacts are important	Rules are equally applied
Shared interests are important	Individualism is paramount

ness as is claimed by the loss of community theorists. In advanced capitalist societies, rural areas are often the adjunct of towns, expressed in the phrase 'dormitory village', where social relationships are often as soulless as those supposedly in the towns. Moreover, there is tension between newcomers and those who find their living in the countryside often leads to conflict and a lack of identity rather than the solidarity associated with rural life.

Moreover, the idea of the city as inhabited by a mass of individualised isolates has also been criticised. Not only have communities been found in city areas, but neighbourhoods, suburbia and the new towns also form

Producing summaries of articles not only develops your skill of interpretation but can be the first step *before* you apply and evaluate material.

From your reading, detail the features of the Chicago School approach and its main criticisms.

ESSAY QUESTION

Ensure that the studies used in your answer are applied to the issue at hand and not just described.

Evaluate the evidence for and against the idea that urbanisation leads inevitably to a loss of community.

the basis of social life for many people. Ethnic groups often form the basis of identifiable communities in the cities, but it may also be working in the same industry or sharing the same social class position which forms the basis of identity for some individuals.

In postmodern societies, the development of fibre optics and satellite technologies has created the possibility for dispersed communities to exist, and already some cities, such as Biarritz, have experimented in linking homes to a number of interactive services. The idea of housing classes has been put forward as a possible basis for communities in towns, as people sharing the same material conditions have a solid basis for identifying with each other.

Implications

The existence of communities in towns has been capitalised on by the new practices of the political parties. Here, the emphasis is on *community politics*, building up a political base through action in a locality. This can undermine support for opposing parties in an area and create networks of supporters. Also, several councils have been decentralising their operations to the local community, empowering local organisations to make decisions concerning community provisions. In the 1980s central government has been both centralising powers away from local authorities and decentralising powers to community representatives, such as parents, school governors, industrialists and local hospital boards.

Application can consist of examining your own and your peers' experiences.

1 List the organisations that you belong to and the leisure activities that you engage in.

2 Compare them to your colleagues in your class or at work. How similar or different are they?

Although the debate continues about whether there has been a loss of community or not, the empirical evidence suggests that there is wide variation in both rural and urban areas as to lifestyle and focus of identity. However, some sociologists suggest that there is increasing variation in the way that individuals live their lives. It is argued that advanced capitalist societies are characterised by strong senses of personal identity and individual self-assertion which tend to undermine the collective identity of individuals, whether in the community at large, trade unions or even the nation-state.

To satisfy the need for belonging, the media now form a crucial role in allowing individuals to access transnational networks that offer a form of community, and which go beyond class, race, gender or national culture. This *bonding* on a global scale can be seen first and foremost in media events such as the Band Aid concerts, and these communities are seen as typical of the postmodern age, a replacement for the traditional community of the village.

3 Housing

The issue of housing has been an area where sociological interest has grown since the Second World War. This partly reflects the growing variety of types of housing and housing area in modern Britain, but also the growing understanding of the forces which shape the modern city. As the average size of the city has increased, the complexity of its housing provision has also developed. These changes do not just affect the urban areas, but the rural areas as well. So, while cities have been characterised by the appearance of suburban areas, large council estates, gentrified inner cities and the absorption of outlying villages, villages themselves have been transformed by new housing developments, including in-fill housing, new private estates and overspill population.

Housing and social problems

One area of concern has been the description of housing as a social problem. This takes several forms but can be summarised in the phrase

---

Thinking of criticisms of material you are reading is a good practice for evaluation.

Read *Sociology Review*, vol. 1, no. 2, pp. 6–9. (See [67], p. 338.)

INTERPRETATION

1 Outline the development of cities, according to Jewson.

EVALUATION

2 What criticisms would you make of this typology?

Thinking about social problems is an important aspect of sociology.

How far do you agree with the idea that urban problems are primarily social, and not simply urban?

E VALUATION

housing crisis. This is usually seen in terms of a housing shortage, though it has other aspects as well. Homelessness undoubtedly grew in the 1980s and there have been furious debates concerning the social policy causes of homelessness. For example, changes to the rules governing Income Support claims for young people have been suggested as one reason for an increase in young people sleeping rough in the 'cardboard cities' of Britain's main urban areas.

The collapse of the privately rented sector and the sale of council housing has also produced strains in the housing market. Nevertheless, home ownership continues to be an attractive proposition to many families, even when high interest rates caused more repossessions. However, when property 'booms' and the prices of houses increase faster than average wages, the investment value of buying your own home becomes apparent. The down-side of home ownership can be seen in the situation where many house owners have mortgages larger than the collapsed prices of their houses.

But there is another dimension to the social problem aspects of housing, which is the associated difficulties it often gives rise to. Bad housing conditions have always been associated with poor health, early child death and higher levels of family disorganisation. This may be made worse by social policy decisions which concentrate families with difficulties into 'sink estates', creating pockets of poverty and crime in the midst of a wealthy urban society. The lack of amenities in such areas compounds the problems.

While middle-class suburban areas may also suffer from a lack of amenities, the inhabitants usually have the means to travel to entertainment or shopping centres. However, even in these areas, certain cate-

Using other resources in addition to sociological textbooks is important for the A level student.

1 Carry out a newspaper search for articles on homelessness.

I NTERPRETATION

2 How might a sociologist make use of the articles you find?

A PPLICATION

EXERCISE

Housing supply and demand

How else might you present this information to highlight the similarities between countries?

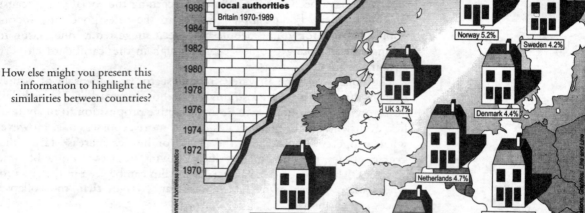

Housing supply and demand

Households accepted as homeless by local authorities
Britain 1970-1989

SOURCE: Government homeless statistics

Norway 5.2%
Sweden 4.2%
UK 3.7%
Denmark 4.4%
Netherlands 4.7%
W Germany 5.1%
Average excluding UK 4.7%
France 4.4%

Percentage of a country's income (GDP) which is spent on housing
1987, selected countries

SOURCE: Isabel Lydons. Graphics: Line and Line

(Source: Edward Pilkington, the *Guardian*, Tuesday 8 January 1991)

What is the City Council doing?

Q How many houses does the Council own?
A We currently own about 30,000 houses, but that number is always falling. Since the 'Right to Buy' was introduced, the Council has had to sell houses to tenants, but cannot use the money from council house sales to build more houses.

Q How many people are on the council house waiting list?
A Currently there are about 14,500 people registered for accommodation. Of these, almost 11,000 are on the housing waiting list and the remainder are existing tenants requesting a move.
The waiting list has remained about the same in recent years but, as homelessness has increased, applicants on the waiting list face longer waits for rehousing. Families are now having to wait years before being

allocated a house. Nor does there seem to be any prospect of improvement.

Apply your knowledge of methods here. Suggest reasons why it might not be possible to collect an accurate figure.

APPLICATION

Q How many homeless people are there in the city?
A You can't give an accurate answer to that because the figure can vary so much. However, homeless officers are dealing with between 50 and 75 cases at any one time. In the period April to June 1991, 177 families were accepted as homeless under the legislation. During 1990, the number of families the authority had a responsibility for rose by 30 per cent.

Q Is the Council obliged to house them?
A Yes, we have a statutory duty to rehouse homeless people.

(Source: *Leicester Link*, Leicester City Council, August 1991)

The text suggests a link between social policies and the extent of homelessness. Answer the following:

1 Make the link, as made in the text, explicit in no more than 100 words.
2 Describe the trend in homelessness since 1970, without mentioning any figures.
3 Suggest arguments against the idea that government policies cause homelessness.
4 Find sociological evidence which supports both sides of the argument.
5 Which side is the more convincing, and why?

gories of people, such as the old, may find life on their own difficult to manage without transport or daily support. As the welfare services have cut back on home help for these individuals, there has been a growth in collective provision for the old, through State and private accommodation. These may take the form of sheltered housing or old people's homes.

Power and housing

Certain powerful groups in the housing sector have become the focus of sociological interest in the 1980s. These 'urban managers' have a crucial role in the allocation of housing to particular social groups, and in the type of housing that is actually built. These groups range from local business personnel, whose investment decisions may influence the type of employment available, and the zoning of urban space, to the planners and architects themselves. The decisions of councillors, bank managers, building society assessors, etc. will affect individual family's housing situations, but there are also larger forces at work which affect the amount and type of housing available on the market.

INTERPRETATION

Working out problems by thinking about the real world is an important part of the application skill. Therefore, list the groups who can influence what happens in urban areas, and identify their main powers.

The style of housing available tends to result from a whole number of factors, such as the amount of money available to finance building, architectural fashion and pressures on urban space. However, the human dimension can be lost in this process as the 'streets in the sky' of the 1960s demonstrated. Not only were they not popular among residents, but they tended to have a range of architectural faults built into them. More recently, planners have tried to involve residents and the local community in decisions regarding housing, so that they produce housing with a human face. It is the concern with the human dimension, the decorative aspect and continuity with past traditions which are the hallmark of postmodern architecture.

Although there may be a greater willingness to listen to the community in urban planning, the urban crisis which many sociologists have explored manifests itself most vividly in rising crime rates in the city and the riots in many city areas in the early 1980s. These riots are often associated with inner-city populations, but one interesting facet which sociologists have looked at is the possibility of copycatting, the spread of rioting through mimicking events on the television.

Others argue that the media, especially the music industry, form the basis of new identities for the individualised population, which finds new communities in wider groupings than the locality or an occupational group. This is particularly so for ethnic minorities in Britain, who may find a new community built around particular forms of music, resolving the dilemma in which they find themselves, of being neither fully part of their ethnic background nor fully accepted as British. These forms of music evolve in the inner-city space which ethnic minorities often inhabit.

Read *Social Studies Review*, vol. 5, no. 5, pp. 170–4. (See [68], p. 338.) Often questions involve several skills. For example:

Evaluate the explanations put forward by sociologists for inner-city disturbances.

To answer this, you would need to:

• put forward several explanations from the article;

INTERPRETATION

• use evidence to discuss the strengths and weaknesses of each explanation;

APPLICATION

• come to a conclusion as to which is the most realistic.

EVALUATION

ESSAY QUESTION

You need to identify the residential patterns that you are going to discuss and then evaluate a range of contributions.

Assess sociological contributions to an understanding of residential patterns in cities.

4 The inner city

The inner city is commonly associated with the social problems of bad housing, crime, poor services, urban blight and decay. But this picture has been undermined by sociological research. Sociologists have shown that the patterns of housing in the inner city are much more varied than common-sense suggests.

Variation in the inner city

Apart from the urban poor who are concentrated in the inner city, other groups also live there. In particular, the student and intellectual populations tend to congregrate in the cheaper housing of the inner city, while the very rich often keep town houses close to the commercial centre of the city. In the 1980s, the housing boom and rising prices created the phenomenon of gentrification, where redevelopment involved the pulling down of slum housing, replacing it with expensive housing enclaves, often physically separated from the poorer housing around it.

The housing boom of the 1980s had another effect in that it resulted in London reverting to a 'capital city', with a rich class serviced by a poor class, rather than a city with a developed industrial base, as it had been since the industrial revolution. The process means that postmodern societies become characterised by a two-thirds/one-third structure, in which a new under-class emerges to meet the domestic and service needs of the rich, who have a great deal of disposable income as they inherit the expensive housing of their parents, sell it off and use the proceeds to buy services. But the effect on the poor of the cities is that their incomes become influenced by variations in the housing market. Without steady

Read O'Donnell, pp. 438–40.

INTERPRETATION

Identify the social groups which, O'Donnell suggests, inhabit the inner city, describing their main features.

You need to be aware of developments in society in order to assess some sociological concepts. For example:

1 How far do you agree that an *under-class* is emerging in urban areas?

2 What evidence can you call upon to support your view?

income, life becomes precarious and multiplies the environmental problems that the inner-city inhabitants already face. (See Coursework Suggestion 10.2 on p. 264.)

Policy and housing

Sociologists have tried to contribute to solutions to the problems of the inner cities over a number of years. Inevitably, there are disagreements among sociologists as to the proper way to tackle the problems of the inner city. Some sociologists have argued for specific programmes to break the cycle of deprivation, and these have usually been aimed at inner-city children's education. They have been criticised for failing to deal with the multiple deprivation that the inner cities face, and for being unintentionally racist in effect, as they tend to be geared towards underachieving black children.

Others have suggested that there ought to be a much more comprehensive attack on inner-city problems, which examines the economic dimension and the effects of government initiatives on the inner city. It was claimed that this attack was bureaucratic and interventionist without achieving much, except providing jobs for the middle-class providers of the programmes. Yet another approach argues that the inner cities should be deregulated, with market forces allowed to create wealth which will 'trickle down' to the poor in the area. The creation of the enterprise zones in the 1980s was a central part of the strategy to solve the problems

Sociology is often connected to social policy.

1 Which policies have been tried in order to combat inner-city poverty?

2 Choose one and evaluate its effectiveness.

Thinking about the effects of policies on social groups is an important way that sociology can be applied.

Take one of the policies identified in the paragraph above and suggest what effects it may have on either women or ethnic minorities in the inner city.

of the inner city, but these have come under increasing criticism as economic recession in the 1990s has made private initiatives in the inner city less successful.

Other areas of study which have attracted sociological attention in the city and inner city have been the issues of power and the operation of the urban elite in cities. Moreover, the power of town planners has also come under increasing scrutiny, but on an individual level as their ideologies have been examined, and in particular their use of the concept 'community' to legitimise their activities.

Housing policy has also been looked at for the ways in which it is used to control various groups through segregation, uniformity of provision and allocative power. Another area of interest for sociologists is the different forms of economic activity to be found in the inner city, from the black illegal economy, through the grey semi-formal economy, to the hidden domestic economy of mutual support, which have been the hallmarks of urban communities in the past.

Conclusion

Urban and rural living have been a focus for much comparative work in sociology because the variation and the similarities have been a fruitful source of investigation. The sense of identity which living in a locality can engender has proved to be a potent means of integrating individuals into the wider society. The success or failure of the integration process is important for the creation of social order in society, and so community remains a central concept in modern sociology.

Although some areas of social life may be of great interest to sociologists, they may be hard to investigate. For example:

How might a sociologist begin to investigate the forms of economic activity identified in the paragraph above? What problems would a sociologist face?

Important points to bear in mind

1 There is a great deal of geographical mobility in society and, therefore, many individuals are members of several different local communities during their lifetime.
2 Housing is one of the central needs of individuals and families in society and its provision absorbs a great deal of individual income.
3 Patterns of residence are constantly changing and the desirability of certain districts is subject to such influences as fashion or taste.
4 Because someone lives in the inner city does not guarantee that he or she will end up in some sort of criminal career.
5 Living in the countryside may not be idyllic if you are poor, old, without transport or disabled.

KEY CONCEPTS

It is important that you are familiar with and are able to use the concepts in this section in appropriate ways if you are to apply them effectively in the examination. Check your understanding of the concepts by carrying out this exercise.

Fill in the missing spaces with the concept which is the most appropriate fit:

Gemeinschaft	*Gesellschaft*	Modernity
Myth	Anomie	Urban planning
Suburbanisation	Gentrification	Community politics
Decentralisation	Overspill population	Urban managers
Deregulation	Housing policy	Loss of community
Housing boom and bust		

The process whereby run-down inner-city areas are regenerated is called _____.

The state of normlessness is called _____.
Fluctuations in the price of accommodation are called _____.
Systematic development of a built-up area is called _____.
The idea of a golden age of the village community is a _____.
People who moved from over-crowded inner cities to new towns are called _____.

The process whereby people move to the edges of towns is called _____.

The concentration of political parties on local issues is called _____.
The process whereby social relations move from warm and close to distant and fleeting is called _____.
The amount and type of houses built in a society will be influenced by its _____.

The situation where social relations are distant and fleeting is called _____.

Groups such as architects, finance planners or housing officers are collectively known as _____.

The process whereby power is dispersed to more and more people is called _____.

The opposite of traditionalism is _____.

The process whereby organisations are subject to fewer rules is called _____.

The situation where social relations are close and warm can be called _____.

COURSEWORK SUGGESTIONS

10.1

You could devise a questionnaire to find out which communities people feel part of. You will need to devise an appropriate hypothesis to investigate. In testing for which communities people identify with, you should be careful to include as many options as possible. You will also need to find some way of allowing respondents to rank their choices in order of importance. The statistics which result may seem complicated, so they will have to be analysed carefully, not just reiterated, to relate them to your hypothesis.

You will need to consider the following points:

1 What system will you employ to rank-order respondent's choices: 'order of importance', 'most important to least important', 'numerically'?
2 How will you distribute the questionnaire and collect it in?
3 Have you access to a statistics package on a computer and the expertise to use it? If not, can you get someone else to process the statistics for you?
4 Can you find a vivid way of presenting your results, so that the important points you wish to make stand out from your diagrams and charts?
5 Make sure that you evaluate your efforts, pointing out the strengths and weaknesses of your chosen methodology, and how other approaches might have been useful.

Make sure that you interpret your statistics in terms of your hypothesis and do not just describe them in a different format.

10.2

Cities and towns are conveniently divided by local government into areas or wards, and statistics are gathered about these wards by many agencies. It is, therefore, possible to carry out a statistical comparison between two or more wards, which might show very different profiles. You will need to decide which variables you are going to compare, and relate these to a hypothesis or aim that you have in mind. It is important that you do not end up just describing the different words, but actively compare them in terms of your chosen variables, to establish the truth or otherwise of your hypothesis. You will also need to locate your work clearly in the tradition of urban sociology and will, therefore, have to do some reading beforehand.

Make a list of statistics which may be useful for your comparisons and a list of those which are easily available. How similar are they?

Here are some aspects to think about:

1 Much information of this kind is now kept on computer, so do not ignore this as a possible resource.
2 You might consider the geography department in your institution as a source of information.
3 Presentation of your statistics will be crucial for the success of your project, so this must be fully thought out.
4 Your commentary on the statistics and their implications for the hypothesis will also be important.
5 Photographs might also be useful as evidence, depending on the points you wish to make.

CHAPTER 11

Organisations

In this chapter we will examine the arguments surrounding:

1 bureaucracy;
2 formal and informal organisations;
3 other forms of organisation;
4 organisations, groups and individuals;
5 trade unions and professional associations.

Before you begin any of the exercises you should have studied and should be familiar with at least one of the following texts:

Giddens, A. *Sociology* (Polity 1989), chapter 9.
Haralambos, M. and Holborn, M. *Sociology: Themes and Perspectives*, 3rd edn (Collins Educational 1991), chapter 7.
Morgan, G. *Organisations in Society* (Macmillan 1990).
O'Donnell, M. *A New Introduction to Sociology*, 3rd edn (Nelson 1992), chapter 12.

In addition, you should have your notes on organisations in good order.

Introduction

Organisations are unavoidable in modern society. Most individuals will spend a great deal of time in organisations or a large amount of their lives dealing with them. This is because organisations are the major way in which individuals cooperate to achieve certain aims, and they form a central part of the individual's experiences in society. Most people in industrial societies are born in a complex organisation, a hospital, and will leave life with the help of some religious organisation.

However, organisations are especially interesting to sociologists because they combine the two levels of analysis which make up the core of sociological study – the individual and social structures. While organisations are by definition collective endeavours, in that they consist of relationships between people, they are inhabited and given meaning by individuals acting in particular ways. To achieve individual and organisa-

You need to be able to extract key items of information from texts by using the skill of interpretation.

Read Haralambos and Holborn, pp. 405–6 and answer this question:

According to Haralambos and Holborn, what two social features does a specialised division of labour generate?

tional aims, the individual must agree to act in a constrained and partly determined way.

Individuals, therefore, seek to control their lives more fully by joining organisations, and yet organisations will to some degree increase the amount of control in their lives. It is this potential conflict between the individual and the collective which is at the heart of sociological interest in organisations. Hardly a day goes by without most of us coming into contact with a formal organisation. They are a central feature of modern industrial societies.

1 Bureaucracy

We tend to think of organisations as being bureaucracies, although bureaucratic arrangements are only one way in which individuals can formally relate together in an organisation. This identification of organisations with bureaucracy comes about because bureaucracies have until now been the dominant form of organisation in modern society. (See Coursework Suggestion 11.1 on p. 287.)

Applying sociological techniques to your own life will help you to understand the subject.
1 Make a list of all the organisations you 'inhabit'.
2   Select appropriate criteria for categorising them (for example, formal/informal, large-scale/small-scale) and produce a typology of the organisations you are involved in.

1 What do sociologists mean by *ideal type*?

2 What are the advantages and disadvantages of this technique?

From your reading, you should be able to apply your knowledge of organisations to specific issues. For example:

List the features which separate bureaucratic organisations from charismatic and traditional organisations.

Weber

There have been many attempts to describe the essential features of a bureaucracy, the most famous being that of the early sociologist, Weber. Weber's ideas about bureaucracies have been the starting point for much of the debate which surrounds bureaucracies. This debate centres around the concept of *efficiency*. Weber believed that the bureaucratic organisation was dominant in the world because it was the most rational form of organisation, and as such was the most efficient way of relating individuals in organisations.

However, there has been a great deal of disagreement over what Weber actually meant by efficiency. Some believe that Weber was suggesting that bureaucracy was the most efficient way of 'getting things done'. This is sometimes known as the *technicist* approach. Others believe that he was referring to bureaucracy's efficiency in controlling the individuals who worked in this type of organisation. This is sometimes referred to as the *power* approach.

The technicist approach

This dispute is important because, depending on which approach is adopted, different questions will be asked concerning bureaucracies. With the technicist approach, research was directed to examining the features of bureaucracies to see how they might be made more efficient. Some sociologists argued, for example, that the very features which Weber identified as being efficient, such as having a set of rules or a hierarchy, could, under certain circumstances, lead to dysfunction or a lack of efficiency. The role of the sociologist in examining bureaucracy was, therefore, to identify ways in which bureaucracy could be made more efficient in getting things done.

It is never enough just to know a piece of sociology. You also need to know how to use it and how it fits in with related pieces of work. For example:

For each of Merton, Burns and Stalker, Gouldner and Blau, spell out the implications of their work for Weber's theory of bureaucracy; that is, in what ways does each writer undermine, support or extend Weber's work?

INTERPRETATION   APPLICATION

EVALUATION

KNOWLEDGE   UNDERSTANDING

With many questions, you need to bring together all your skills. For example:

To what extent do you agree that bureaucracies control individual lives?

To answer this question you will need to:

- be able to describe the evidence for and against the idea;
- show how you are going to use it to answer the question; and
- come to a conclusion which assesses the idea.

The power approach

The power approach argues that the important feature of bureaucracy is its ability to control the movements and actions of those at the lower level of the hierarchy; that is, bureaucracies are designed to coordinate the activities of many individuals through direct but limited control over the members of the organisation. So, the features that make for efficiency are those which direct the activities of members of the bureaucracy in particular ways. Discipline is the major characteristic of bureaucracies and it has been the focus of research in this approach. Therefore, bureaucracies are not just instruments for achieving goals, but potentially dangerous structures threatening the freedom of the individual.

An alternative approach

A third approach to bureaucracy suggests that the other two are *reified* accounts of this type of organisation, treating bureaucracy as if it were a real thing rather than made up of thousands of individual day-by-day actions. This approach focuses on the individual's experiences in the bureaucracy, arguing that the features of the bureaucracy are resources to be used and manipulated by all the individuals within them, in pursuit of their individual aims. For example, individuals follow bureaucratic rules when they suit their purposes, and bend or break them if that is more likely to help them achieve their ends. So, research has been directed to investigating individual experiences of bureaucracies and their role as active manipulators of the structures they inhabit.

APPLICATION

Read Haralambos and Holborn, pp. 446–8.

How can the findings on psychiatric hospitals be applied to other types of organisation, such as schools or factories?

In applying the findings you should consider similarities and differences between the types of organisation, in which ways the findings might be relevant and in which ways they are not.

ESSAY QUESTION

'Relative' merits implies that you should look at the advantages and disadvantages of both views.

Assess the relative merits of viewing bureaucracies as technically efficient as opposed to being efficient in controlling members.

These differences in approach are a reflection of the paradoxes inherent in bureaucracies themselves. The means used to help an organisation to achieve its goals efficiently do not always enhance efficiency because the means include human beings who may have different goals from the management. Therefore, all organisations are faced with potentially destructive contradictions which they may seek to neutralise by increasing control, changing personnel, changing the operation of the bureaucracy or moving away from a bureaucratic structure altogether.

2 Formal and informal organisations

Sociologists of organisations have, therefore, often focused on the distinction between the formal structures of an organisation and the informal structures. Formal structures describe what is supposed to happen in an organisation – who relates to whom and how – while informal structures describe what actually goes on. Much sociological research has been directed to investigating formal and informal features of organisations, so that policies can be evolved to increase the efficiency of organisations. Indeed, this area of sociological research has been the most heavily funded by industry as individual firms seek to maximise the efficiency of their operations.

E VALUATION

A PPLICATION

One of the most difficult types of assessment is where you have to compare two phenomena and come to a conclusion about them. For example:
1 What is the relative importance of formal and informal organisations for the efficient functioning of organisations? You might consider, among other things, rules, commands, peer pressure, solidarity, dysfunctions, rewards.
2 What evidence supports your conclusion?

From your knowledge of different types of organisation, you should be prepared to assess them.

Which type of organisation do you think is the most effective and why? You could start by defining what is meant by effective.

Organisational policies

Early examples of this approach were scientific management (Taylorism) and human relations or self-actualisation theories. The former tried to resolve the contradiction between formal and informal organisations, by seeking to increase the control of the formal managers over the informal workings of the workers. This tightening of discipline, through time and motion and increasing specialisation, has met with resistance from those it seeks to control and there is much dispute as to how far it has been used by industry.

The latter seeks to use informal organisations and the desire of workers to control their own work by trying to harness their energies to the formal organisation's aims. This has included such tactics as creating work teams, bringing work tasks together, rather than breaking them down, and giving workers opportunities to contribute positively to the production process.

Another approach argues that both these tactics represent ideologies of control and are geared towards the wishes of management. They do not take account of what workers want from work. The overriding aim of both Taylorism and human relations, it is argued, is the greater profitability of the organisation; a profitability of which workers will not see a fair share. This third approach examines the de-skilling effects of these tactics and worker resistance to attempts by management to gain greater control, or greater effort with no increases in reward. These strategies of resistance are many and varied, but sociologists of organisations from this perspective have been particularly interested in the ways in which workers develop informal methods of working that do not conform to management wants, but reflect workers' ideologies about what constitutes a fair day's work.

1 What empirical evidence can you discover about the workings of both scientific management and human relations theory?

2 Does your evidence support or criticise the theory that it writes about?

3 Other forms of organisation

While bureaucracies have been a dominant form of organisation since industrialisation introduced mass production methods as the main way in which society produced the goods that it needed, bureaucracy existed before the industrial revolution, as did many other forms of organisation. Since then, other forms of organisation have existed alongside bureaucracy and new forms have developed in reaction to technological and social developments. Moreover, different types of society have emphasised different features of organisation, depending on their political priorities and ideologies.

For example, the Chinese Communists have tried to develop communes as a distinctive type of social organisation and a basis of agricultural production. Communist societies have tended to develop large bureaucracies to produce their goods, with an additional political element in the shape of Party control of organisations. The collapse of the Communist system of production in Eastern Europe demonstrates that bureaucracy is not necessarily efficient and that new forms of organisation may be needed as technology becomes more sophisticated.

Organisational environments

Sociologists have recognised that bureaucracy is not always the best form of organisation, depending on the environment which the organisation faces and the tasks that it needs to perform. Much research has been carried out into the challenges which organisations face and their response to conditions of uncertainty and change. While bureaucracies may be efficient when the demands made upon the organisation are routine, different types of structure may be more appropriate when there is a situation of challenge.

Some sociologists have argued that bureaucracies can be successfully adapted to meet conditions of change, while others suggest that a different type of organisational structure is necessary to deal with constant uncertainty. This contrast between *mechanistic* types of organisation like bureaucracy and *organismic* networked organisations is an important and developing one.

1 List the features of mechanistic and organismic organisations.

2 Which features of mechanistic organisations may hinder the emergence of organismic systems?

3 Why do these features act as barriers to change?

1 Where do you think you can find out more about the theories described in the paragraph below?

2 Which of the two do you think more closely corresponds to social reality? Give reasons for your answer.

Is this third approach any more convincing? Is there any evidence for your answer?

More recently, a debate has arisen between those who argue that organisations are similar to species in biology, affected by their environment but unable to affect it themselves – the *population ecology* theory – and those who argue that organisations can affect their environments in direct ways – the *resource dependence* theory. The former argue that organisations are natural phenomena, which live and die according to principles of natural selection, and their survival or death is only slightly influenced, if at all, by the intentions and actions of individuals within them. The latter see organisations as the means by which managements seek to control their environment by devising strategies to increase their independence from other organisations, and increase the reliance of other organisations on their own.

A third modern approach emphasises the power relations between organisations, as they network in an attempt to control their environment. The relations between organisations can take many different forms, but they all have in common a desire to restrict the unforeseen consequences of an environment which is constantly changing. One aspect of this 'network' theory stresses the stability of capitalist networks in controlling the environment in which they operate.

Future environments

As modern industrial societies move into the post-Fordist era, some sociologists argue that there will be a changeover to more flexible organisations in industry and elsewhere. The fragmentation of demand for products has meant that industrial firms have to respond quickly to changes in the market and, therefore, need a flexible form of working. This will be reflected in new types of organisation, where members of the firm, both workers and managements, will be much more skilled and work together as teams rather than divided into rigid hierarchies. Hierarchies will also be under threat from advanced information technology which strips away the traditional communication functions of middle management.

Thinking about the future is a good way of practising applying your sociological understanding.

1 Write a paragraph supporting each of the three views of the future put forward in this section, giving three paragraphs in total.

2 Search the newspapers and sociological literature for any evidence about these three views and attach any relevant pieces to the appropriate paragraph. This will ensure that your ideas are supported by evidence. However, consider the different type of evidence you will get from newspapers as opposed to sociological works.

However, some sociologists reject the idea that sophisticated, automated technologies mean that there must be a change to a different form of organisation, arguing that this is only so for a very small proportion of modern industry, while the vast majority remain more efficient by using bureaucratic methods. Moreover, individual bureaucrats, who have gained much prestige and income from bureaucratic organisations, can resist the change to more flexible organisations precisely because they have the power and interest to do so.

Others believe that the development of new technologies and new forms of organisation herald a 'golden age' of production, where individual needs will be met, both as consumers and as workers, because individuals will gain an increased commitment to the organisation for which they work. On the other hand, other sociologists take a more pessimistic view of these developments, suggesting that the increased exercise of skill in post-Fordist organisations will be for relatively few workers. The great majority of workers will continue to be involved in routine and bureaucratic procedures, controlled by management as they perform repetitive and largely meaningless tasks.

Trade unions

It is not only industrial firms which face conditions of change, nor is it only new technology which creates those conditions of change. For example, the traditional bureaucratic structures of the trade unions have come under increasing strain during the 1980s, as the decline in manufacturing and the growth of flexible specialisation have caused the traditional areas of trade union strength to contract.

There was also a parallel attack on trade union powers by Conservative governments in the 1980s, and trade unions faced conditions of uncertainty and change. They are now having to adapt their organisation and strategies to these circumstances by finding new ways of working and reaching new types of worker.

Traditionally, trade unions have been strong among male, full-time industrial workers. To reach the growing numbers of part-time and

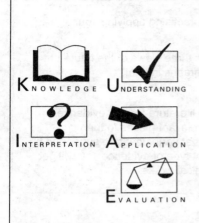

You should be aware of political events because they often provide the raw material of sociological study.

1 What measures did the Conservative governments of the 1980s and 1990s take to restrict union power?

2 Did any other factors restrict union power?

3 What is the relative importance of government actions and these other factors in restricting the trade unions?

female workers in the service sector, trade unions will need to find a more flexible structure. Moreover, it is argued that the unions are going to have to adapt to the conditions of post-Fordist industrial societies and provide more personal services for their members, such as health insurance. The Electrical, Electronic, Telecommunications, and Plumbing Union (EETPU) is often cited as an example of the 'new unionism', though white-collar unions have also been associated with the development of new structures and policies.

Professional associations

Some sociologists have suggested that bureaucracy has not been the dominant form of organisation for certain groups of workers, especially for middle-class workers. For certain professional groups, a different type of organisation was introduced in the nineteenth century – the professional organisation, in which highly skilled workers took control of their own profession and introduced a more collegiate form of organisation. Here, the professional was responsible only to other professionals for the exercise of his or her skill, and was not subject to the minute-by-

Most individuals have had experience of a professional in some capacity and, therefore, have some common-sense knowledge of professionals.

1 Describe one encounter you have had with a professional (such as a doctor).

2 How might a sociologist explain this event?

Controversial issues need to be considered in the light of the evidence.

What evidence is there for the de-professionalisation thesis? Is there any counter-evidence?

A P P L I C A T I O N

minute control which characterised the bureaucratic control of the industrial manual worker.

However, sociological attention has increasingly been focused on the experiences of professionals as they have become more involved with bureaucratic organisations. The growth of bureaucracies in traditional professions has been most marked in the medical profession as the National Health Service developed large hospitals and bureaucratic procedures to run them. While there are still many elements of professional organisation in the Health Service, it is the potential conflict between the two forms which has intrigued sociologists.

Some suggest that the professionals have been strengthened by bureaucratic organisations as they give them access to much larger resources. Others suggest that professionals lose their independence and control in bureaucracies and effectively become 'de-professionalised' by the bureaucrats. An alternative view is that professionals in bureaucracies are in a constant state of role uncertainty as they seek to juggle the demands made on them by the different aspects of the organisations to which they belong. The changes to the Health Service introduced by the government in 1991, had a profound effect on the organisational forms of the medical profession and will be examined by sociologists for their effect on the professionals' position in bureaucracies.

Total institutions

Another type of organisation which has attracted sociological attention has been that which seeks to exert the greatest amount of control over individual lives, such as the prison. These *total institutions* have been investigated because they are an extreme form of organisation, and they

Applying your understanding of methodology to an area is an important skill.

A P P L I C A T I O N

1 Suggest ways in which sociologists might seek to investigate total institutions.

E V A L U A T I O N

2 Which is likely to be the most effective method, and why?

**ESSAY
QUESTION**

Note that the question requires you
to have some examples to apply to
the issue.

'Professional associations are just trade unions with middle-class status.'
Using examples, evaluate the evidence for and against this view.

highlight the conflict between the needs of the individual and the control
of the organisation most clearly. It is this relationship between individuals and the structures they live in which is one of the central issues in
sociology, and so total institutions constitute a strategic case to study.

While some sociologists have focused on the structural components of
total institutions, isolating features which are unique to them and separate them from bureaucracies, others have focused on the individual reaction to total institutions and how the institutions come to deal with the
demands made upon them. Still others focus on the aspect of control, and
the ways in which many controllers of organisations seek to introduce
totalistic features into non-total organisations to extend their control
over subordinates. For example, post-Fordist organisations have adapted
many totalistic features, demanding primary loyalty from their work-
force in exchange for providing many services which employees would
normally find outside of work.

4 Organisations, groups and individuals

As the issue of control is the crucial dimension in the sociological debate
about organisations, there has been a great deal of attention directed
towards whether organisations can ever be democratic. Michels, an early
sociologist, argued that, as soon as people set up organisations, they were
setting off down a road which could only lead to a minority dominating
the majority within the organisation. This has led to much investigation
into the democratic or oligarchic potentiality of organisations. While
bureaucracies have superiority and inferiority built into them, some sociologists argue that this does not prevent them from being democratically
accountable.

Read *Social Studies Review*, vol. 2, no. 5, p. 13. (See [69], p. 338.)

Identify and define the sociological concepts employed by Goffman.

INTERPRETATION   APPLICATION

EXERCISE

The breeding of abuse

Experimental research has also looked at the effects on people of being placed in positions of power in [total] institutions. Haney, Banks and Zimbardo (1973) set up a simulated prison and assigned 24 volunteers to the roles of guards and of prisoners. The 'guards' were led to believe that the focus of the research was on the behaviour of the 'prisoners'. The regulations of the 'prison' were explained, and the guards were then given the authority to run the prison within these rules.

Are there any ethical problems that you can identify with this experiment?

The experiment ended, however, after only six days because of the reaction of both guards and prisoners. Some prisoners were retreating into apathy by the second day, and some had to be released early because of emotional stress. Many of the guards showed enjoyment of the power they had been given and abused it, mainly through insulting the prisoners, and by transforming their rights into privileges – then arbitrarily withdrawing them.

The prisoners welcomed the early end of the experiment, but the guards were reluctant to give up the extreme power and control which they had exercised. There were individual differences in the behaviour of the guards, ranging from the relatively passive, through the 'tough but fair', to those who engaged in 'creative cruelty and harassment'. But no guard ever challenged the behaviour of another guard, which meant that the behaviour of the toughest guard became the norm for that shift.

(Source: adapted from Patrick McNeill, *Society Today 2*, Macmillan 1991)

To what extent do you think that experiments like this tell us anything about life in a real prison?

To answer the question, you must exercise the skill of evaluation and make sure that you respond directly to it.

Make a list of the arguments for the validity of this type of experiment and a list of arguments against.

KNOWLEDGE   **U**NDERSTANDING

What do sociologists mean by:

- oligarchy;
- democracy;
- hierarchy;
- bureaucracy?

APPLICATION

In examining whether the iron law of oligarchy exists or not, you need to apply the evidence on both sides of the argument. Therefore:

1 List the sociologists who support the idea of an iron law of oligarchy and those who oppose it.
2 Write down the main points of their work alongside the details of their book. Use the following format:

Iron law of oligarchy	
Supporters	**Main points**
Opponents	**Main points**

The iron law of oligarchy

The evidence concerning this debate is taken from many sources, from the highly oligarchic organisations in the Communist societies to the democratic structures of trade unions and voluntary associations. While some sociologists see the evidence pointing conclusively to the inevitability of elite control, others suggest that there are ways in which the members of organisations can control their leaders. Still others suggest that there is a constant struggle between oligarchic and democratic tendencies within organisations, and it is individual choices which influence the type of control exercised in an organisation.

Trade unions have been investigated by sociologists as crucial examples of democratic organisations. This is because trade unions strongly put forward an ideology of democracy, both in terms of their own organisations and in their demands for workers' democratic rights in their workplace. As might be expected, trade unions exhibit a wide range of characteristics from the very oligarchic to the very democratic.

Successive governments, however, have introduced laws to try to make trade unions more democratic; for example, by insisting on ballots before industrial action. Although the intention has been to reduce the amount of strike action, democratic accountability has not always led to a peaceful resolution of disputes. But trade unions are also faced with the dilemma common to all organisations. They claim to represent their members,

Categorisation of your own knowledge is a good way of applying your understanding to problems.

Make a list of all the trade unions you know. Divide them into categories in a systematic way. For example, 'Large' (over 1 million members) and 'Small' (under 1 million members) might be one way. Use another.

but they also control their members, having the power to expel or discipline them. (See Coursework Suggestion 11.2 on p. 287.)

Types of control

Of course, control by superiors in organisations does not have to be by coercion or force. In fact, organisations use a variety of techniques, both formal and informal, to control their members. These may range from the giving of monetary rewards to the promise of promotion. The particular combination of techniques employed will be affected by many factors, such as the goals of the organisation, its size and the technology it employs, among others. However, the actions of control will also be affected by government policy, which through its laws sets limits to the types of control that may legitimately be employed. This does not stop organisations ignoring such restrictions, whether deliberately or by omission.

Control is usually exercised by superiors over inferiors in organisations. In bureaucracies this order of people is formally laid out, and involves some groupings which have attracted sociological attention. It is the older members in bureaucracies who tend to have positions of power, as they have moved up the hierarchy. This means that there is an age differentiation in bureaucracies. However, in more networked organisations, power is given to those with expertise, regardless of age, so that the phenomenon of the 'yuppies' may appear.

Social groups and organisations

Similarly, there is a gender and ethnic distribution within organisations with women and ethnic minorities being concentrated at the bottom. This distribution has been explained in many different ways by sociolo-

Clegg and Dunkerly are important writers on organisations. But you must always be critical of any study as a first step to assessing it.

Read Haralambos and Holborn, pp. 438–40.

What arguments could you put forward against Clegg and Dunkerly's ideas?

Read *Social Studies Review*, vol. 4, no. 2, pp. 50–3. (See [70], p. 338.)

Describe the distribution of women in organisations, using the information in the article.

gists from outright racism to the ideology of domesticity. The position of women in organisations has been the subject of particular research, as the 'glass ceiling' which prevents many women's promotion is marked. Moreover, women tend to adopt particular roles within organisations as support workers rather than decision makers, so that they are said to 'do the office housework'.

Some sociologists have argued that it is women's primary responsibility for housework which is the major reason for their lack of career ambition . Others suggest that it is sexist assumptions in society at large. Still others put forward the idea that women and ethnic minorities constitute a reserve army of labour, who are brought into organisations when there is a need for labour, and dismissed when there is a need for the organisation to save money. It is this ability to give or take away a livelihood

In comparing and contrasting two phenomena, you are engaging in a form of evaluation. For example:

Professional associations and trade unions
Similarities
1 Both have rules controlling members
Differences
1 Professional associations are predominantly middle class. Trade unions are predominantly working class

List the similarities and differences between professional associations and trade unions. The first ones are done for you.

which gives employing organisations their ultimate control over their members.

5 Trade unions and professional associations

Both trade unions and professional associations have been the subject of sociological investigation over their nature and role in modern industrial societies. Although both are combinations of individuals who share certain features in common, they differ in the crucial sense that trade unions emerged among manual workers and professional associations are linked to higher status occupations. It is not that professionals are skilled and trade unionists unskilled, but that they have different types of skills and different powers over their own occupations.

Differences and similarities

Although the differences between trade unions and professional associations are often stressed by sociologists, others argue that there are, in fact, remarkable similarities. The underlying difference between the two is that professional associations have much more power and status than trade unions in society. Both types of organisation seek to pursue the interests of their own members, although they are associated with different strategies to protect them. Trade unions are associated with militant industrial action as the main way of achieving benefits for members, while professional associations rely on accreditation and high levels of knowledge as the basis of a claim for high benefits for their members.

However, the growth of bureaucratic organisations in modern societies has blurred the distinctions between trade unions and professional associations to a certain extent. The major area of growth in the trade union movement since the Second World War has been in white-collar organisations and among professional or semi-professional people, such as teachers. Even the decline in trade union membership during the 1980s has disproportionately hit manual workers rather than white-collar workers. As more and more professionals are employed in bureaucratic organisations, their traditional independence has been eroded and they have become subject to the strict rules and controls of a hierarchical organisation. One response of some groups has been to turn to trade unions to protect their declining standards of living.

E VALUATION

Read Haralambos and Holborn, pp. 320–2.

Which view of the professions do you find most convincing, and why? Make sure that you consider all the views in terms of their strengths and weaknesses.

INTERPRETATION

APPLICATION

Taking information from your reading and using it is an important habit to develop.

Read *Social Studies Review*, vol. 4, no. 4, pp. 146–9. (See [71], p. 338.)

1 What does Hyman suggest has happened to the unions during the 1980s?

2 How might this change in the 1990s?

The role of occupational associations

During the 1980s, both trade unionists and professionals came under increasing attack as 'privileged' members of society from Conservative governments concerned to free the market from the restrictive practices of such groups. There have been major legislative attempts to change the working practices of doctors and lawyers, and numerous changes to the powers that trade unions are allowed to exercise. While the professions have been somewhat successful in blunting these attacks on their powers, the trade unions found the 'enterprise culture' of the 1980s a difficult time, with declining membership and several notable industrial defeats.

Different sociologists have varied views on the role of trade unions and professional associations in society. Some see their role as essentially defensive, and concerned with the living standards and conditions of work of their members. Others see them as more harmful organisations. In the case of the trade unions, this takes the form of viewing them as one of the main causes of Britain's industrial decline, as they force wages up without a corresponding increase in productivity. For professional associations, the attack centres on the use of professional power to protect the interests of professionals against the interests of their clients, through their mystification of knowledge.

Individuals and groups

Other sociologists concentrate on the individual within the organisation and the power that trade unions and professional associations exercise over their members. Membership of these organisations is not always

KNOWLEDGE

UNDERSTANDING

What do sociologists mean by:

- code of conduct;
- elitist;
- exploitation?

EXERCISE

Professional foul

Professionals, of course, are always better at it. Whatever the "it" may be, drama, football, medicine or life, they are definitely superior. Professionals are the people who guide us through life's crises; make decisions about our bodies, our children and ourselves. They write letters to each other about us, withhold information from us and wield power over us. Since my closest friends and many helpful strangers are described as professionals, why do I hate the concept so? Lately, it has acquired the aura of a religious faith, or at least a very strong code of conduct, to many concerned and responsible people. I hate it because it is elitist and divisive. It simultaneously creates an illusion of superiority and coerces people into complying with unreasonable demands . . . I hate the idea of professionalism because it is a class system within the working environment, a way of being superior and at the same time submissive to exploitation. It is fast becoming a concept we do not question, enshrining the idea that those who need help and those who give it are fundamentally different types of human being.

(Source: Sheila Windsor, *Observer Magazine*, 19 May 1991)

This extract expresses a very forceful but personal point of view about the concept of professionalism. However, it is mirrored by a certain sociological view. Your task is to find studies or sociologists to support the idea expressed here. This will develop your skill of interpretation, by making you work out which viewpoint it is, and then your skill of application, as you have to apply that knowledge to the studies you read.

You should then attempt an evaluation of this idea. To make a sociological judgement, you need to know the arguments for and the evidence against the idea. Therefore, you will need to read about the alternative viewpoints about professionalism, and then come to a conclusion about which is the most convincing and why.

Professionals are often seen as part of management in organisations.

EVALUATION

1 How far do you agree with this?

APPLICATION

2 Cite evidence in support of your answer.

You may be asked to engage in debates on controversial issues. Although you should always use evidence, you need to be clear about the arguments you can apply to issues. For example:

Discuss the view that there is a contradiction in employees being given more freedom in order to control them more. Concentrate on the arguments, not the evidence.

voluntary and the reactions of individuals to enforced membership, either through the closed shop or through the compulsory joining of professional bodies, have been a major source of sociological interest. It has also been a focus of research that different social groups are disproportionately represented in these types of organisation.

In particular, women do not join trade unions in the same numbers as men, and the situation is even worse in the professional associations. In the latter case, sociological interest has focused on the interview and selection procedures of the professions which tend to discourage women from applying or being accepted if they do apply.

Similarly, ethnic groups are not represented in these organisations in the proportions that might be expected. For trade unions, it is the presence of ethnic groups in the secondary labour market of part-time and temporary work, in which trade unions are weak, which constitutes a major factor in their absence. Some also argue that ethnic workers are the main labour component of the illegal and sweat-shop parts of industry, where the power of the employer over the marginal and sometimes illegally entered immigrant is virtually total.

For professional associations, sociological attention has focused on the educational achievement of such groups and their under-achievement compared to indigenous groups. Even where ethnic minority groups are educationally successful, many individuals find it easier to join the family business than gain entry to the professions. This, of course, does not mean that individuals do not enter the professions or join trade unions, but that they are not represented in the same proportions as might be expected.

Nevertheless, the composition of both the trade unions and the professional associations is changing as more ethnic minorities and women join them. This reflects both the need for the economy to involve more women workers in the labour market as the demand for skilled labour grows, and also the need for the increasing assimilation of ethnic minorities into the whole range of occupations available. Moreover, the nature of the occupations that these organisations seek to represent is also changing, as developments in industry, technology and knowledge increase specialisation and the potential for control of employees.

Look through the sociological literature or *Social Trends* to find some up-to-date figures on the composition of trade union members.

1 Assess *either* the concept of de-professionalisation *or* incorporation.

2 Use appropriate evidence in your response.

Sociologists have tried to explore the consequences of these changes, employing such concepts as the professionalisation of work, the de-professionalisation of the professions, and the incorporation of the trade unions into capitalism to explain developments in these areas. The acceleration of these changes in the post-Ford era has become a major focus of sociological concern and a way forward for the future investigation of work.

Conclusion

Organisations are pervasive. We are born in them and we go to our final resting place through them. But, more important, the central aspects of our lives are shaped and moulded by organisational forces. While many people work in large formal organisations, the informal group of the family lives its public life through contact with formal organisations, both private and of the State.

Organisations are also the focus of the central contradiction of individual existence, which is the relationship between the individual and the collective. By inhabiting an organisation, the individual gives up part of his or her individuality to the social. Moreover, the form of organisations is subject to the forces of change, which alter the conditions in which the individual relates to the collective. It is this which sociologists continue to find a rich area for research.

Important points to bear in mind

1 Bureaucracies are an important part of modern societies but they are not the only type of organisation which exists.
2 While individuals often have power exercised over them in organisations, they are not helpless, even in subordinate positions.
3 What is supposed to happen in organisations and what actually happens are not always the same thing.
4 Organisations are the main way in which human goals are achieved, although this often has a cost attached.
5 Organisations can be flexible as well as rigid and can be satisfying as well as alienating environments.

KEY CONCEPTS

It is important that you are familiar with and are able to use the concepts in this section in appropriate ways if you are to apply them effectively in the examination. Check your understanding of the concepts by carrying out this exercise.

Each of the following concepts has a definition attached to it. Only ten of them are correct sociological definitions.

Decide whether each definition is true or false. For those that you think are false, provide a true one.

Bureaucracy – a system of organisation which relies on strict allocation of duties among individuals placed in a system of superiority and inferiority.

Informal organisations – organisations which are not properly organised.

Reification – treating abstract things as concrete.

Taylorism – another name for scientific management.

Deskilling – making machines simpler.

Mechanistic organisation – the way in which technology is organised.

Organismic organisation – an organisation which is not organised hierarchically, but based on the contributions of those with relevant expertise.

Networking – connecting up computers.

Professionalisation – the process whereby occupations become professions.

De-professionalisation – the process whereby an individual loses professional status.

Human relations – a theory of management which stresses the giving of responsibility for production to the workers.

Total institutions – organisations in which members carry out their whole lives.

Unionisation – the bringing together of two organisations.

Iron law of oligarchy – the argument that democratic control of organisations is impossible.

Glass ceiling – an architectural feature.

Racism – discrimination on grounds of ethnic origin.

Democratisation – the process of voting.

Formal organisation – the structure of an organisation.

COURSEWORK SUGGESTIONS

11.1

You could carry out an exercise using Weber's ideal type of bureaucracy to determine how bureaucratic your school or college is. To be an effective project, it would not be enough just to describe the organisation of your institution, but you would need to provide evidence of its operations, and give examples to support your points. More importantly, you would need to come to a conclusion as to how bureaucratic the organisation is, and this would need to be done with some sociological sensitivity.

You will need to bear in mind the following points:

1 You need to find a full description of Weber's ideal type and isolate all the elements in it.
2 Who will be the major informants in your organisation who will supply you with the necessary information, and how will you get that information out of them?
3 How are you going to decide how bureaucratic your organisation is – purely numerically, or using your judgement as to the importance of different elements of the ideal type?
4 How are you going to collect examples to illustrate the points you make? What supporting documentation can you provide?
5 You will need to know more than just Weber's ideal type to identify ways in which your organisation might be different from it. How will you know what alternatives to consider?

11.2

Do you know which teachers' associations there are? Do they consider themselves to be trade unions?

One of the few groups of trade union members whom you meet on a regular basis is your teachers. They are likely to be members of one of the teachers' associations or unions. You could explore their degree of participation in their organisations, for instance their voting in national and local elections, attending meetings and awareness of union issues. You will need to work out exactly what measures of participation you are interested in and which questions will elicit the appropriate responses. You will also need to make sure that your hypothesis, results and conclusions are linked firmly together.

You will need to consider the following points:

1 Who will be the 'gate-keepers' you approach to gain access to organisation members? How will you secure their cooperation?
2 Will you explore only one organisation or carry out a comparison of two or more?
3 How will you measure awareness of union issues? What are the current concerns of the unions? How can you find out?
4 Will you need to involve the local or national levels of the organisations?
5 Will you interview the teachers or will a questionnaire be sufficient? What if the level of response to a questionnaire is low?

CHAPTER 12

Politics

In this chapter, we will examine the arguments surrounding:

1 legitimacy;
2 political involvement;
3 voting behaviour;
4 power;
5 the State and democracy.

Before you begin any of the exercises you should have studied and should be familiar with at least one of the following texts:

Bilton, T., Bonnett, K., Jones, P., Stanworth, M., Sheard, K. and Webster, A. *Introductory Sociology*, 2nd edn (Macmillan 1987), chapter 6.
Giddens, A. *Sociology* (Polity 1989), chapter 10.
Haralambos, M. and Holborn, M. *Sociology: Themes and Perspectives*, 3rd edn (Collins Educational 1991), chapter 3.
O'Donnell, M. *A New Introduction to Sociology*, 3rd edn (Nelson 1992), chapter 14.

In addition, you should have your notes on politics in good order.

Introduction

Politics is concerned with the exercise of power and the organisations and structures which societies develop to permit the practice of power. Although we tend to think of politics in connection with government, the exercise of power occurs in most areas of social life, from the places where we work to our families. Power is, therefore, a daily feature of everybody's life, for nearly every day we exercise power over someone else, or have power exercised over us. So, politics is an everyday experience which makes it of interest to sociologists.

However, the more formal aspects of politics, in terms of the government of the country, also affect our daily lives in myriad ways. For example, decisions taken by a small group of people in government or industry can determine our income. With the globalisation of the economy and the growth of the European Community, decisions taken many miles away from Britain can affect the way that we live.

Being aware of the social world around you is the first step to a sociological imagination.

List the formal political structures which influence life in modern Britain in order of size and beginning with the smallest.

INTERPRETATION

1 Legitimacy

One of the more interesting questions which sociologists have addressed in looking at politics and power is why people obey other individuals or the instructions put out in the name of organisations. For example, individuals may be called on by the government of their country to give up their normal activities and take up arms and fight other individuals, with the possibility that they may lose their own lives. It is this obedience unto death as well as everyday obedience which sociologists have tried to explain.

Factors in legitimacy

Although sociologists agree that the legitimation of political structures in society needs to be explained, there are different emphases placed on certain factors, depending on which perspective the sociologist adopts. Some stress the use of force by those in power to ensure the obedience of those with little power. It is force, or the threat of force, which is the glue that cements society together. Others suggest that moral systems bind people in a society together, so that there is a general agreement about who has authority in society and therefore should be obeyed. Still others argue that there is a rational calculation at the bottom of an act of obedience. Conforming to the law of the land is in everybody's interest because it safeguards an individual's life and property, as well as everybody else's.

From your reading, answer the following questions:

1 What may be the sources of legitimation of societies?

KNOWLEDGE   UNDERSTANDING

2 Which do you think is the most stable, and why?

EVALUATION

Working out how to apply sociological concepts to descriptions will develop your skill.

Of the positions described above in the text, which would you label as 'utilitarian', which 'coercive' and which 'consensus'? Why have you allocated the labels in the way you have?

Obedience is usually associated with the law and legitimate political authority, but in fact we obey others in many situations where the relationship between the law and an individual's obligations are less clearcut. For example, it is fairly clear that the power of an employer is supported and reinforced by laws which have been passed to define the rights of property.

However, the powers of teachers are less well defined by laws, and rest on tradition, on the agreement of those in the classroom, and also on the bureaucratic office of teachers. Moreover, the power of teachers changes over time, so that, in the past, corporal punishment has been an accepted weapon for teachers to enforce obedience, but is now in a state of legal limbo and hardly ever used at all. Moreover, individuals often obey parents, or brothers and sisters, when there is no legal requirement that they do so, although some reformers would like to see a set of children's rights enshrined in law. The Children Act 1990 may be an early step in this direction.

Political socialisation

Part of the reason why we obey non-statutory authority is the way that individuals are brought up. Political socialisation is the way in which young people are introduced to political ideas and values through a variety of institutions. The process of political socialisation involves an acknowledgement of the legitimate sources of authority in individual lives. The absorption of political ideas by young children is a complicated process, which sociologists have tried to examine in a variety of ways.

Some suggest that there is no specific political socialisation going on at all, but the *enculturation* of a whole culture of a society by the young. Others argue that political socialisation is all about the control and channelling of anti-social drives, such as violence, into politically acceptable

In assessing an argument, you need to be able to apply the case against it. Therefore:

What arguments would you put forward against the idea that political socialisation is the most important determinant of the way in which people vote?

APPLICATION

Applying sociology to your own life can be an important way of 'making sociology come alive'. Therefore:

How closely do your views on politics resemble your parents'?

forms, while still others stress the importance of learning roles as the central aspect of political socialisation.

The institutions which socialise the young politically are various, but it is usually recognised that the family is the most important. This is mainly because the family is the first institution in which individuals live, and so it has control of the children from a very early age. This does not mean that those children brought up in non-family situations are not politically socialised, as there are alternative institutions available. Nevertheless, the family does not directly encourage political ideas or values, but tends to present an atmosphere and environment which encourage the development of particular political attitudes and breed hostility to others. The process is, therefore, a long and complicated one, which is neither obvious nor without contradictions. Because the process is not consciously carried out by parents, children will often receive contradictory messages, which they seem to assimilate with little difficulty.

This process is further complicated by the often contradictory messages that children will receive from other institutions with which they come into contact. In modern times, it is the media which seem to be the most important channel for passing on political ideas and values to future generations. Variously, schools, the workplace, peer groups, religion and the neighbourhood have been suggested as possible sources of political socialisation.

It is difficult to isolate the effects of each of these institutions or structures, or to calculate their importance. It is likely that at different times of an individual's life, different factors may be more prominent than others. Moreover, political ideas and values are never fixed, but tend to change in response to events both in our lives and in the wider world. So, in one sense, political socialisation continues throughout our lives as we respond to political developments and personal circumstances.

EVALUATION

List the political ideas with which you firmly agree. Can you think of any arguments against those ideas?

This is important because, as a sociologist, you should try to be balanced and objective, while recognising the difficulty of doing this.

ESSAY QUESTION

You should not just describe the ideas but assess their importance and come to a firm conclusion.

Evaluate competing explanations of why individuals obey the State.

---

2 Political involvement

Despite the fact that sociologists find politics interesting and pervasive, many individuals in society do not. Not only do large numbers of citizens find politics extremely boring and actively avoid formal politics, but many would also deny that politics have much effect on their lives at all, as 'politicians are all the same, out for themselves'. While such individuals might recognise the exercise of power in their daily lives, by bosses or family, they might regard the workings of the European Parliament, or the decisions of the American President, as too remote to have any impact on their lives.

Social groups and participation

Therefore, the level of involvement of individuals in formal politics tends to be limited. Only a minority of individuals are members of a political party, or are active as members. Most people's political activity is restricted to voting in national elections, and even fewer vote in local

---

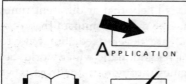

Application is often based on knowledge. For example:

In what ways could the concept of *empowerment* be applied to a discussion of political participation?

To do this, you will need to know what empowerment is.

When interpreting figures, look for both trends and omissions. For example:

Read *Social Studies Review*, vol. 3, no. 2, pp. 46–7. (See [72], p. 338.)

1 What do the figures in the article tell us about female participation in politics?
2 What do they not tell us?

elections. But the participation of individuals in politics is not random; it shows systematic variations along several social dimensions.

Much sociological attention has focused on the role of women and their lesser degree of involvement in politics than men. Despite the high profile for women as a consequence of the ten years of Mrs Thatcher's premiership, few women get into the top level of politics. Fewer women than men get into the Cabinet, are elected to Parliament or selected as candidates for elections. It is ironic that women are more prominently represented in the unelected House of Lords than in the elected House of Commons. Similarly, it is only relatively recently that ethnic minority members have been elected to the House of Commons, although more Asian and Afro-Caribbean candidates stand than are actually elected.

Explanations for this disproportionate lack of involvement in politics are varied. Some point to the traditional position of men in public life and the concentration of women in the private sphere of the family. Women are said to be socialised into these traditional views of themselves and, therefore, do not put themselves forward. Others suggest that women are more likely to find their opportunities for involvement restricted by being given the prime responsibility for housework and childcare.

Always support your assessment with evidence.

EVALUATION

1 Which of the views expressed in the paragraph above best explains the levels of women's involvement in politics?

APPLICATION

2 Have you any evidence as to why your choice is a good one?

Further, it is argued that there are institutional barriers to women being selected as candidates, from traditional sexist attitudes which suggest that women have greater difficulty being elected than men, to newer versions of sexist attitudes which categorise women as more emotional and less rational than men. In the case of ethnic minorities, racist attitudes have been suggested as a reason why members of such groups have not been selected, although in areas of high ethnic concentration, ethnic minority members have been elected with both black and white votes, with little evidence of voter bias against ethnic candidates. Moreover, Ashok Kumar was elected in a by-election in the predominantly white constituency of Langbaurgh in November 1991.

Non-voting

One of the ways in which bias against a particular candidate might manifest itself is through abstention by voters who usually vote for the party with the female or ethnic minority candidate. However, although there is

APPLICATION

In solving problems like the following, you will develop your skill of application:

Reasons for non-voting		
Positive abstention	**Negative abstention**	
	Avoidable	**Unavoidable**

Place the following in the correct column:

It was raining.
The elector was dead.
The elector was ill.
EastEnders was on.
I don't like my usual party's candidate.
They are all the same.
Democracy is a con.
I'm not on the register.
I forgot.

Which one does not go in any column? Give reasons why it does not.

little suggestion that this is statistically or electorally significant, there has been sociological interest in the rate of abstention in elections as differential turnout might influence the result of elections. If the supporters of one party fail to turn out more than a second party's supporters, this could be fatal to the first party's chances. The focus on voter volatility has been increasing since the 1980s as voter loyalty to a particular party has been eroded.

The actual significance of levels of abstention is hotly disputed. In technical terms, the debate concerns the difference between gross volatility and net volatility. Some suggest that there has been a real increase in those who change their vote from one election to the next, or use abstention as a weapon to express displeasure with a particular party. Others argue that the main reasons for apparent voter volatility are the disappearance of voters through death, and their appearance on the register at

18. These *enforced abstainers* make up the largest number of individuals who change their votes between elections.

Nevertheless, there are still individuals who do not vote in elections, even though they are entitled to and are capable of voting. Some sociologists have examined negative abstentions, looking at the reasons why people may neglect to vote even though they do not make a conscious decision not to do so. Others have examined the positive abstainers, those who, for one reason or another, decide that they will withhold their vote. The patterns of abstention contribute to the outcome of elections and it is this which has been of interest to sociologists.

3 Voting behaviour

Sociologists have traditionally looked for social factors which influence the way in which people vote by examining statistics concerning different social characteristics and the voting patterns associated with them. Often the evidence for this research is obtained from opinion polling. However, opinion polls have been criticised for producing inaccurate results and, more importantly, for creating movements in political behaviour through causing a bandwagon effect.

You can interpret information in articles as part of an evaluation. For example:

Read *Social Studies Review*, vol. 6, no. 2, pp. 47–52 (see [73], p. 338), and answer this question.

With reference to the information in the article, how useful do sociologists find opinion polls?

1 Apart from ICM Research, what other major polling organisations exist?

2 Search the newspapers to find out any other polling organisation you may not know.

3 Give reasons why they might produce different figures from ICM.

EXERCISE

The *Guardian* publishes a poll of the state of the political parties every month. Conducted by ICM Research, it bases its results on interviews with 1,500 voters across the country. The sample of 1,500 must be totally representative of the voting population as a whole, and so 48 per cent of the people questioned are male and 52 per cent female. Each interviewer speaks to 15 different people every month, and is briefed on their age, sex and social class. The interviews are conducted at 103 locations, each of which is in a different Parliamentary constituency. Results from 100 of the interview points are used; the extra three sets of interviews are always carried out in case something goes wrong. A typical problem is that one or two parcels of questionnaires may get lost in the post and so interviewing may not be completed on time.

When the interview results are returned to ICM's headquarters, in London, they are fed into a computer. The computer refines the results, making up for any deficiencies in the interviews – for example, the interviewer may not have spoken to the required number of first-time women voters. The computer then gives the results of the poll in percentage form.

The *Guardian*/ICM poll has a margin of error of 2.5 per cent. According to ICM's managing director, Nick Sparrow, this means: "If we were to do the survey all over again in the same way we would be 95 per cent sure that we would not record an answer more than 2.5 per cent different to the one we have already got." In practice, the *Guardian* poll has been more accurate than that. During the 1983 General Election it was within 1.25 per cent of the eventual result and in the 1987 election it was within 1.5 per cent of the result.

(Source: adapted from Sean O'Neill, the *Guardian* 23 October 1990)

Write a paragraph on the reliability and validity of the opinion poll using only the information in the extract.

Through researching opinion polls, add any other factors which might affect the reliability and validity of opinion polling.

What are the uses that opinion polls can be put to?

List the advantages and disadvantages of opinion polling and come to a conclusion as to their worth.

Social class and voting

During the 1950s and 1960s, it was generally agreed that, in Britain at least, social class was the most important influence on the way people voted. However, this does not mean to say that there was no disagreement about the effects of social class. For example, some sociologists suggested that Britain was the exception rather than the rule, as few other democratic countries showed the same social class effects. Other sociolo-

On central issues, like the effects of social class on voting, you need to have worked out your attitude to the problem. For example:

1 How far do you think social class still influences voting behaviour?

2 Use appropriate evidence in your response.

gists argued whether objective or subjective social class was more important in determining the votes of the classes.

Nevertheless, the idea that working-class people vote Labour and middle-class people vote Conservative did have some sociological support, and it also has a powerful common-sense presence in individual lives. While there may have been a general recognition that social class was important in the immediate post-war period, human beings are not automatons, and individual voters do not automatically vote the way that their social class suggests they should. Individuals are partly the product of their environment but they also have an element of free will. Moreover, individuals are subject to social forces other than social class and much research was directed towards identifying other influences on the way in which individuals voted.

Some sociologists examined other social characteristics which might be important, notably people's gender, religion, age and ethnicity. Others looked at experiences or contacts which might cut across class loyalties, such as peer groups, work, or trade union membership. Another idea was to assess the effects of ideological and political forces themselves, such as the mass media or the election campaigns which led up to people's voting. The evidence about these effects was often contradictory and certainly complex. But these influences helped to build up a picture of voting which avoided the simple 'class = party' model.

A good exercise to develop your interpretation and application skills would be to search the sociological literature to find out how each of the factors in the above paragraph affect voting.

Make a list of the studies which investigated them.

APPLICATION

As an application exercise, which of the groups of working-class voters described in the following table is:

- traditionalist;
- deferential;
- instrumentalist;
- secularist?

A	B	C	D
Tory Ascription-oriented described by Nerdlinger	Tory Achievement-oriented described by McKenzie and Silver	Labour Achievement-oriented described by Goldthorpe and Lockwood	Labour Opposition-oriented described by Tunstall

Deviant voting

In particular, sociologists were concerned with deviant voters – those voters who did not conform to the voting patterns that their class membership would suggest. These working-class Conservatives and middle-class radicals were the subject of much research. These groups were important because they helped to explain how the Conservative Party, supposedly representing a minority of the electorate, has dominated politics in Britain during the twentieth century.

In the case of the working-class Tories, various reasons were put forward to explain their existence. Some suggested that they were the product of a hierarchical society, in which they recognised their inferior social status compared to the upper class. Others suggested that they calculated that they would be financially better off under the Conservatives and voted Tory for instrumental reasons. Another view was to see the working-class conservative as responding to the dominant middle-class values of society, which were put forward through a network of social institutions, such as schools and the media.

The middle-class radicals were also seen as being the product of different forces. On the one hand, middle-class Labour voters were concentrated in the public sector, and it was suggested that they were voting according to their material interests, as Labour was more sympathetic to public service. On the other hand, it was suggested that it was middle-class workers whose salaries and working conditions were under threat who turned first to the trade unions and then to the Labour Party in an attempt to reverse their fortunes. Lastly, some middle-class radicals were seen as *ideologues*, people who despite a privileged background were convinced of the rightness of socialist ideas and voted accordingly. (See Coursework Suggestion 12.1 on p. 312.)

Before you use your other skills, you should have a good basis of accurate knowledge. Therefore:

List the main types of middle-class deviant voter, giving a clear definition for each and showing the differences between them.

The decline of class

During the 1970s, interest in the idea of deviant voters declined, as changes in voting patterns suggested that social class was no longer the most important factor in deciding people's votes. Increasingly, voter volatility in the 1970s and 1980s led sociologists to believe that the old class loyalties were dying. The growth in support for third parties, and changes in the composition of the class structure, led some sociologists to believe that class de-alignment was occurring and new alignments were emerging, which linked groups to particular ways of voting.

The theories put forward to explain these new patterns of voting were many and varied. Some suggested that new social cleavages were emerging which represented the development of a postmodern sector in the economy. This explanation tended to emphasise regional variations in voting, with the Labour-voting North and the Celtic fringe representing older, traditional economies and the South, dominated by the Conservatives, more connected with the emerging global economy associated with the sunrise industries of the new technologies.

Other social divisions, which were identified as being important in developing working-class support for the Conservatives, were the growth of home ownership among the working class and the increasing proportion of workers in the private sector through the Conservative government's privatisation programmes. A more radical view of this process suggested that the growth of the State since the Second World War had created a constituency for the Labour Party which could be undermined by the selling off of State industry, council estates and making people less 'dependent' on the State.

Other explanations put forward concentrated on voter motivation, developing a view of the voter as a consumer shopping around for the party which best fits his or her value systems. Still others suggested that the degree of Conservative dominance in the 1980s had been exaggerated by splits in the opposition parties and that social class still remained the best predictor of an individual's vote. Naturally, all these theories have

Read Haralambos and Holborn, pp. 171–82.

Using the figures in the extract, write a report on changing patterns of voting since 1984. Do not just repeat the figures but identify the trends in words.

ESSAY QUESTION

Though the focus of your response should be around class and region, you should not automatically exclude other factors. But you need to ensure that any comments on other factors are directly related to the question.

'Social class has been replaced by region as the main factor influencing voting behaviour.' To what extent do sociologists agree with this statement?

Using material in articles as a basis of evaluation is a good skill to develop.

Read *Social Studies Review*, vol. 5, no. 1, pp. 24–9. (See [74], p. 338.)

INTERPRETATION

1 List the main explanations for recent developments in voting behaviour.

APPLICATION

2 What psephological (voting) evidence can you apply here?

EVALUATION

3 Which do you find the most realistic, and why?

come under sociological scrutiny and have been criticised for one reason or another. But the most important level of criticism directed against these theories is the evidence of General Elections themselves, which offer firm statistical evidence with which to evaluate the accuracy of the theory.

4 Power

The concept of power is a central one in sociology, mainly because it operates at many different levels, from the day-to-day ordinary level to the macro-social, life-threatening level. Although we usually associate power with governments in some form or another, power is operative in many situations, not just political ones. This is because there are many different types of power, which are important in different spheres of social life.

Identifying the differences between sociological writers is an important part of the skill of interpretation.

Read Haralambos and Holborn, pp. 117–20, 122–3.

How does *Lukes's* definition of power differ from Parsons's?

Types of power

Sociologists of different persuasions tend to emphasise one type of power at the expense of the others. For example, some have stressed that owners of factories have important economic power, although the effects of their power may be indirect. For example, investment decisions made by a Board of Directors can create jobs in some areas and destroy them in others. In the past, military power has been a crucial aspect of British society and, while still important, it is much less visible than it was in the past. The exception to this is, of course, Northern Ireland, where military power is an everyday experience for many citizens.

In postmodern society, cultural power is seen as the most important aspect of power, as it is the manipulation of images in the media which is claimed to 'create' reality and have political consequences in the post-modern world. Power need not be as a result of formal position, but rather it is networked into all social situations. It is shifting and filled with reversals and resistances. For example, labels which attempt to stigmatise a social group can be taken by that social group and be used to re-affirm identity and create new cultural forms of power out of the label; the Black Power movement in the United States took the concept of 'black' and, through using it in positive ways ('Black is Beautiful'), helped to create a Black industry in the cosmetics, fashion and cinema fields among others.

Nevertheless, political power has been the main focus of sociological work in this area, and sociologists have concentrated on trying to understand who has, and wields, power in modern democratic societies. The question of 'who rules?' in society is, in fact, a difficult one to operationalise (or investigate properly), mainly because the practice of power is often hidden from view and its effects are not always as the exerciser of power intended them to be. If powerful people want to resist investiga-

Reflecting on how your own life can be interpreted in sociological terms is an interesting exercise in application.

List the different types of power that you will be subject to throughout the course of your life, with accompanying definitions.

What implications do the comments in the above paragraph have for sociologists' views of the world?

Answering this question will improve your skill of application.

tion, they have the power to do so. Given the opaqueness of many aspects of power, sociologists often rely on secondary data to carry out their studies. It is the powerless who tend to be the easier subjects of sociological investigation, while the activities of the powerful tend to remain hidden or can only be inferred from the effects of their power.

Who rules?

As might be expected with such an important issue as 'who rules?', there are many different sociological answers to the question. They can be divided broadly into three types of response. The first emphasises the importance of economic power, and concludes that a small class of owners of factories and businesses are so powerful that they dominate the political world. Though there are several variations in this approach, they all accept that economics is the key to power.

The second approach, also with variations, accepts that there is a small elite which rules, but they are composed of the key decision-makers in several areas of social life. It is thus the political sphere which is most important, although the holders of top institutional posts in the military, the civil service, industry, the universities, etc., have many links with the political elite. There is an emphasis in this approach on the strategies which the elite adopts to hold onto power and pass it onto their children.

Read *Social Studies Review*, vol. 2, no. 1, pp. 2–7. (See [75], p. 338.)

1 Outline the 'managerialist' position, stating its strengths and suggesting criticisms of it.

2 Use information both from the article and elsewhere.

3 Do you think that the evidence you have produced supports or undermines the managerialist theory?

Theories of Power

	Marxist	Elitist	Pluralist
Who rules?			
Distribution of power			
Nature of power			

Use your skill of application to place the following in the appropriate cells:

no-one, institutional, ruling class, power elite, concentrated, diffuse, economic, political.

Which one appears twice?

So that you will be able to evaluate the three theories in this section, begin by drawing up six columns:

Three approaches to power

Ruling class		Power elite		Pluralism	
Main points	**Criticisms**	**Main points**	**Criticisms**	**Main points**	**Criticisms**

Identify the main points and the main criticisms of each of the three approaches to power.

ESSAY QUESTION

'Ruling-class power remains as entrenched as ever in Britain.' Evaluate the evidence for and against this statement.

Write a paragraph on the role and importance of pressure groups in modern democracies. Support your ideas with evidence.

The third approach argues that no one group holds power, but that many different power groupings and pressure groups influence the government to make social policies fit their interests. Again, there are many variations within this approach, from those who accept that some elements have much more power than others, to those who argue that each individual has a certain amount of power to exercise in social relationships.

The role of different types of pressure or interest groups is important in this approach, as they represent the major way in which individuals in democratic societies can seek to influence decision-making. Joining a political party is another important way in which individuals may seek to exercise power, but this is done by only a small minority of the population. Therefore, it is pressure groups which have been claimed to be the main avenue of democratic practice.

Globalisation and empowerment

While traditional sociological approaches have centred on national political power, more recent events have shifted the focus of research in two ways. Firstly, as the globalisation of the world's economy has proceeded, and national boundaries begin to dissolve, either through the grouping together of national states in larger units, such as the European Community, or the break-up of states through ethnic or cultural tensions, attention has switched to cross-national aspects of power. In particular, institutions such as the European Parliament and The European

Common-sense understandings tend to go unchallenged. You need always to apply a critical outlook to any phenomenon. For example:

What limits to the power of multi-national and trans-national companies might sociologists identify? You might consider law, competition and recession as possible areas of interest.

Assessing the claims of political parties is an important aspect of sociological thought.

EVALUATION

1 How far do you agree that the State has empowered citizens during the 1980s and 1990s?

APPLICATION

2 What evidence can be applied to this debate?

Commission have begun to figure in sociological accounts of power. Similarly, the activities of the trans-national Companies have come under scrutiny, especially over their operations in the Third World.

Secondly, attention has also focused on individual power and the claimed dispersion of state power to individuals over the 1980s and 1990s. The effect of social policies over this decade is a matter of sociological dispute, centring around the concept of empowerment. While there is agreement that policies such as council house sales, privatisations and the Education Reform Act have changed the balance of power between the citizen, the local authorities and central government, there is no consensus as to the effects of these changes. Some argue that there is a dispersal of power to individuals, while others argue that there has been a centralisation of power under the rhetoric of 'power to the people'.

The notion of empowerment is an important one because it implies that there are those who need to be empowered. In other words, there is also a contradictory concept of powerlessness which has interested sociologists. Many individuals are said to experience powerlessness in many situations; for example, in relation to government agencies with which they have dealings. So, among many people in high-rise estates or the unemployed or those in routine, boring jobs, feelings of hopelessness and a belief that they are unable to change their circumstances are said to be dominant. It is these groups which, it is claimed, have not been empowered by the reforms of the 1980s, but which constitute a powerless underclass in society. Moreover, many members of ethnic minorities, and women who are said to experience similar feelings of powerlessness, employ political actions to try to alleviate their situations.

5 The State and democracy

Political action may take many forms, from violence to voting. In democracies, desired changes are supposed to be achieved through peaceful persuasion and the exercise of the ballot, not the bullet. However, there are many different forms of democracy, and the word itself has become associated with 'good' and anything which can be shown to be 'anti-democratic' takes on an aura of 'evil'. Therefore, many totalitarian

You should also use evidence to support debates. For example:

What evidence can you find to support the claim that no social group dominates decision-making, and what evidence to undermine the claim?

states claim to be democratic, because they seek the legitimacy of representing the 'people', even where the government only represents a minority of the people.

The forms that democracy can take are many and, even in advanced democracies associated with the capitalist West, there are disagreements as to how democratic such societies are. For example, there is debate concerning the role of the media in democracies and how far market forces, left to their own devices, can guarantee a balanced press and television service. Similarly, the notion that certain groups in society are effectively disenfranchised has been a subject of discussion. Attention has focused especially on ethnic minorities and 'guest-workers' in western Europe. In the United States, it is the Latinos and Chicanos who have been the object of research.

The role of the State

The role of the State in modern democracies has been a recurrent theme in sociological debate. The State is a much wider concept than government, encompassing the military, the judiciary, the education system and the civil service, and not just the legislature. Some sociologists argue that the State is merely the creature of the dominant ruling class, which owns the means of production.

Although they may differ as to the precise way in which the State serves the interest of this group, sociologists agree that social policies serve their interests primarily. Even social policies which overtly seem to help working-class interests are said to have a hidden agenda of creating legitimacy for the capitalist system and thus benefiting the ruling class. The problem with this approach is that it is difficult to show how the

Applying your understanding to contemporary society is one of the most important aims of sociology. From your reading:

1 To what extent do you agree that there is a ruling class in Britain?

2 Use evidence to support your arguments.
3 Make sure that you come to a conclusion which directly answers the question.

EXERCISE

The political allegiances of newspaper readers
(April–June 1990)

Convert this table into a graphical format to practise your skill of interpretation. In it, highlight only the different political allegiances of the readers of the *Mirror, Mail, Guardian* and *Telegraph*.

INTERPRETATION

	Con	Lab	LD	Green
The Sun	33	54	6	4
The Star	16	67	9	4
Daily Mirror	13	77	7	3
Daily Express	58	29	8	4
Daily Mail	60	27	8	4
Today	43	37	12	7
The Times	53	29	10	5
The Guardian	12	70	8	8
Financial Times	56	27	11	3
The Independent	28	46	13	8
Daily Telegraph	70	15	9	3

(Source: MORI, in the *Guardian* Monday 23 July 1990)

Revenge of the mind benders

Do the Tory tabloids make the slightest difference to how their readers vote? For 30 years, academic researchers have chorused: "No, or anyway much less than what you would think". . . . Now a team led by William Miller of Glasgow University has published *How Voters Change*, an elegant and rigorous study of the Conservative revival between the Westland affair and the 1987 election. It fatally undermines the "reinforcement, not change" argument . . .

The evidence for this reinforcement position was:

1 television is more important than the papers
2 tabloid readers were uninterested in politics
3 newspapers followed their readers' politics not vice versa
4 cross-readers stayed unconverted because they were either too sophisticated or too unsophisticated to be influenced
5 any effect happened equally to Labour and Conservative voters, so cancelling each other out . . .

After Westland, the really big swing to the Conservatives occurred among readers of the Tory tabloids – 30 points among *Star* readers and an even more massive 36 points among *Sun* readers. "Irrespective of the readers' initial party preference," Miller *et al.* conclude, "the more tabloid the paper, the more its readers swung to the Conservatives . . ."

These figures blast a large hole through the assumptions underlying the original "reinforcement not change" position. Miller *et al.* show that the *Star* and the *Sun* were not mobilising latent Conservative partisans with Conservative opinions but converting readers with pro-Labour attitudes on the economy and defence, however likely and inchoately held.

(Source: Ivor Crewe, the *Guardian*, Monday 19 November 1990)

Answer the following questions on no more than two sides of paper:

a) How convinced are you by the Miller study?
b) How might sociologists criticise the study?
c) Does the Miller study mean that the 'reinforcement, not change' thesis is false?
d) What other evidence concerning the effects of the newspapers on voting behaviour can you find from your own reading?

ruling class actually dominates the State, though this does not mean that it does not do so.

Others suggest that the State should have a minimal role in social policy, creating only the minimum conditions for the successful pursuit of profits. Intervention by the State which is not geared to defence or law and order tends to distort social relations and create a dependency culture, in which social groups become habituated to State financial help, sucking in public money while the social problem remains unsolved. Thus, the operation of the free market, unhindered by State regulation, becomes the basis of all liberty in society.

One problem with such a position is that it tends to stigmatise groups who, through no fault of their own, may need State support, such as the unemployed, and ignores other groups who do receive State support – such as mortgage relief recipients – but who are not labelled as scroungers.

Another approach suggests that the market cannot resolve all social problems if left to itself. Indeed, many social problems are created by the workings of the market, as some groups are disadvantaged in the marketplace. This approach suggests that the State needs to intervene through social policies to redress the injustices of the market and provide necessary support to disadvantaged groups. However, this can be criticised because, despite many years of State intervention, social problems, far from being solved, have become more deeply entrenched in the social structure.

A further approach is to see the State as a neutral decider of social policy issues. It examines the cases put to it by pressure groups and social interests and decides which is the best for the country as a whole. The State neither represents one particular interest nor has an interest in expanding its own power. Rather it is responsive to the wishes of society, expressed through many political actions by its citizens. One way of criticising this approach is to look at the actual workings of the State and see if the State is as neutral as is suggested.

In making up your mind about alternative approaches to a problem, you will be developing the skill of evaluation.

1 Which of the attitudes towards the State identified in the text best describes the way in which the British State operates?

2 What evidence will you use to support your choice?

3 What will you not be able to find out?

The State and social policy

Although the operations of the State are often shrouded in secrecy and difficult for sociologists to examine directly, the effects of the actions of the State are everywhere and can be examined empirically. It is in the working out of social policies that sociologists have examined the functions of the State. This has happened not only on the physical level, but also on the ideological and cultural levels. For example, social policies concerning one-parent families are influenced by the ideological formation of the nuclear unit as the 'proper' family in modern societies. Therefore, the individual is affected not just by the power of the State in the physical or legal sense, but also in its ideological and cultural effects.

The links between ideology and the law are many and subtle, but the outcomes of those links intimately affect individual lives, from the income that an individual enjoys to his or her sense of worth and place in society. It is the potential of the State's power, its ability, for example, to call up its citizens to bear arms and possibly die, which makes it so dangerous to individual liberty, and it is the contradiction between the State and the individual which forms the basis of much sociological interest.

Conclusion

The exercise of power occurs every day in many situations, from parents and children to the gaoling of a convicted criminal. It is the pervasiveness

Read Haralambos and Holborn, pp. 152–4.

Add to the criticisms of Marxism, drawing upon your knowledge of theories generally and applying them to the specific problem identified by Haralambos and Holborn.

of relationships of power which make them interesting to sociologists. While voting seems to be the most obvious way in which citizens exercise political power in a democracy, the experience of other kinds of power is much wider than this. Without power, it would be very difficult to carry out social life, and yet, by its nature, power holds the potential for conflict. It is this contradiction, between its necessity and its potential for the destruction of social order, which makes it such a fascinating subject for sociological investigation.

Important points to bear in mind

1 While British people tend to think of power as the peaceful exercise of legitimate authority, for many individuals, force, coercion and violence are their main experience of power. War is the ultimate exercise of power.
2 Voting is often taken for granted but democracy is a relatively recent development, even in Britain.
3 The way in which an individual casts his or her vote is the result of a myriad of factors, not just his or her social characteristics.
4 Voting studies by sociologists offer a constant stream of new evidence each time there is an election. Voting theories are, therefore, not very stable.
5 If a group does rule in society, does it know it rules or does it just happen anyway?

KEY CONCEPTS

It is important that you are familiar with and are able to use the concepts in this section in appropriate ways if you are to apply them effectively in the examination. Check your understanding of the concepts by carrying out this exercise.

For both of the following paragraphs, choose the appropriate concept for the missing words from the list attached:

Elections in modern Britain have usually resulted in one of two parties becoming the Government – a situation known as the _____. This stability is partly the result of _____, because children tend to follow their parents' preferences in voting behaviour, which leads to _____ in voting behaviour. Yet, not everyone in Britain shows an active _____ in politics beyond voting at elections, and even then there are high rates of _____, although the reasons why people may not vote are varied. While social class has been the main factor affecting voting behaviour, this connection has never been absolute. There have been two types of _____, where people do not vote according to their class interest, the _____ and the _____. Members of the working class who vote Conservative habitually can be identified as those who believe they will be financially better off under the Conservatives (the _____), and those who believe the higher social class status of Conservatives means that they are born to rule (the _____). However, more recent elections have shown that electors are more willing to change their political allegiance, a situation of voter _____.

Political socialisation	Involvement	Abstention
Duopoly	Pragmatists	Middle-class radicals
Traditionalism	Volatility	Deviant voting
Working-class Tories	Deferentials	De-alignment

Although in a _____, _____ is supposed to be held by the people, many sociologists have argued that the reality is that the organs of government which make up the _____ are controlled by a few. Some identify the few with the owners of the means of production, which they call the _____; others see a _____ composed of the people in key institutional positions in society. Both positions are concerned with the ways in which the many are controlled by the few, so that the _____ of the masses is ensured. A central concept here is _____, a process whereby the many accept the few's right to rule. Other sociologists believe that society is truly democratic, through the activities of pressure groups and individuals – a situation they describe as _____. Their main concern is how to widen the influence of individuals on the political process, through _____.

Power	Legitimation	Obedience
Empowerment	Ruling class	Power elite
Pluralism	Democracy	State

COURSEWORK SUGGESTIONS

12.1

One of the advantages of investigating voting behaviour is that new evidence emerges every time there is an election. You should be able to gather a formidable amount of evidence from the newspapers in a fairly short space of time. The problem that you will face is what to do with all the evidence you have collected. The important part is, therefore, to establish very clearly what it is you want to investigate about the statistics you have collected. For example, it could be the effect of a particular event on voting intentions, although this might be difficult to isolate; or you could focus on the changing intentions of a particular social group; or you could look at the ways in which different newspapers present the results.

Here are some points for you to bear in mind.

1 You can easily be proved wrong when the next set of opinion polls comes out, so put forward your conclusions conditionally.
2 You must ensure that you meet the evaluation requirements of the skills domain, by being critical about the way in which you have gone about your study.
3 Remember that voting intentions are not the same as voting behaviour, so be careful how you frame your comments.
4 The literature on voting is huge and you will need to place your findings in a particular theoretical framework in order to focus your work.
5 Will you be able to carry out your project entirely with secondary data, or might it be better combined with some primary research?

12.2

You will need to be sensitive in your handling of this issue.

Although power is difficult to investigate because of its very nature, there is one area where you may gain access. The sociology department that you are in has a system of power embedded in it and is worth investigating. You will need to devise a strategy to examine the exercise of power in the department and whether there is any discrepancy in the views of superordinates and subordinates.

Here are some points for you to consider.

1 Will there be any ethical or practical problems with your investigation and how will you resolve them?
2 How will you gain the cooperation of the members of the department?
3 What are the crucial issues that you will focus on? Decision-making? Financial control? Time-tabling?
4 Who will be allowed to read your final project? Will it matter?
5 What concepts will you use? Democracy and oligarchy? Elitism and pluralism? Participation and exclusion?

CHAPTER 13

Religion

In this chapter, we will examine the arguments surrounding:

1 definitions of religion;
2 functions of religion;
3 secularisation;
4 religious organisations;
5 modern religious movements.

Before you begin any of the exercises you should have studied and should be familiar with at least one of the following texts:

Beckford, J.A. *Religion and Advanced Industrial Society* (Unwin Hyman 1989).

Bilton, T., Bonnett, K., Jones, P., Stanworth, M., Sheard, K. and Webster, A. *Introductory Sociology*, 2nd edn (Macmillan 1987), pp. 405–27.

Giddens, A. *Sociology* (Polity 1989), chapter 14.

Haralambos, M. and Holborn, M. *Sociology: Themes and Perspectives*, 3rd edn (Collins Educational 1991), chapter 11.

O'Donnell, M. *A New Introduction to Sociology*, 3rd edn (Nelson 1992), chapter 17.

In addition, you should have your notes on religion in good order.

Introduction

Religious experience has been a central part of the human condition throughout history. Religious institutions have often taken a central position in societies and have attracted the loyalty of millions of people to the point where individuals have been prepared to die for their faith. For many individuals, their spiritual lives constitute the most important aspect of their existence, while others have little connection to or feeling for the religious life.

Religious leaders often claim to speak with authority on moral issues and this has an effect on the social policies of governments, especially on issues such as abortion or divorce. The role of the Shi'ite clerics in Iran is

In your reading, you should have come across the 'evolutionary' approach to religion. Read Haralambos and Holborn, pp. 645–7 if you have not. You should make up your mind whether you agree with this approach, and in doing so you will be developing your skill of evaluation. Of course, you may be undecided about this approach because your evaluation should be based on sociological evidence, and this may be inconclusive.

Can any sociological evidence be applied to the evolutionary theory of religion?

a good example of the way in which religion can still determine what happens politically and economically in a society. Because religion has been, and still remains, a central aspect of so many people's lives and societies' histories, sociologists have been interested in both its individual effects and its social consequences.

1 Definitions of religion

It is not always easy to define what constitutes religion or a religious experience. It is not enough to refer to some supernatural or spiritual world to define religion. Religious authorities do not agree among themselves as to which organisations may be legitimately considered religious,

By summarising your notes systematically, you will be practising the skill of interpretation because you will be identifying the main points from a mass of text. Therefore:

In three columns, list the main features of the functionalist, Marxist and phenomenological approaches to religion.

Approaches to power		
Functionalist	**Marxist**	**Phenomenological**
1 Religion provides value-consensus	1 Religion is the opiate of the masses	1 Religion provides meaning for activity
2	2	2

The first ones are done for you.

From your own knowledge and experiences:

1 List as many variations of the main religions as you can. Check with another colleague, if you can, to produce as large a list as possible.

2 How are the main religions geographically dispersed around the world?

3 What does this tell us, as sociologists, about religion?

as opposed to vehicles of superstition. There are many examples of non-physical experiences, such as ghost-sighting, which would not usually be called religious. Yet spiritualism, which many would consider to be a religion, claims to be able to contact a non-physical world. Others deny that spiritualism is a proper Christian religion. Each of the major contemporary religions has had groups within it which have been considered 'heretical', or not 'properly' part of that religion, and many groups have been persecuted for it.

Sociologists have had similar difficulty in coming to an agreed definition of religion. This is not unimportant for sociology for, in defining religion, sociologists are determining what should be investigated as a religious organisation and what should not. Generally, sociologists have adopted a broad or a narrow definition of religion.

Broad definitions

In the wide definition, there is no mention of a supernatural being as such, so that as many beliefs and organisations as possible can be included. The reason for producing a wide definition is because religion is seen as performing an important function in society, and some societies, such as Communist ones, operate without a traditional religious belief at their centre. This leads to the conclusion that religion, whether it identifies a God or not, will always be an important part of social life, and cannot decline. Instead, religious organisations are said to adapt constantly to changes in society and will thus take different forms in different times. Therefore, what might be seen as the 'death of religion' in the postmodern world can be interpreted as a blossoming of religion as different groups and individuals seek to practise their religiosity in many new and various ways.

Narrow definitions

The narrow definition seeks to exclude the more exotic organisations which claim to be religious and limit the definition to the more mainstream and common-sensically defined religious organisations. By so doing, sociologists seek to identify the importance of religion at different times, and especially to examine whether religious influence has declined in modern times. Less traditional forms of religion are often seen here as

The classical sociologist Weber has had an important contribution to make to a sociological understanding of religion.

Write a paragraph on how Weber's work has helped sociologists to understand religion, stating whether you think his contribution is greater than that of Marx, and why.

'not really religious', but concerned with discovering meaning, regardless of whether this includes a conventionally defined deity or not. More critical sociologists emphasise the enormous wealth of some of the leaders of the more exotic religious groups.

In accepting one of these two definitions sociologists will tend to ask different questions and be interested in different aspects of the religious experience. Nevertheless, sociologists are united in focusing on the real rather than the spiritual effects of religion; that is, sociologists are interested in the empirical effects of religion in society rather than the spiritual dimension. Sociologists do not pronounce on the existence or non-existence of God, but they do wish to investigate the effects on society of those who claim to be doing His work in the world.

2   Functions of religion

Religiosity

Firstly, sociologists have been interested in the relationship between individuals and religious experience. For some sociologists, all individu-

For some sociologists, religiosity is an important concept; for others, it is not. You must make up your own mind by evaluating the concept. Therefore:

1 How far do you agree that everyone has religiosity?

2 Does your personal experience have any bearing on your answer?

3 What are the limitations of personal experience as sociological evidence?

4 What sociological evidence can we offer for the existence of religiosity?

also have a need for religious experience to fulfil their religiosity, which is the spiritual dimension which we all share. Thus, attendance at religious services or private religious observance functions satisfies the yearning in individuals for some meaning in their lives. In attaching themselves to religious experiences, it is claimed that individuals are fulfilling some deep-seated need in their lives.

Others, however, deny the existence of religiosity as an essential part of the human personality. Rather, they point to the uncertainty and lack of purpose that individuals face in their lives, which may be countered by turning to the supernatural or to other beliefs and activities. However, religiosity is not the only answer to the great unknown questions of the human condition (Who am I? What is the meaning of life?, etc.), and many non-religious alternatives exist. While the religious dimension is a feature of all human societies, this does not mean that every individual in these societies has religious feelings or pays more than lip service to religious observance.

Religion and groups

Sociologists have also been interested in the functions of religion for different groups in society. In contemporary Western societies like Britain, one of the most obvious features of religious observance in the mainstream Christian Churches is that the congregations are ageing. This can be seen in a variety of ways, such as the decline in Sunday School attendance or the average age of those who attend church services. On the other hand, others suggest that young people are more attracted to the livelier celebrations of the evangelical movement in the traditional Churches or the new charismatic movements, which emphasise commitment and joy in worship rather than traditional rites and sermonising.

Similarly, the congregations of church-goers are predominantly women and some sociologists have suggested that this is because of women's marginality in society. As women cannot gain status in the secular world to the same extent as men, some women turn to religion to 'find a place'. The debate concerning the ordination of women priests is in part concerned with female dominance in church attendance. While the majority of attenders are women, the Church of England and the Roman Catholic Church continue to be dominated by men in their hierarchies. While the debate in the Churches concerns the theological justification for the ordination, or denial of ordination, of women, sociolo-

---

More specifically, on Weber's contribution to an understanding of religion, your reading will have introduced you to the idea of religion as a vehicle of social change. However, not all sociologists agree with this.

Assess whether religion can produce social change, referring to the pros and cons of Weber's work.

EVALUATION

What do sociologists mean by:

- secular;
- industrialisation;
- demographic shifts;
- respectable working class;
- enthusiasm?

gists have been more interested in the reflection of secular male–female relations and the patterns of dominance and subordination along gender lines within the Churches.

Similarly, social classes have been a focus of sociological concern. Since industrialisation, the working class has had limited connection to the established Church of England, or to any of the other Christian denominations. Sociologists have attempted to explain this non-attendance in various ways, some emphasising the slowness of the Churches to react to demographic shifts and others stressing the work and leisure patterns of the working class itself. Equally interesting have been those groups within the working class who have been attracted to specific forms of Christian worship, such as Primitive Methodism, the Salvation Army, etc. The religious attraction of these organisations to the 'respectable' working class seems to have been their 'enthusiasm' and commitment, but the sociological attraction is to be found in these organisations' potential for working-class control over their own lives, separate from the upper- and middle-class dominated Church of England. (See Coursework Suggestion 13.1 on p. 337)

In the case of ethnic minorities, their position as marginal groups in society has provided the focus for much sociological research. Undoubtedly, religion has proved to be a focal point for them, giving identity and meaning in a society which may at times be hostile. The local temple, mosque or synagogue forms a central part of the lives of many ethnic minority individuals, whether deeply religious or not.

However, religion may also be a focus for hostility, as the Salman Rushdie affair has shown. The social arena where religious differences have attained the most importance has been in education. Whereas the State supports various Christian schools, it has not so far given financial support to non-Christian religions, which may also wish to establish their own schools. This has created much debate among the religious sections of the ethnic minorities.

In developing hypotheses, you are applying your sociological sense to a particular problem.

Apart from the two hypotheses in Coursework Suggestion 13.1 (see p. 337), produce two hypotheses to test concerning the religious beliefs of men and women.

It is important that you should provide a sociological approach to contemporary issues.

1 Develop two sets of arguments, one supporting State help for religious schools and one opposing it.

2 What do your arguments lead you to conclude about State help for Muslim schools?

Society and religion

In examining the societal functions of religion, the same dichotomy between cohesion and conflict emerges. One viewpoint argues that the central function of religion is to bind individuals to society. This approach tends to ignore the individual's reasons for observing religious rites and focuses on the social importance of rituals. These serve to integrate individuals and re-affirm the solidarity of the society as a whole. The best example of this is perhaps the role of the monarch as head of State and head of the Church of England. However, this implies that those who do not attend Anglican services are somehow less integrated than others.

A second viewpoint highlights the potentiality for conflict which religion poses. There are many historical and contemporary examples where religious differences have led to conflict, although these are often also mingled with political, ethnic and economic conflicts. The situation in Northern Ireland is perhaps the closest example of religious division.

A criticism of both these positions is that they ignore what individuals think they are doing when they attend religious services. While the effect of attendance may be integration or division, these are unintended consequences of observance. The primary function of religion is, therefore, to

You will recall from your reading that some religious organisations are said to support the status quo and some oppose it. The Church of England is an example of the former and the Baptist Church in Communist Russia an example of the second.

1 Provide other examples in which religious organisations may be conservative or radical, stating why you have put them in the specific category.

2 Are there any which do not fit easily into the categories? Why is this?

To what extent do you agree that religion serves social functions, such as integration? Use examples in your response.

Remember that evaluations should always be supported by evidence applied to the specific question.

satisfy individual demands, not society's. Nevertheless, both these positions take an ideological view of the function of religion, believing that religious institutions serve a purpose in society, either to integrate individuals into the collectivity or provide a justification for the activities of the ruling class.

Another approach argues that religion does not perform functions for society at all, but rather is a matter of individual belief and choice. The acceptance or rejection of religious belief and attendance at religious services are matters of free will and personal commitment. For example, many individuals attend religious marriage or funeral services, without necessarily exhibiting a great deal of belief or even knowledge about the service they are attending. However, this approach has been criticised for ignoring the social pressures which accompany attendance and non-attendance, as well as the official links between those in power in societies and particular forms of religious expression.

3 Secularisation

One of the major disputes in the sociology of religion concerns how important religion continues to be in an age of industrial and scientific progress. This debate is interesting not only for its religious importance, but also for the methodological issues that it raises.

Two broad positions

In looking at the issue of the influence of religion in modern industrial societies, two broad positions have emerged. On the one hand, there are those who suggest that religion has gone through a massive decline, from a 'Golden Age of Religiosity' to a situation where religion has a limited and often formal importance in those societies. This decline is most spectacularly seen in the decline in the numbers attending religious services over the past century.

The issue of secularisation is a complex one. It will be easier to handle if you use your skill of interpretation to pick out the major points.

Summarise the arguments for and against the claim that modern societies have undergone a process of secularisation.

By doing this, you will be preparing the way for the evaluation of the idea.

ESSAY QUESTION

You have to be clear which factors make up the institutional level and which form part of individual consciousness.

E VALUATION

'Religion may be losing its power at the institutional level, but it still retains immense influence over individual consciousness.'

Evaluate the sociological evidence for and against this view.

Nevertheless, the formal acknowledgement of religion continues in the way that individuals use the Churches for baptisms, marriages and funerals, without seeing regular attendance as a necessary accompaniment to them. But even these 'rites of passage' are no longer celebrated in church as much as they were in the past.

On the other hand are those who argue that the evidence is not as clear-cut as secularisation theorists maintain. Different industrial societies show different trends, with the United States showing continued high levels of church attendance. Even where attendance has declined, religious belief continues to be strong, as shown by many social surveys. Rather than seeing religion as declining, these sociologists argue that religion is adapting to meet the changing social circumstances of industrialising countries. As traditional methods of worship no longer meet the needs of individuals in the industrialised West, new forms of worship will emerge. Therefore, the splitting of Christianity into many different groupings, and the growth in alternative non-Christian religions in the West, are not signs of the disintegration of religion but symbols of religion's continued growth and vitality.

Different levels of secularisation

The debate about secularisation occurs at different levels, and ends up as a complicated inter-mingling of these different levels. Some stress the

K NOWLEDGE U NDERSTANDING

I NTERPRETATION

1 Using *Social Trends* or another statistical source, collect together some statistics on at least two measures of religious observance.

2 What do your figures tell you about secularisation, if anything?

Sociologists sometimes distinguish between disengagement, differentiation and pluralism. You need to be able to apply these concepts to sociological issues.

What are the implications of these processes for the power of religious institutions?

formal, societal level, examining what economic and political power the Churches have lost and what they still retain. Issues such as land ownership and the composition of the House of Lords have also figured here.

The debate centres around whether the Church has lost important functions in modern societies. The withdrawal of the Church from education and welfare services, from political life and from some economic activity is undeniable, although, of course, vestiges of the Church's influence in these areas remain. However, the interpretation of these changes may differ. Some argue that this represents a decline, but others suggest that the Church has been purified by its withdrawal from secular areas of life, so that it can concentrate on its central functions in the spiritual dimension.

In addition, the level of culture has been considered, examining the continuing ideological and ritual importance of religion. For this level, issues of church attendance, baptism, marriage and death – discussed earlier – have been important aspects of the dispute between secularisation and anti-secularisation theorists. But there has also been much dispute about the statistics used to measure any fall-off in attendance at rites of passage and church services on Sundays. Some argue that these do actually chart a real decline in religious attendance and, therefore, in religious belief.

Others question the reliability and validity of the statistics, throwing doubt on the method of collection. They thus suggest that the statistics do not tell us much about real levels of attendance, especially in the past, and, therefore, we cannot chart any decline as easily as some might suggest. Another view puts forward the argument that statistics about attendance tell us nothing at all about belief, as people attend or do not attend church services for a variety of reasons other than belief.

As we have seen, evaluation may involve assessing the methodological soundness of particular approaches.

How useful are statistics in examining secularisation? What do the statistics not tell us about religion?

EXERCISE

Steady fall from grace

The fall from grace has not been swift – more a steady decrease in the number of people prepared to give up their Sunday morning lie-in.

The number of Northerners attending church fell by 15 per cent between 1979 and 1989.

Part of that decline can be attributed to the death of older members of the congregation but that begs the question, why are younger people not taking their place?

A census of England's 38,000 churches shows that Free Churches, such as the Baptists and Independents, are the only ones whose attendances are increasing.

The rise of such churches is in stark contrast to the thinning

INTERPRETATION

Charts like this convey much information but, to interpret them properly, you need to understand what they do not do. Which figures are missing from the charts?

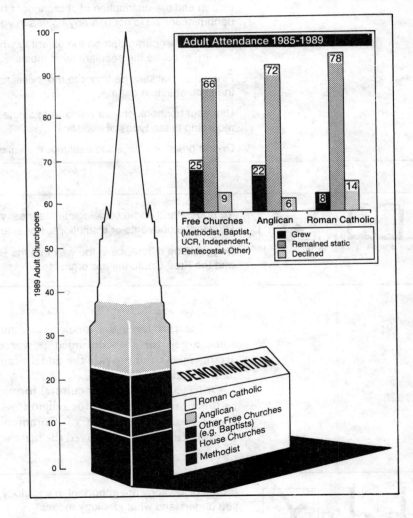

numbers at Anglican and Roman Catholic services . . .

In an increasingly secular society it seems that churches based on lively and informal get-togethers in front rooms and school halls are meeting needs more readily than traditional churches. The number of Catholic churchgoers fell by 15 per cent over the last ten years, the number of Anglicans by 9 per cent and Methodist attendance – which counts for almost half of the Free Church – was down more than 33 per cent. Baptists, meanwhile, grew 20 per cent after 1985 and the Independents witnessed a staggering 80 per cent increase.

(Source: Sarah Oliver, *The Journal*, Saturday 30 March 1991)

In a paragraph, describe the pattern of change in adult attendances at church and the distribution of churchgoers between the different denominations. Do not use any figures in your paragraph.

Write another paragraph on the extent to which these figures help to confirm or refute the secularisation thesis.

Find other statistics pertinent to the thesis and discuss their contribution to the secularisation debate.

Use your textbook or your notes to examine the problems of collecting and recording these types of statistics.

On the basis of your work, evaluate the validity of the secularisation thesis.

To understand some sociological theories, you need some basic knowledge of events or institutions. For example:

Suggest one difference in the way that the Roman Catholic, the Anglican and the Free Churches are organised.

Still at this level, the ideological dimension is also important. Here, some argue for the continued power of religion to legitimate social arrangements and provide the underpinning for particular forms of domination and subordination.

Others argue that other cultural formations have emerged which stand as functional equivalents for religion, while having no religious content themselves. The collapse of Communism in the Soviet Union and Eastern Europe has destroyed the main secular alternative to religion, but

Issues of ideology are important in sociology, so you need to check that you understand what ideology means.

Write a paragraph on what sociologists mean by ideology.

INTERPRETATION

EVALUATION

To summarise your reading usefully, you can often categorise information logically.

Read Haralambos and Holborn, p. 688–93 and draw up a table like the one below.

To prepare for evaluation, you should list the pros and cons of each category.

Generalisation		Individuation		Transformation		Desacrilisation	
Pros	Cons	Pros	Cons	Pros	Cons	Pros	Cons

humanist thought has provided alternative legitimations, for example in France. In modern industrial societies, it is argued, meritocracy provides a more important ideology for capitalism than religious ideas.

At another level of the individual, questions of belief and the mind-set of individuals have been raised, with the notion of scientificity central to the debate between those who argue for the continued importance of religion and those who argue that its influence has declined. Surveys of individual belief show the readiness of most people to express a belief in God, even though these same individuals may have no contact at all with religious organisations.

While this has been claimed to be evidence of the continued vitality of religious thought, others argue that positive responses to questions about belief in God represent a 'normative' reaction – people answering what they think they should be thinking rather than what they actually think. On the other hand, the claim that science has replaced religion as the main system of thought held by individuals has also been challenged. Although we live in a scientific age, few people understand the details of scientific thought but tend to take it on faith, in the same way that individuals take theological thought on board, without really understanding the details.

Clearly, science and religion are not exclusive alternatives, with most people accepting both and all their contradictions quite happily. Indeed, much belief in magic and superstition also remains in modern 'rational'

Sociology touches upon issues in your own life.

1 List the superstitions that you believe in.

2 Do you really believe in them or are they just a bit of fun?

3 What evidence is there about the importance of superstition in modern societies?

societies, with a great deal of individual belief in astrology, the para-normal and other non-religious superstitions.

The secularisation debate will continue as the ebb and flow of religious sentiment and belief continue. In one sense, the debate represents a deep-seated disagreement between, on the one hand, those who see progress as inevitably bringing about the death of religion, as individuals increasingly gain scientific understanding of the world around them, and, on the other, those who see religion as a necessary and inevitable part of human societies, without which social arrangements would disintegrate and individuals be without any anchor in their lives.

Yet both sides are united in the way that they seek to explore the importance of religion in modern societies, looking to empirical evidence to back up their arguments. They may disagree on the interpretation of the evidence, but they are agreed that it should be on the basis of evidence and not personal opinion that the importance of religion should be assessed.

4 Religious organisations

Sociologists, in examining the appeal of different religious organisations to various sectors of society, have evolved typologies of religious organisations, which seek to define different types systematically.

Church and sect

The crucial distinction accepted by most sociologists concentrates on the people whom religious organisations attract. Those organisations which

Sociologists seek to apply evidence to support their ideas. From your reading:

1 List the studies which have empirically investigated secularisation.
2 Which studies have supported the secularisation thesis and which have undermined it?

K NOWLEDGE   U NDERSTANDING

A PPLICATION

Religious organisations are often divided into church, sect and denomination. You should know the differences between them.

1 Fill in the following chart on the main features of religious organisations. The first ones are done for you.

Main features of religious organisations		
Church	**Sect**	**Denomination**
1 Has links with State 2	1 Opposes State 2	1 Accepting of State 2

2 At the end of your chart, give an example of each.

receive support from the higher social orders, and have political connections with the State, are deemed to be 'Churches', while those which attract the allegiance of the marginal or lowly in society are called 'sects'. However, this is not the only distinction of importance because there are religious differences between them as well. Churches tend to emphasise the ritual nature of worship with the authority of the Church coming from tradition. Sects, on the other hand, stress that members have to 'live the life' of the Christian, with salvation dependent on commitment, not ritual, and authority stemming from the congregation, not the past.

Thus, some sociologists have stressed the conservative nature of religious organisations acting as Churches, highlighting the personal links between the powerful in society and the leaders of these religious organisations, the ideological connections between Church and State, and the general support that Churches give to social arrangements or the status quo through the legitimation process. Sects, on the other hand, have been associated with social change. Some religious organisations have been the catalyst for social change, promising their followers 'heaven on earth' through introducing the changes proposed by the sect. Various revolutionist sects in Africa used the religious beliefs of adherents to forge anti-colonial movements, sometimes to the extent of armed rebellion.

However, this basic distinction has come under much criticism from some sociologists. They argue that it is far too simple a division, presenting complex distinctions in dichotomous terms. Moreover, the church–sect distinction is ethno-centric, relying on Western Christian tradition and ignoring non-Christian religious organisation, which does

You can also practise the skill of application by making decisions about which examples are appropriate for which category.

1 Using the same chart as the previous exercise, place the following in an appropriate column;

- Methodism;
- Jehovah's Witnesses;
- Shia Islam;
- Roman Catholicism;
- Church of England;
- Moonies;
- Sunni Islam;
- Baptists;
- Alawite Islam;
- Greek Orthodox;
- Pentecostal.

2 However, application also involves judgement and it may be that some of the examples are not easy to categorise. Which ones, and why?

Notice that in answering the last 'why' you are practising evaluation.

not fall easily into the dichotomy. The distinction also ignores the dynamic nature of any religious organisation, which changes over time, sometimes having the characteristics of a Church predominant, and at others showing sect-like habits.

Also, to classify Churches as conservative and sects as radical is over-simple. At times, Churches can behave in radical, even revolutionary ways, such as the Catholic Church's oppositional role in Communist Poland, and sects can be very conservative, such as the ruling Alawite sect in Syria. Because of this, sociologists have produced increasingly complex typologies of religious organisations to try to deal with the various attributes that empirical observation of them discovers.

Other types

One additional type introduced has been the denomination, a sort of half-way house between Church and sect and representing the change that often comes over sects when, for example, members begin to have children. Whereas Churches accept individuals as members when they are baptised as infants, sects have usually demanded some form of public, adult acceptance as proof of their commitment. Denominations are, therefore, those sects which compromise on the need for adult baptism and allow their children to be accepted into the organisation at an early age.

Moreover, sects themselves have been subdivided into several different types as sociologists have explored various examples of sects and

ESSAY QUESTION

In order to evaluate, you must look at the arguments and evidence both for and against the proposition, and then come to a conclusion.

Assess the argument that the only function of religion is to provide a justification for the existing social arrangements in society.

attempted to place them in some systematic order. Examples have been taken from history, such as the Methodist movement, and from contemporary events, such as the Moonies. But, more interestingly, sociologists have investigated many sects in the Third World, from many different cultures, such as the Cargo Cults of the Micronesia or anti-colonial sects in Africa.

Some sociologists have argued that the variety of religious organisations is so great that any attempt at typology is doomed and that it would be better to examine the details of religious organisations, rather than trying to force them into artificial divisions. Nevertheless, one further type of religious organisation has been proposed – that of the cult. Cults are highly individualistic, short-lived organisations, drawing their religious inspiration from a variety of cultural traditions and often proving attractive to those on the margins of society.

5 Modern religious movements

Sects and cults have formed the majority of what are described as the New Christian Right, or the Fundamentalist movement or new religious movements, although features of these organisations are increasingly found in the more traditional Churches. These movements are also associated most strongly with the United States, where individuals have been more attracted to religious observance generally. Much of the media

To be a good sociologist, you need to be aware of the nature of the society in which you live and ask questions about it. This will inevitably involve your sociological skills.

EVALUATION

1 How important are sects in modern societies?

APPLICATION

2 Provide evidence to support your answer.

You can use information from many sources to address sociological questions, and this involves the skill of application. Therefore:

Read *Sociology Review*, vol. 1, no. 2, pp. 23–5. (See [76], p. 338.)

What are the implications of the information in the article for the influence of religion in modern societies?

I NTERPRETATION   A PPLICATION

interest in them has focused on their more disreputable aspects, such as alleged brain-washing, sexual permissiveness or their ability to exploit members.

There is also an assumption that these movements attract the poor and marginalised in society. However, the phenomenon is much more varied than this. Some attract the rich seeking to explain their good fortune to themselves; some are rich; many use modern methods of communication to reach their potential members and not all of them are as sinister as has been suggested.

The media and religion

It is the modern communications used by more recent religious movements which have allowed them to reach wide audiences and grow wealthy. The appearance of 'Radio Christianity' has been a focus of sociological concern. Some see this as religion adapting to the industrial age, and, therefore, pointing the way for all religious organisations to go. Others see the development of religious broadcasting as providing the opportunities for charismatic individuals to reach large audiences and become media 'stars', not just preachers.

Still others argue that there is a band-wagon effect, with more unscrupulous individuals using religion to create a lifestyle of some wealth for themselves. The exposure of certain preachers' malpractices in the late 1980s seemed to suggest that there was an element of exploitation in some TV ministries, without diminishing a section of the public's enthusiasm for these ministries.

Another important aspect of tele-evangelism during the 1980s was the New Christian Right's increasing political power in America. Associated with the New Right political agenda of anti-abortion, anti-welfare, homophobic and pro-choice policies, its power arose from its ability to mobilise a potentially large electorate in support of particular candidates in American elections. Sociologists disagree about the political importance of the New Christian Right. Some argue that it was a significant component in the interest groups which supported Presidents Reagan and Bush, and others believe that it was important in creating a conservative agenda of ideas in the 1980s.

EXERCISE

The weaker sects

The degrading treatment of women in many religious cults today reads like a chapter from the dark ages. Yet, 200 years ago, women were leaders of a number of sects, asserting female equality (and even superiority) within them. What on earth went wrong?

In *The Secret World of Cults*, Jean Ritchie fills in the dismal detail of the contemporary picture. The Krishnas believe women to be "prone to degradation, of little intelligence and untrustworthy". In the Central London Church of Christ, women are not allowed to speak in church and have no place in its hierarchy. Among the Children of God, women bear large numbers of children to unidentified fathers and are open to every disease going, thanks to their leader's ban on contraception and instruction that women must "share" sexually . . .

Mormon women have to rely on their husbands to call them from the grave on resurrection day; if the man doesn't make it to heaven, neither does the wife. And many a cult leader does his young female followers the honour of using them for his personal gratification.

Jean Ritchie describes the most common cult recruit as white, middle class and male. Often his motives are idealistic; he is looking for a spiritual dimension to his life and for a sense of purpose – also the starting point for several cult leaders. Only as they gathered more followers and greater power did they become greedy and corrupt, and the history of many sects provides lurid evidence of the corrupting effect of such corrupting power.

Given that most twentieth-century sects are male led and that many are based on the fundamentalist view that the male is superior to the female, it is not surprising that the women within them fail to rise to positions of power. Yet it is surprising when you look back to their role in the past.

Female religious leaders flourished. There was Mother Ann Lee, who led the Shakers to the New World where they founded societies based on female equality, communal property and complete celibacy.

(Source: Jane Rogers, the *Guardian*, Thursday 9 May 1991)

Through reading or contacting an 'expert', find more examples of female cult leaders in the nineteenth century.

What does the article suggest is the role of women in most sects?

What does the article suggest is the main motivation for joining a sect?

Produce a list of the positive aspects of cult life and a list of the negative aspects, drawing on information in the article.

Find sociological studies to support the points you make by researching in your sociology or institutional library.

What do sociologists mean by:

- cult;
- fundamentalist;
- communal property?

K NOWLEDGE U NDERSTANDING

Still others suggest that the New Christian Right political role is much exaggerated, mainly to boost the self-importance of its leaders. Most would agree that any influence that the New Christian Right did have, has waned under the impact of various financial and sexual scandals which have hit its leaders. Nevertheless, several of the important leaders of the New Christian Right have important links with politicians in Washington and continue to have some influence there. The New Christian Right also had an important input into the Republican Party's manifesto for the 1992 election.

The importance of the new religious movements

Sociologists also disagree as to the importance of these movements for the sociology of religion. To begin with, the range of movements included is wide, from the new religious movements, such as the Divine Light Mission, or the Hare Krishna movement, to more mainstream fundamentalist religious institutions of the 'Moral Majority'. Some see them as a further sign of the disintegration of religious belief in society, as Christianity splinters into smaller and smaller groupings.

Others suggest that they represent a re-kindling of religious feeling in society and a revival of interest in the supernatural because people have lost faith in science as an explanation of the natural world. Still others argue that human beings seek rewards and when they are scarce or unavailable, they settle for compensators instead. Religion constitutes one of the major compensators in life because it offers intangible rewards. (See Coursework Suggestion 13.2 on p. 337.)

Although you will be focusing on Great Britain, the United States is often used as an example in sociology. So, you also need to be aware of developments there. Finding out about another society can be exciting, but you must be sure that you use your skills to make sociological judgements about it. For example:

E VALUATION

1 How important is the influence of the New Christian Right on American politics?

A PPLICATION

2 What evidence can you suggest concerning this issue?

Be careful to look for evidence both for and against the New Christian Right's importance.

Read *Social Studies Review*, vol. 1, no. 1, pp. 3–7. (See [77], p. 338.)

What factors in the article are suggested as influencing the origins and the development of the new religious movements.

Present your answer in two columns, as below:

New religious movements	
Origin	**Development**

When deciding on a method, you need to be aware of its strengths and weaknesses, so that you can evaluate its success or otherwise.

List the advantages and disadvantages of in-depth interviews in two columns, as below. This will give you an organised basis on which to evaluate them.

In-depth interviews	
Advantages	**Disadvantages**

Therefore, as the mainstream Churches have reduced the emphasis on the spiritual and mysterious in their practices, many individuals have turned to the new religious movements as they offer more appealing compensators. However, the statistics do not suggest that the numbers involved in the more exotic of the new religious movements are large and, if they do provide compensators, it is for a relatively small number of people. Also, the numbers involved in these movements tend to fluctuate, as the more exotic movements tend to be less stable, with members constantly moving in and out.

Probably more important for the long-term development of religion has been the growth in fundamentalism throughout many religions. The return to more fundamental versions of religion, with an emphasis on lit-

You may know someone or have heard of people who have joined a new religious movement. Therefore:

EVALUATION

1 To what extent do you agree that sects offer compensation to, rather than exploit, individuals? To evaluate this issue adequately, you need to deal with compensation and exploitation.
2 Is your own knowledge sufficient evidence?
3 What other types of evidence are available to the sociologist when studying this issue?

APPLICATION

Because religion is a continuing issue in sociology, you need to build up a good base of knowledge on it.

INTERPRETATION

1 Carry out a newspaper search to build up a dossier on fundamentalist religious movements in different parts of the world. You might want to do this with a few friends.
2 But note that newspaper evidence is not sociological evidence and you need to use it carefully by analysing the information, not just accepting it. You should make a start by noting the similarities and differences between the various movements.

APPLICATION

eral interpretation of holy script and 'traditional' values, has been a world-wide phenomenon. The re-emergence of religion in the former Communist states of Eastern Europe has been a major triumph for the persistence of religious organisations in the face of hostility. But Islam and Hinduism have also experienced fundamentalist revivals throughout the 1980s. The political and social consequences of this revivalism have still to be played out fully, and sociologists will be following its development as keenly as they have studied religion in the past.

Conclusion

Religion seems to be a profound feature of the human experience and, although sociologists cannot test the validity of the spiritual claims of religion, they can examine the social and individual impact of religious organisations. The resurgence of religious fundamentalism throughout the world provides new challenges for sociologists of religion as they attempt to explain the renewed interest in more militant forms of traditional religions.

Important points to bear in mind

1 Religious feeling is experienced by an individual but is usually practised as part of a congregation, i.e. as a social phenomenon.
2 Religion is connected to power, both in society and over individuals.
3 The definition adopted for religion will affect the type of questions asked and also the answers that emerge.
4 Religious organisations are difficult to categorise because they are constantly in a state of flux.
5 Some religious organisations are not always seen as providing spiritual comfort, but as a threat to the integrity of either individual members or current social arrangements.

KEY CONCEPTS

It is important that you are familiar with and are able to use the concepts in this section in appropriate ways if you are to apply them effectively in the examination. Check your understanding of the concepts by carrying out this exercise.

Fill in the blanks with the most appropriate concept from the list which follows:

1 While a _____ is usually connected with the ruling group in society, a _____ attracts those who oppose the status quo. A _____ stands somewhere in-between. A _____ is much more individual and beyond the mainstream.

2 _____ usually refers to recent developments in religious organisations generally, while _____ refers to those with a particular ideological stance. However, radical religious groups are not just a Christian phenomena, because _____ is a world-wide movement.

3 The process of _____ where religion loses its influence on society takes many forms. While individuals may retain their religious feelings or _____, supporting the Church is no longer a way of expressing them, because _____ is common. While the Church has loosened its connections to many other institutions in society (_____) and thus loses its importance, religion has become a matter of personal choice (_____). Some sociologists argue that, while there has been a loosening of ties between religious organisations and society, this allows a much 'purer' form of religion to appear, a situation that Parsons call _____.

4 The Church is supposed to perform the function of _____, but this is difficult where there are many different faiths in society, a situation of _____.

Religiosity	Non-attendance	Church Integration
Multi-culturalism	Cult	Secularisation
New Christian Right	Structural differentiation	Fundamentalism
Individuation	Disengagement	Sect
Denomination	New religious movements	

COURSEWORK SUGGESTIONS

13.1

It is possible to investigate differential religiosity by gender through a variety of variables. You could devise a questionnaire which seeks to establish the religious behaviour and beliefs of men and women. If the sociological literature is correct, your hypothesis could be something along the lines of 'Women attend religious services more frequently than men' or 'Women are more likely than men to express faith in God', or whatever.

Here are some aspects for you to consider:

1 What sort of questions will draw out the information you require?
2 What size of sample do you need to make your research worthwhile?
3 How will you deliver the questionnaire, through the post or face to face? What are the advantages and disadvantages of these alternatives?
4 Will you concentrate on religious behaviour or on religious attitudes? Which would be more difficult to research, and why?
5 Where will you find the literature to provide the context for your work? Who can you ask for help in this?

13.2

It may be possible to study members of the new religious movements, if you can find them. Through an in-depth interview methodology, you could try to establish whether there is a consistent social and political set of attitudes associated with these members. You will need to be aware of the traditional attitudes with which they are usually associated in order to explore these issues during the course of the interview.

Here are some problems that you may encounter:

1 Finding enough subjects will be your main problem, and you will need to explore a number of avenues to build up your contacts. This will take time.
2 The literature on the new religious movements is recent and may be difficult to get hold of. How can you ease this problem?
3 Which social and political attitudes will you focus on, and what strategy will you adopt to get your subjects to talk about them?
4 If your subjects are relatively young, as they are likely to be, how does this affect the generalisability of your results?
5 You will need to be sensitive as your subjects are likely to be marginal to mainstream religions. Any hostility to the views expressed might finish off the interview.

List of resources

38   Research Roundup, 'The nation divided?' *Social Studies Review*, vol. 3, no. 2, pp. 67–70

39   Wyn Grant, 'Corporatism in Britain' *Social Studies Review*, vol. 2, no. 1, pp. 36–40

40   John Scott, 'The debate on ownership and control' *Social Studies Review*, vol. 1, no. 3, pp. 24–9

41   Richard Scase, 'Theories of convergence and the comparative study of society' *Social Studies Review*, vol. 4, no. 4, pp. 153–5

42   Dick Hobbs, 'A bit of business' *Social Studies Review*, vol. 5, no. 2, pp. 66–8

43   Howard Parker, 'Heroin: a solution with a problem' *Social Studies Review*, vol. 2, no. 2, pp. 2–6

44   Paul Rock, 'New directions in criminology' *Social Studies Review*, vol. 5, no. 1, pp. 2–6

45   John Williams, 'In search of the hooligan solution' *Social Studies Review*, vol. 1, no. 2, pp. 3–5

46   John Williams, 'England's barmy army' *Social Studies Review*, vol. 4, no. 1, pp. 6–10

47   Steve Redhead, 'Rave off: youth, subcultures and the law' *Social Studies Review*, vol. 6, no. 3, pp. 92–4

48   Gordon Hughes, 'Taking crime seriously?' *Sociology Review*, vol. 1, no. 2, pp. 20–3

49   Michael Clarke, 'Business crime' *Social Studies Review*, vol. 4, no. 3, pp. 106–10

50   David Smith, 'Crime prevention and the causes of crime' *Social Studies Review*, vol. 3, no. 5, pp. 196–9

51   John Muncie, 'Much ado about nothing?' *Social Studies Review*, vol. 3, no. 2, pp. 42–6

52   Geoffrey Pearson, 'Hooligans and youthful crime' *Social Studies Review*, vol. 3, no. 4, pp. 160–4

53   Steve Taylor, 'Beyond Durkheim: sociology and suicide' *Social Studies Review*, vol. 6, no. 2, pp. 70–4

54   Aidan Foster-Carter, 'Development sociology: whither now?' *Sociology Review*, vol. 1, no. 2, pp. 10–14

55   Ray Bush, 'Explaining Africa's famine' *Social Studies Review*, vol. 2, no. 3, pp. 2–6

56   Becki Walker and Ivan Waddington, 'AIDS and the doctor–patient relationship' *Social Studies Review*, vol. 6, no. 4, pp. 128–30

57   Ivan Waddington, 'Inequalities in health' *Social Studies Review*, vol. 4, no. 3, pp. 116–20

58   Research Roundup, 'Counting up the poor' *Social Studies Review*, vol. 5, no. 3, pp. 115–16

59   Michael Banton, 'The culture of poverty' *Social Studies Review*, vol. 5, no. 3, pp. 112–14

60   Mike O'Donnell, 'Ideology, social policy and the welfare state' *Social Studies Review*, vol. 2, no. 4, pp. 36–40

61   Research Roundup, 'Active Citizens Unite' *Social Studies Review*, vol. 4, no. 3, pp. 110–11

62   Stephen Wagg, 'Mass communications: the debate about ownership and control' *Social Studies Review*, vol. 2, no. 4, pp. 15–20

63   Kenneth Newton, 'Making news: the mass media in Britain' *Social Studies Review*, vol. 6, no. 1, pp. 12–15

64   Greg Philo, 'Seeing is believing?' *Social Studies Review*, vol. 6, no. 5, pp. 174–7

65   Research Roundup, 'The Glasgow Media Group' *Social Studies Review*, vol. 2, no. 1, p. 8

66   Stephen Wagg, 'Politics and the popular press' *Social Studies Review*, vol. 5, no. 1, pp. 17–22

67   Nick Jewson, 'The development of cities in capitalist societies' *Sociology Review*, vol. 1, no. 2, pp. 6–9

68   Nick Jewson, 'Inner city riots' *Social Studies Review*, vol. 5, no. 5, pp. 170–4

69   Research Roundup, 'Hoffman's "Asylums"' *Social Studies Review*, vol. 2, no. 5, p. 13

70   Research Roundup, 'Doing the business, female style' *Social Studies Review*, vol. 4, no. 2, pp. 50–3

71   Richard Hyman, 'What's happening to the unions?' *Social Studies Review*, vol. 4, no. 4, pp. 146–9

72   Parliamentary report, 'Women in parliament' *Social Studies Review*, vol. 3, no. 2, pp. 46–7

73   Ivor Crewe, 'Matters of opinion' *Social Studies Review*, vol. 6, no. 2, pp. 47–52

74   Michael Riley, 'Theories of voting' *Social Studies Review*, vol. 5, no. 1, pp. 24–9

75   John Scott, 'Does Britain still have a ruling class?' *Social Studies Review*, vol. 2, no. 1, pp. 2–7

76   Steve Bruce, 'Pray TV: observations on mass media religion' *Sociology Review*, vol. 1, no. 2, pp. 23–5

77   Roy Wallis, 'The sociology of the new religions' *Social Studies Review*, vol. 1, no. 1, pp. 3–7

Index